ON TRIAL

ON

The Soviet State versus "Abram
Tertz" and "Nikolai Arzhak"

TRIAL

Revised and Enlarged Edition

TRANSLATED, EDITED AND WITH AN INTRODUCTION

by Max Hayward

HARPER & ROW, PUBLISHERS

NEW YORK AND EVANSTON

LIBRARY OF CONGRESS CATALOG CARD NUMBER: 67–23281

H-R

Contents

v

II. APPENDIX

ON TRIAL

Introduction

THE TRIAL in February, 1966, of the two Soviet writers Andrei
Sinyavsky and Yuli Daniel (Abram Tertz and Nikolai Arzhak) is, as
one of the defendants pointed out to his judges, unprecedented in
the annals not only of Russian literature but of world literature. The
case has shaken Soviet society more profoundly than anything since
the revelations about Stalin at the 20th Party Congress in 1956.

This volume consists of an almost complete transcript of the court
proceedings and a number of other documents relating to the trial
and its aftermath. Most of this material reached the West by
undisclosed channels, and, apart from a few items taken from the
Soviet press, none of it has been published in the Soviet Union.

From internal evidence it seems clear that the transcript of the trial
was taken down in note form by somebody present among the hand-
picked and carefully vetted spectators in the courtroom. It is possible
that parts of it were reconstructed subsequently from rough notes,
but the bulk of it appears to be a verbatim record with only minor
defects where the unknown observer was unable to catch a name
(these are sometimes garbled) or left out words and phrases here and
there, thus occasionally obscuring the sense of a passage, or the
logical sequence in an exchange between the defendants and the
prosecutor or judge. Also, whoever it was who made this record of the
proceedings did not always take down quotations from the works of
the two defendants, evidently hoping to be able to insert these
afterward. This has rarely been done, and it is therefore not always

1

easy to "place" quotations referred to, but not given, in the text. In many cases, however, there are sufficient clues (e.g., the first words of the quotation or a brief description of what it is about) to enable one to locate it.

The other documents, which have been widely circulated in Moscow intellectual circles, consist of statements by the wives of the two defendants, protests against pretrial newspaper attacks on them, testimonials offered in evidence for the defense and several open letters protesting against the sentences imposed on the two writers. There is also a letter from one of the defendants, Daniel, written from the hard-labor camp in which he is confined, to the newspaper *Izvestia*. This is a retraction of a partial admission of guilt made at his trial. Finally, a protest by a group of faculty members of Moscow University throws light on an attempt to victimize the only defense witness.

The purpose of this Introduction is to give as much information about the work of the two writers as is necessary to follow the trial proceedings, and also to give a general outline of the whole Sinyavsky-Daniel "affair."

THE DEFENDANTS AND THEIR WORK

Both defendants were born in 1925. Andrei Donatovich Sinyavsky is a Russian. His wife, Maria, is an art historian, and he has a young son. Yuli Markovich Daniel is a Russian Jew—probably the son of the Yiddish short story writer Mark Daniel-Meerovich, who died in 1940. He is also married and has a fourteen-year-old son. As appears from the transcript, Daniel is a veteran of World War II, at the end of which he was invalided out with a pension after being severely wounded. The evidence on Sinyavsky's war record is not quite clear—the judge implied that he had a relatively easy time during the war, but he nevertheless appears to have served in the army, at least toward the end of the war, and according to the testimony of Helène Peltier-Zamoyska: "Although he was in it only for a short time, because of his youth, it was for him his first chance of contact with the ordinary people of Russia, and he retained from this time a deep feeling of solidarity with the simple, nonintellectual people with whom he rubbed shoulders there."*

He was a student at the Philological Faculty of Moscow University in the postwar years. It was here that he first got to know Madame Zamoyska, whose father was at that time French naval attaché in Moscow. She was one of the two or three foreigners who were allowed in those years to study at Moscow University, and it was she who on subsequent visits to Russia, beginning in 1956, brought out the first works of "Abram Tertz" and arranged for their publication abroad—in *Esprit*, a left-wing Catholic journal, and later in *Kultura*, the distinguished Polish-language journal edited in Paris by Mr. Jerzy Giedroyc. He obtained the degree of "candidate of philological sciences" (roughly corresponding to a doctorate), and for the last few years, until the moment of his arrest, he was a senior staff member of the Gorky Institute of World Literature in Moscow. A person of unusually wide literary culture with a special interest in the history of art, he has a considerable public reputation in Moscow intellectual circles as a teacher, scholar and critic. His major work (in collaboration with A. Menshutin) is a book on the poetry of the early revolutionary years.† The French scholar Michel Aucouturier reports (*Tribune de Genève*, February 8, 1966) that Sinyavsky once told him that, for him, "destalinization" meant above all a return to the creative vigor unleashed by the Revolution. In his first work published abroad under the pseudonym Abram Tertz he wrote: "The image of the Revolution is as sacred, both to those who took part in it and to those who were born after it, as the image of a dead mother." His views are certainly nonconformist, but there is nothing in his published work to suggest that he is anti-Soviet or "counter-revolutionary" in any reasonable definition of these terms.

It is true that, like most Russian intellectuals of his generation, he was deeply affected by Khrushchev's revelations at the 20th Party Congress in 1956 about the horrors of the Stalinist past, and reacted with all the inevitable outrage of one who had, albeit with some

---

* Le Monde, April 17, 1966.

† *Poeziya pervykh let revolyutsii; 1917–20*, Moscow, 1964. This work was picked out by the *Times Literary Supplement* as one of the best critical studies to have appeared in 1964 in a language other than English.

qualms of intellect and conscience, believed. This was a turning point for many young Russians, who had hitherto tended to excuse the excesses of the Stalin era on the grounds of revolutionary expediency. The disclosures of 1956 opened their eyes (for some the shock came earlier—at the time of Stalin's funeral—see Evtushenko's *Precocious Autobiography*). The naïve young Communist, Seryozha, in Sinyavsky's first novel *The Trial Begins* no doubt contains elements of self-portrait. Zamoyska says that when she knew him at Moscow University in the years 1947–50 he was a convinced member of the Young Communist League (Komsomol):

The son of a militant revolutionary, he could not conceive of his country having any other structure than that created by 1917. The very word "revolution" . . . had for him an emotional quality, the ring of something holy which portended the coming of a more just social system, a new humanism which would bring renewal to the universe. . . . Was he shocked by the cruelty employed to establish this new order? Certainly less than I was, as a foreigner. . . . He would tell me that, unfortunately, the law of historical progress demanded human sacrifices. Nevertheless, he was not easy in his conscience with this complacent argument. It is significant that one of our first discussions was about the dilemma posed by Ivan Karamazov: Can one build a crystal palace on the body of a child? . . . Then came the shock of Stalin's death. The famous "secret" speech by Khrushchev at the 20th Congress was an event of incalculable significance for the whole of the U.S.S.R., and particularly for the generation of my [Moscow University] friends. "A world has collapsed," Pasternak said to me, "a new one will be born." One witnessed a complete change of values. My old friends from the University, for example, had suddenly become aware of the tragedy lived through by millions of innocent people in the concentration camps, and they felt themselves personally answerable for, and accomplices in, these crimes, since they had allowed them to happen in the name of a patriotism synonymous with conformism. Their sense of shame gave birth to a determination not to remain passive or indifferent to the slightest injustice. People who had had the rare courage not to bend their consciences to the slogans of the day became heroes. For this generation a new concept of Soviet patriotism was taking shape. This was the reaction of Sinyavsky and Daniel, and it is this that impelled them to write. In 1956, the year of the 20th Congress, Sinyavsky wrote his essay *On Socialist Realism* and his first short novel *The Trial Begins*. Manuscripts began to circulate all over the country, which was seized by the need to tell of those years which had passed by in tears, blood and terror. The abscess had to be lanced—not only by the leaders, but by simple mortals as well—a right that was granted to them very reluctantly. The brutal attacks on Dr. Zhivago (1958) soon came as a reminder that, in practice, the burning questions of the day were still taboo and that one couldn't treat them in a spirit different from that imposed by official dogma. This attitude on the part of the authorities only enhanced Pasternak's prestige among the youth, whetted their appetites to express themselves by any possible means, and reinforced their skepticism as to the possibility of doing this through official Soviet publishing houses. Hence, Sinyavsky's first work to be published abroad came out in 1959. His "fantastic stories" came out in the same way between 1959 and 1961—that is before the appearance of Solzhenitsyn's remarkable *One Day in the Life of Ivan Denisovich*, the first work on the concentration camps to appear in the Soviet Union. This subject could not be broached until eight years after Stalin's death.‡

As a result of the experiences of the last decade, Sinyavsky, like many other young Soviet intellectuals, had found Marxism increasingly irrelevant to the "existential" problems raised and brought into sharp focus by the catastrophic events of his own lifetime. Such a loss of confidence in Marxism is not incompatible, needless to say, with acceptance of, or even reverence for, the Russian Revolution of 1917, and with a generalized belief in a "Communism" loosely defined as the attainment of social and economic equality within a framework of essential and absolute moral values. Sinyavsky freely avowed his belief in an un-Marxist Communism at the trial, and particularly in his final plea when he said that he wrote from an "idealist" (in the philosophical sense) point of view. Nonacceptance of Marxism or materialism is not a crime in the Soviet Union. Belief in Marxism, or lip service to it, is incumbent only on party members. In his general philosophy Sinyavsky accepts roughly the same scale of values as Pasternak; he never concealed his attachment to these values, which was symbolized by the fact that he (with Daniel) was one of the pallbearers at Pasternak's funeral. There could have been no clearer public confession of faith.

For many Russians his name is now, indeed, linked with that of Pasternak, since it is he who wrote the long and scholarly introduction to an important edition of Pasternak's poetry which was recently

---

‡ Helène Peltier-Zamoyska, *ibid.*

published in Moscow—evidently after many delays and battles over what could or could not be included.§ Even though it does not include such a key poem as "Hamlet" from the Zhivago cycle, this volume is a great step forward over the very parsimonious selection which appeared in 1961. Sinyavsky first made his mark as a critic by reviewing the latter volume for the "liberal" literary journal Novy Mir in March, 1962. He pointed out then that the selection was biased and unrepresentative, and that individual poems had been censored: "A number of memorable verses are missing, others have been changed, in some poems the ending is missing." In the recent edition, perhaps in some measure due to Sinyavsky's efforts, much of this damage was repaired, so that, for example, the opening stanzas of Pasternak's famous poem about Blok, discreetly replaced by asterisks in the 1961 edition, have now been made available in full to Russian readers.*

Sinyavsky's interpretation of Pasternak, as expounded first in his 1962 article and at greater length in his introduction to the 1965 edition, is probably the most sophisticated to have appeared so far in any language. Both essays illuminate Pasternak's difficult poetry for the reader with unequaled scholarship and critical sensitivity. He shows us how Pasternak sought profound, though unobtrusive, poetic sermons in humble everyday activity, the humdrum and the commonplace, in nature and in all other things taken for granted by man in the heat of his "historical" pursuits. It is interesting to note that Sinyavsky found that Pasternak was in many ways a kindred spirit to the late Robert Frost, on whom he wrote a perceptive essay in Novy Mir for January, 1964.

Sinyavsky outraged the "influential yes-men" still in control of Russia's literary establishment (who perhaps inspired the trial, and

---

§ Boris Pasternak, Stikhotvoreniya i poemy, Vstupitelnaya statya A. D. Sinyavskogo, Moscow-Leningrad, 1965.
* The first of these stanzas is:

> Only the influential yes-men know
> Whom critics are to propagate
> With praise, or criticize
> And liquidate.
> (translated by Michael Harari)

whose spirit certainly dominated it), not only by his subtle advocacy of Pasternakian values, but also by occasionally taking issue with these natural enemies of them. For example, he reviewed in the December, 1964, issue of *Novy Mir* an almost unbelievably scurrilous novel, *The Blight* by Ivan Shevtsov, lampooning Soviet artists along the lines of Khrushchev's notorious outburst during his visit to an art exhibition in Moscow in 1962. The novel, which appeared somewhat belatedly around the time of Khrushchev's fall in November, 1963, was intended to whip up popular feeling against Soviet artists who had deviated from "socialist realism."

At first sight Sinyavsky's review of this particularly grotesque neo-Stalinist fantasy appeared to be just another blow in the running fight that has now been going on for several years between the "liberals" and "conservatives" (or whatever one chooses to call them) in the Soviet press. This factional struggle has been legitimized by the "cultural" powers-that-be and, apart from the brief interlude at the end of 1962 and the beginning of 1963 when Khrushchev temporarily upset the balance between the two sides, the polemic has gone on as monotonously as a ping-pong match. The "liberals" have generally played the game by advancing rational arguments. In his review of Shevtsov's novel, Sinyavsky implied that the "liberals" are in fact dealing with minds impervious to reason. He suggested that instead of polemicizing with them, it would be better to exercise charity: "Perhaps, rather than attack Ivan Shevtsov, it would be better to pity him, to sympathize with him. . . ." In his last "legally" published article, a review in *Novy Mir* for March, 1965, of a collection of poetry by E. Dolmatovsky, Sinyavsky examines more in sorrow than in anger the work of this representative of the conservative camp, and takes it as the starting point for a witty and enlightening disquisition on the nature of poetic mediocrity in general.

In his fiction and essays published abroad—*On Socialist Realism, The Trial Begins, Fantastic Stories, The Makepeace Experiment (Lyubimov), Unguarded Thoughts* and "Pkhentz"—he took a stage further some of the ideas implicit in the work published under his real name in the Soviet Union. He had demonstrated his interest in modern art in a study of Picasso (published in Moscow in collaboration with I. Golomshtok),§ and there is often in his fiction a conscious application of the surrealist technique to literature.† As regards their content, there is much in his work which would shock the susceptibilities of "right-minded" Soviet citizens. His language is unconventional, and he pokes fun at such august institutions as the secret police. (Often, however, his portraits of individual policemen are remarkably sympathetic—as, for example, Colonel Tarasov in "The Icicle.") But there is nothing seditious in any reasonably defined legal sense.

Only three of his works actually figured in the indictment—*The Trial Begins, On Socialist Realism* and *Lyubimov*. His *Fantastic Stories,* his collection of aphorisms, *Unguarded Thoughts,*‡ and an unfinished "Essay in Self-Analysis," confiscated during the search of the apartment, but not available in the West, and the short story "Pkhentz" (which was published in the West in Polish and English) were mentioned at the trial, and sometimes quoted in evidence both by the prosecution and the defendant, but, as was stressed by the judge on one occasion (see page 110), these formed no part of the charges. To take the first three works in chronological order of their appearance in the West:

On Socialist Realism (1959) is an attempt to study this official Soviet literary doctrine in its relation to the past and present of Russian literature. It also offers something in the nature of the author's own literary credo, of which his subsequent short novels and stories are a kind of illustration. "Socialist realism" has been the obligatory literary doctrine in the Soviet Union since the first Congress of Soviet Writers in 1934, when acceptance of it was declared to be binding on all Soviet writers, and indeed a condition for membership of the Union of Soviet Writers. Briefly defined, it is an attempt to apply the artistic and literary style of nineteenth-century Russian realism as a means of propagating the ideology and the political and social aims of the ruling party of the Soviet Union.

---

§ According to a report from Moscow in the New York Times of May 4, 1966 (p. 10), Golomshtok received a "suspended sentence" of six months for his refusal to give compromising evidence in court. See page 148.

† The best example is his story "The Icicle" in *Fantastic Stories,* New York, Pantheon Books, 1963.

‡ Published in the West first in Polish in *Kultura,* and then, under the title "Thought Unaware," in the New Leader, July 19, 1965.

The main point of Sinyavsky's article is that the nineteenth-century realist method is ill-adapted to the expression of the purposeful march of society toward a given social and political goal. He points out that Soviet society is a teleological one (in the indictment, as Sinyavsky indicated, this word was confused with "theological"). Teleological (from the Greek "*telos*"—"purpose") implies conscious striving on the part of individuals, or society as a whole, toward a certain aim. Sinyavsky does not quarrel with the aim in question, namely, that of the creation of a Communist society. Neither in his essay nor in his testimony during the trial does he cast doubt on the goal itself, although he points out that it is a matter of historical record that the methods employed in its pursuit have rarely done credit to it.[§]

What troubles him most, however—and this is the main point of the essay—is that if one has a Purpose and one lives in a teleological society, in which art and literature are necessarily the handmaidens of the Purpose, then it is important that adequate forms should be found to express the Purpose, whatever it may be. Literature in nineteenth-century Russia was a literature of skepticism, doubt and irony, and the great realist writers (whom the socialist realists of the Soviet Union are supposed to emulate) had no sense of purpose, but were engaged rather in an anguished quest for the answer to apparently unanswerable ontological questions—not to speak of the more mundane social and political ones. They were self-doubting, inward-looking, and, insofar as the society in which they lived was concerned, their irony and skepticism were corrosive. How, Sinyavsky asks, can one use this style in the literature and art of a society which supposedly knows exactly where it is going, where there is no room for introspection, and the sort of speculation which might raise metaphysical questions as to what happens after the Great Purpose has been achieved? In other words, there is a contradiction between the method which Soviet artists and writers are obliged to employ and the "message" they are supposed to put into their work.

Sinyavsky says that art does not necessarily suffer from being harnessed to a Purpose. What is intolerable, however, and indeed

---

[§] E.g.: "So that not one drop of blood should be shed, we killed and killed and killed." This particular phrase, together with a number of others, was repeated obsessively by the prosecution, as "proof" of Sinyavsky's "anti-Soviet" attitude.

fatal, to art is eclecticism, or the failure to find a means which gives adequate expression to the end in view. He voices his regret that the Soviet period, because of the artificial imposition in the 1930's of a derivative realist style, has not found appropriate aesthetic expression —in a word, it has not created its own style; it has only, as he says, succeeded in mixing a "monstrous salad" in which content is grotesquely out of keeping with artistic form:

The characters [of Soviet fiction] torment themselves almost à la Dostoyevsky, grow sad almost à la Chekhov, arrange their family life almost à la Tolstoy, and yet at the same time vie with each other in shouting platitudes from the Soviet press: "Long live peace in the whole world" and "Down with the warmongers." This is neither classicism nor realism. It is semi-classical demi-art of a none too socialist demi-realism.

He concludes that, if the art of the socialist era must be derivative, then it would be better to go back to the eighteenth century and imitate the classical style of Derzhavin (the Russian poet laureate of his day), who could write about the Russia of his time in an exalted and self-confident manner which was foreign to the skeptical and ironical nineteenth-century realists, and who was not concerned with the more unpredictable aspects of human behavior. As Sinyavsky says, the verse of Derzhavin, when he writes in praise of Catherine the Great, has a contemporary ring:

Like the socialist system, so eighteenth-century Russia conceived of itself as the Center of Creation. Inspired by the plenitude of its virtues— "self-created and self-fortified"—it proclaimed itself as an example to all peoples and all eras. Its religious self-conceit was so strong that it did not even admit the possibility of the existence of other standards and ideals.

Sinyavsky feels that the Soviet era was given adequate expression by a return to the tradition of Mayakovsky (who committed suicide in 1930), whom he regards as the only Soviet poet to have created a style in tune with the era. Finally, as for his own credo, Sinyavsky says he can only put his hope in

a phantasmagoric art with hypotheses instead of a Purpose, an art in which the grotesque will replace realistic descriptions of ordinary life. Such an art would correspond best to the spirit of our time. May the fantastic imagery of Hoffmann and Dostoyevsky, of Goya, Chagall, and Mayakovsky (the most socialist realist of all), and many other realists and nonrealists teach us how to be truthful with the aid of the absurd and the fantastic. Having lost our faith, we have not lost our enthusiasm about the metamorphoses of God that take place before our very eyes, the miraculous transformations of His entrails and His cerebral convolutions. We don't know where to go; but, realizing that there is nothing to be done about it, we start to think, to set riddles, to make assumptions. May we thus invent something marvelous? Perhaps. But it will no longer be socialist realism.*

The Trial Begins is his first attempt at a "phantasmagoria." Actually, in order to achieve an effect of hallucinatory unreality, all he had to do—and indeed all he does—is to describe in a quite realistic vein the events and atmosphere of the last years of Stalin's life. The story is set in the period of the "Doctors' Plot" (1952), which was the nightmarish culmination of that time when, as Khrushchev has told us, Russia was ruled by a man suffering from acute paranoia. Most of the characters in the novel are highly unpleasant, such as the anti-Semitic Public Prosecutor Globov who is rigging up a case, concerning an alleged abortion, against a Jewish doctor, Rabinovich. Equally nasty is the cynical lawyer Karlinsky, who indulges in nauseating fantasies which the prosecution, during the trial, quoted in evidence against Sinyavsky, attributing Karlinsky's sentiments to him. In particular, the following passage was constantly quoted:

Karlinsky suddenly felt sick. To take his mind off his stomach he thought about Malthus. In every theory there was some truth: how could you let the human race increase and multiply *ad infinitum?* One day the Antarctic would be populated, so would the Sahara, but what then? Some universal remedy would have to be discovered. Now, it was well known that the human embryo, at some early stage of its development, had much in common with the fish. Why should the country waste its potential fish reserves? In the Splendid Future, the fishlike embryos would be turned to good account. Carefully extracted from the womb, they would be conditioned to a separate existence in pools set aside especially for them. There they would grow scales and fins under the supervision of the State, in charge of some colleague of Globov's. And next door to the abortarium there would be a canning factory producing tinned fish in vast quantities. Some embryos would be turned into sardines, others into sprats—all according to their ethnic origin. And it would all be strictly in keeping with

---

* *On Socialist Realism*, New York, Pantheon Books, 1961, pp. 94–95.

Marxism. Admittedly, it meant a return to cannibalism, not, however, to the consumption of our fellow men as practiced by primitive tribes—but to cannibalism on a more refined and higher level. Spiral development.[†]

Squalid daydreams such as these, as Sinyavsky contended in his replies to the prosecution, were part of the characterization of the sort of cynical careerists who had their heyday in the last years of Stalin's life. It should be quite clear to any unprejudiced reader, Sinyavsky wearily insisted, that the author's own attitude to these creatures of his own imagination is far from sympathetic.

Sinyavsky's third novel, *Lyubimov* (translated into English as *The Makepeace Experiment*[‡]), is his best work, in which he shows himself to be a Russian writer of the first rank. If his earlier works demonstrated talent and a gift for imaginative experiment quite new to Soviet prose, they also appeared to be a little contrived, and perhaps too self-conscious in their concern to illustrate the literary formula suggested at the end of *On Socialist Realism*. *Lyubimov* is a much profounder work, in which irony, fantasy and wit are employed, not for their own sake (as one finds in some of the *Fantastic Stories*), but as a means of taking the reader into serious realms of speculation.

The town of Lyubimov is a dreamy backwater perhaps modeled on a real town known to the author. It could well be the one mentioned by Michel Aucouturier in the article cited above:

Andrei Sinyavsky made frequent trips to the North of Russia where popular folklore and tradition are better preserved: he brought back wonderful photographs, icons and ancient manuscripts. One day he took me to Pereslavl, a small town off the tourist beat with an ancient monastery and several churches built between the 13th and the 16th centuries. He wanted to show me and let me appreciate, as a foreigner, this little-known gem of the Russian land.[§]

Sinyavsky pointed out at the trial that the fictitious name of the town itself is derived from the word "beloved" and that his attitude to it and its inhabitants is wholly benevolent. The prosecution alleged that he was satirizing and slandering the U.S.S.R. and its

---

[†] *The Trial Begins*, New York, Pantheon Books, 1960, p. 32.
[‡] *The Makepeace Experiment*, New York, Pantheon Books, 1965.
[§] *Tribune de Genève*, February 8, 1966.

people, much as Saltykov-Shchedrin had satirized Czarist Russia in his *History of the Town of Glupov* (1869–70). It is true that there is an external resemblance of plot, but the tone is very different. As Sinyavsky told the court, the very name "Glupov" (derived from the word for "stupid") was itself an indication of the difference between the two works. Saltykov's satire is a ruthless history of Russia up to the time of Nicholas I, in which both rulers and ruled appear in a most unfavorable light. (The work was nevertheless passed for publication by the Czarist censorship.) Sinyavsky hotly denied, under cross-examination, that he was satirizing the Soviet Union through this portrait of a small town. An impartial reader can see that this is indeed so, and that the work has a significance that goes beyond the bounds of the time and place in which it is set. It is an Aesopian comment on the meaning of history in general, and it echoes *Doctor Zhivago*, in suggesting that, while man is a captive of his age, both he and his history are transcended by eternity.

In *Lyubimov* Sinyavsky uses a favorite device which involves the acquisition by somebody of supernatural powers (as in "The Icicle," one of the *Fantastic Stories*, where the hero, to his embarrassment, suddenly finds himself endowed with the gift of clairvoyance and the ability to read people's minds). Lenya Tikhomirov (Lenny Makepeace in the English translation) starts life as a humble bicycle mechanic, but owing to certain peculiar circumstances he acquires mesmeric powers which enable him to impose his will on others. He takes over from the local Soviet authorities during May Day celebrations, proclaims himself the new ruler, removes Lyubimov (by surrounding it with a kind of psychic curtain which makes it invisible to the outside world) from the surrounding space-time continuum of Soviet reality, and sets up his own regime in the "free town" of Lyubimov. His hold over the population—and hence their faith in him—is based on a promise of unlimited material well-being and, by virtue of his extraordinary powers, he is able to suggest to people that they are already enjoying the fruits of unheard-of prosperity—water tastes like champagne, and inedible red peppers are turned into delicious sausages—only the dogs are not deceived.

Insofar as this is "political," it is making fun of political demagogy in general and, as Sinyavsky said at the trial, of "voluntarism" in particular. "Voluntarism" is one of the main faults of which the present Soviet leaders accuse their predecessor, Khrushchev. It may be defined as the delusion that objective problems can be solved by the mere application of will power. For example, Khrushchev believed that by urging the peasants to grow corn—even beyond the Arctic Circle—the agricultural crisis in the Soviet Union could be solved. Hence, if one is to read a direct and contemporary political meaning into the scene of Tikhomirov miraculously feeding the masses, then it does not go beyond what the present Soviet leaders now say about Khrushchev. But since the conversion of water into champagne occurs on the occasion of Tikhomirov's marriage, one could equally well interpret the episode as a parody of the wedding feast at Cana.

This is of some significance, since there is evidence in Sinyavsky-Tertz's work—particularly at the end of *Lyubimov* and in *Unguarded Thoughts*—that, apart from having some personal religious creed (no doubt rooted, like Pasternak's, in Russian Orthodoxy), he certainly has respect for religious belief and for the Christian faith. Yet he nevertheless does not hesitate to introduce images or scenes which, theoretically, would appear blasphemous to many Christians (a similar example is the episode involving a monk and necrophilia in "The Icicle"—see page 117). At his trial Sinyavsky countered the prosecution's allegations that he had uttered blasphemies about Lenin by saying that things said about Lenin by his characters, or the mention of Lenin's name in certain contexts, could not be taken as evidence of his lack of piety. The sincerity of this assurance—though he did not himself make the point—is borne out by the fact that he also writes in a "sacrilegious" tone of matters with regard to which there can be doubt of his respect.

Unlike Sinyavsky, Daniel—until his trial—had scarcely any public reputation in the Soviet Union. He was known only as a verse translator (mainly from Yiddish, Caucasian and Slavic languages), and, as we see from the transcript (page 47), his one attempt to publish an original work "legally" in the Soviet Union was not successful. The other basic facts of his earlier career are given in the transcript (see, notably, page 78). As to his character and personality, we have the testimony of Aucouturier in the article cited above:

Yuli Daniel is a cheerful, open-hearted person, full of verve and generosity. I remember visiting him once when I had just bought in a second-hand bookstore the almost complete works of Alexander Blok [the famous Russian poet]—there was just one volume missing. Without hesitation, Daniel took down the missing volume from the complete set in his bookcase, wrote a dedication in it and gave it to me.

Under the pseudonym "Nikolai Arzhak" he published abroad four stories: *This Is Moscow Speaking,* "Hands," "The Man from Minap" and "Atonement." (Only the first two of these have appeared in English.) All four of them were freely used in the prosecution's case against him.

Daniel is a very different writer from Sinyavsky, although he betrays his influence, particularly in his first work, *This Is Moscow Speaking,* and in the comic extravaganza, "The Man from Minap," which could serve as illustrations of Sinyavsky's literary technique of "fantastic realism." In his other works Daniel writes in a more straightforwardly realist manner, which, from the point of view of style, puts him on a par rather with the "new wave" young Soviet fiction writers. At certain junctures in the last few years, when the atmosphere has been favorable to the liberal writers (e.g., in the summer and autumn of 1962, when Solzhenitsyn's *One Day in the Life of Ivan Denisovich,* with its description of life in the concentration camps under Stalin, was allowed to appear in print), there would have been nothing particularly startling about the publication in a Soviet literary magazine of "Hands" and "Atonement." The latter would probably have been cut, but it is certainly no more outspoken, from a political point of view, than such "legally" published works as Stadnyuk's *People Are Not Angels,* with its horrifying description of the famine in the early thirties and police brutalities against innocent people, or Bondaryov's *Silence,* with its frank revelations about false denunciations and police frame-ups in the Stalin era.

On the whole, Daniel-Arzhak writes in a more somber vein than Sinyavsky, and his satire has a bitter edge which is absent from the more serene Sinyavsky-Tertz; the description of the latter by the unknown author of the transcript as "a good-natured goblin" fits the style of his work as well as it does his appearance.

The prosecution's prime exhibit against Daniel-Arzhak was his story, *This Is Moscow Speaking*, which is a macabre fable very much along the lines of the Italian film, *The Tenth Victim*. As Daniel told the court, he invented the situation described in the story, partly as a comment on what he felt was a resurgent "cult of personality" (this time of Khrushchev) and partly as a speculation in literary form on how people might behave if they were officially allowed to kill by decree of the government. The story opens with an announcement over Moscow Radio that the Presidium of the Supreme Soviet has decreed that August 10, 1960 (the story was written, according to Daniel's testimony at the trial, in 1960–61) would be declared "Public Murder Day." On this day, all citizens of the Soviet Union above the age of sixteen would have the right between the hours of 6 A.M. and midnight to kill any other citizen, with the exception of certain categories, such as members of the police and armed forces, etc., listed in an annex to the decree. Reactions range from initial incredulity to apathy. Somebody suggests that it would all be explained, as everything is always explained, in an editorial in *Izvestia* (the prosecution was to make much of this particular detail at the trial). When the day actually comes, the response of the population is somewhat languid—as it has tended to be in actual fact to government appeals and campaigns. There is some slaughter of Armenians by Georgians—and vice versa—in the Caucasus; the Day is bungled by local party officials in the Ukraine; there are only sporadic incidents in Moscow; and in the Baltic States nobody at all is murdered. In a circular letter summing up the results of "Public Murder Day," and drawing lessons from it, the Central Committee of the party deplores the fiasco in the Ukraine, and condemns as sabotage the total lack of response in the Baltic States.

Needless to say, this is sharp political satire, and Daniel at the trial did not attempt to play down the political aspects of the story. Both he and Sinyavsky, however, emphasized that the story as a whole is very much against violence. As Sinyavsky said in his final plea: "It is one long cry of 'Thou shalt not kill!' " There is one crucial passage in this work which was quoted more often at the trial than almost any other. It was to a large extent the cornerstone of the prosecution's case that the works of the two men—who were held co-responsible for their "dangerous thoughts"—were subversive and seditious in a real sense. The hero of the story is a war veteran (like Daniel himself). Shortly before "Public Murder Day" he toys in his imagination with the idea of assassinating those who bear responsibility for the horrors of 1937 (the year of Stalin's great purge) and the insanity of the postwar period—those who, as he says, still sit in judgment and hold sway, i.e., the Soviet Party and Government leaders. This thought, however, is immediately followed by a reminiscence of the war, of what happens when people are blown to pieces by grenades, mowed down by machine-gun fire and crushed by heavy trucks. This sudden recollection is clearly based on the wartime experiences of Daniel himself, who was severely wounded in action. The passage ends ambiguously, but there is no doubt, given the general implications of the story as a whole, that the sudden evocation of the horrors of war is intended by the author to express his hero's (and his own) revulsion against the idea of using terroristic methods or assassination to achieve political ends. Since the passage in question was often mentioned at the trial, it is as well to give it here in a fuller context— the prosecution always attempted to narrow down the context to make it as damaging as possible to the defendants (see page 65).

The passage is in the form of an inner monologue by the hero:

Hatred gives one the right to murder. Out of hatred I might myself . . . mightn't I? Well, obviously, I might. I might definitely. Whom do I hate? Whom have I hated in my life? Well, schooldays don't count, but what about when I was grown up? There was college—I hated one of the teachers who purposely failed me four times in my exams. Well, to hell with him, that was a long time ago. The bosses of different departments in which I've worked. Yes, they were crooks. They certainly made my blood boil. They should be punched in the face, the bastards. Who else? The writer K., who writes in the spirit of the Black Hundreds. [A reference to Vsevolod Kochetov, editor of the literary monthly *Oktyabr* and the *bête noire* of all the liberal elements in Soviet society. The Black Hundreds were ultra-chauvinist, anti-Semitic and anti-intellectual gangs who organized pogroms in the early part of the century.] Yes, I remember I used to say I'd kill him if I knew that nothing would happen to me. That swine deserves to be taught a lesson! So that he'll never take up the pen again . . . And what about the fat-faced masters of our destiny, our leaders and teachers, true sons of the people, receiving messages of congratulations from collective farmers of the Ryazan region, from metal workers in the Krivoi Rog region [a reference to the stereotyped letters from "workers and peasants" which—less now than under Stalin and Khrushchev—are printed in *Pravda* and *Izvestia* on important anniversaries, etc.], from the Emperor of Ethiopia, from a teachers' congress, from the President of the United States, from attendants in public toilets. The best friends of Soviet gymnasts, writers, textile workers, color-blind persons, and madmen? What should be done with them? Should they be forgiven? What about 1937? What about the postwar insanity when the country was possessed of the devil, thrashed about in the throes of its fit, became hysterical and began devouring itself? Do they think that once they have desecrated the grave of the Mustached One [Stalin—the desecration of his grave is to be understood figuratively, since the story was written before Stalin's body was removed from the Lenin Mausoleum], that's all that's required of them? No, no, no, they must be treated differently. Do you remember still how to do it? The fuse . . . pull out the pin . . . throw. Lie flat on the ground. Lie down! Now it's exploded and you run forward, firing from the hip—one round after another, and another and another! . . . They're lying over there, cut to shreds and riddled with bullets. The ground is all wet so that one's feet slip. Who's this? He's crawling along, dragging his guts along the plaster-strewn floor behind him. And who's this man, bedecked with medals, who accompanies the Chief on his journeys? Why is he so thin? Why is he wearing a padded coat? I saw him once before, crawling along a grade, spilling his blue and red stomach into the dust. And these people? I've seen them before! Only then they had belts with the inscription *Gott mit uns* on the buckles, caps with Red Stars, knee boots; Russians, Germans, Georgians, Rumanians, Jews, Hungarians, tunics, placards, medical corps, spades; over the body runs a Studebaker, two Studebakers, eight Studebakers, forty Studebakers, and you lie there flattened like a frog; we've had all that before! I got up from the bed, went to the window, and wiped my sweaty forehead with the curtain.*

"Hands" is, to my mind, the most successful of Daniel-Arzhak's works. It is a brilliant short story which, in its choice of subject and spareness of style, could have come from the pen of Isaac Babel. At the trial Daniel said it was based on a real episode which had been told him by an old member of the Cheka. The hero of the story explains to a chance acquaintance why his hands shake uncontrollably. It is not because of drink, but because of an experience he had as a young man when he served in the Cheka and was a member

---

* Quoted from *Dissonant Voices in Soviet Literature*, New York, Harper & Row, 1964, pp. 278–279. The translation has been slightly changed by me.

of a punitive unit whose task was the liquidation of counterrevolutionaries. One day he had to shoot a batch of priests, but as a practical joke his comrades had loaded his gun with blanks. When he shoots at the first priest, the priest advances on him with arms outstretched, apparently immune to bullets. The narrator was overcome with a kind of superstitious horror which shattered his nerves, so that he had to leave the service, and forever afterward his hands shook. As Daniel said in his final plea, this episode is paralleled almost exactly by a very similar one in Sholokhov's *And Quiet Flows the Don,* for which in 1965 the author received the Nobel Prize with the official blessing of the Soviet Government.

"The Man from Minap" is Daniel's weakest work and he himself said about it at the trial: "I don't like this story; it is poorly written, crude and in bad taste, but it contains nothing anti-Soviet." The idea itself is a good one, but it's the sort of bawdy joke which needs to be treated with Gallic delicacy if it is to succeed artistically. It is about a man who is able to predetermine the sex of the children he sires, by thinking during intercourse of Karl Marx if he wishes the child to be a boy, or of Klara Zetkin† if he wants a girl. This extraordinary faculty becomes known to the Soviet authorities, and is exploited by them in various comic ways. It goes without saying that the introduction of the "sacred" name of Karl Max in this context did not appeal to the sense of humor of the judge and the prosecutor, or to most members of the hand-picked audience in the courtroom.

"Atonement" is set in the year 1963 and is a harrowing tale of somebody (in this instance, too, Daniel claimed at the trial that the story was based on a real case involving a personal acquaintance of his) who is falsely suspected of having denounced people under Stalin. He becomes a social outcast, and his agony is increased by the fact that the suspicion is shared by the supposed victim of his denunciation, who has returned from a long period of imprisonment. He becomes a focus for the generalized guilt feelings among people in his milieu (mainly that of the Moscow intelligentsia) because of their awareness of the fact, which few are willing to face, that none of them can evade moral responsibility for what went on under

---

† Klara Zetkin (1857–1933) was one of the founders of the German Communist Party and the Comintern.

Stalin. The falsely suspected hero of the story thus serves as a kind of scapegoat, and he eventually is driven insane by the ostracism of his former friends. As Daniel insisted at his trial, the main point of the story is that all members of society, individually and collectively, must accept responsibility for what is done in their name.

PRELUDE TO THE TRIAL

The two men were arrested in early September, 1965. Rumors of the arrest began to reach the West at the beginning of October, and Giancarlo Vigorelli, the Secretary-General of the European Community of Writers, first raised the question in public, in the presence of Soviet delegates, at a meeting of the organization in Rome on October 9. For the next two months, numerous anxious inquiries, both public and private, from leading Western writers and organizations were addressed to Kosygin, Surkov (Secretary of the Union of Soviet Writers) and others. They were met by silence. Only on November 22 did Surkov admit the arrests at a press conference in Paris, at the same time giving a solemn assurance that "legality" would be observed.[‡]

The Soviet public had to wait another two months before they were first officially apprised of the arrest of Sinyavsky and Daniel. On January 13, 1966, *Izvestia* published an article about the case by Dmitri Eremin. Entitled "The Turncoats," this article set the tone for the pretrial campaign, and for the trial itself. To call it prejudicial would be an understatement. Eremin expressed regret that certain (unnamed) Western intellectuals should have protested the arrest of Sinyavsky and Daniel, whom he depicted as double-faced agents of Western anti-Soviet propaganda. Behind a façade of legitimate open activity, he declared, they had hidden "hatred for our system, vile mockery of everything dear to our Motherland and people." This amounts to an accusation of sacrilege. "Double-dealing" or "two-facedness" is not covered by the Soviet Criminal Code. There is no specific ban on the use of pseudonyms, publishing abroad, or writing one thing under one name and something else under another.

---

‡ See reports in *Humanité* and *Figaro* of November 24, 1965.

Sacrilege, however, can at a pinch be accommodated under Article 70 of the Criminal Code, which reads:

Agitation or propaganda carried out with the purpose of subverting or weakening the Soviet regime or in order to commit particularly dangerous crimes against the state, the dissemination for the said purposes of slanderous inventions defamatory to the Soviet political and social system, as well as the dissemination or production or harboring for the said purposes of literature of similar content, are punishable by imprisonment for a period of from six months to seven years and with exile from two to five years, or without exile, or by exile of from two to five years.§

Clearly, everything hinges here on proof of *intent*. Eremin and subsequently the prosecution at the trial based their case on the allegation that the defendants' work was consciously intended by the authors to subvert and weaken the Soviet system. In other words, their literary work had to be equated with seditious leaflets or proclamations, even though their work was not available to the Soviet public, not distributed inside the country and could hence scarcely be shown to subvert an audience it did not reach. To prove that the work of Sinyavsky and Daniel was sacrilegious in content and seditious in intent, Eremin and the prosecution constantly quoted passages out of context.†

"The first thing you feel in reading their works," wrote Eremin, "is disgust. It is revolting to quote the vulgar things with which the pages of their works abound. With morbid prurience, both of them delve into sexual and psychopathological 'problems.' Both of them present a picture of total moral degradation. . . . Here is a typical example from the work of Daniel-Arzhak:

You see women walking about the streets, looking like eunuchs—waddling like pregnant dachshunds or as scrawny as ostriches, with swollen bodies, varicose veins, wadded breasts or tight stays hidden under their clothes."

---

§ See *Ugolovny Kodeks R.S.F.S.R.*, Moscow, 1962, pp. 47–48. "Exile" (*ssylka*) means enforced residence in a designated area after the completion of the term of imprisonment, or as an alternative to it. Sinyavsky was given the maximum term of imprisonment provided for under Article 70, but neither he nor Daniel was given the "exile" also demanded by the prosecutor.

† This and the other procedures employed by the prosecution to make their case are well described by Daniel in his final plea.

One would search the works of Daniel-Arzhak in vain for this passage, since it actually appears in *The Trial Begins* by Sinyavsky-Tertz.* It is in the context, not so much as hinted at by Eremin, of the vixenish heroine of the story examining herself in front of the mirror and mentally comparing herself with other women of her age.

Eremin goes on: "They like nothing in our country, nothing is holy for them . . . in her multinational culture, and they are ready to curse and run down everything dear to Soviet man, both in the past and the present. Imagine what they write about Anton Pavlovich Chekhov: 'That Chekhov ought to be taken by his wretched tubercular beard and have his nose stuck in his consumptive spittle.' "

This is quoted from Tertz's *Fantastic Stories*† and is part of the ravings of a semidemented graphomaniac who is jealous of the classics.

Sinyavsky is further alleged to have slandered the Soviet Army, but there are no quotations to back up this particular contention. Finally, and *horribile dictu*, Eremin wrote that there were things said about Lenin which were so terrible that he couldn't possibly reproduce them. The most "terrible" things about Lenin in those works of Sinyavsky available in the West are a passage in *On Socialist Realism* in which he says that it is impossible to replace the cult of Stalin with a cult of Lenin because "Lenin is too much like an ordinary man and his image is too realistic: small, bald, dressed in civilian clothes,"‡ and a reference in *The Makepeace Experiment*, not in the least bit unkindly to Lenin, to the widely held belief that in the last days of his life "he bayed at the moon, our Ilyich, knowing that he was soon to die." (See transcript, pages 101–2 and 108, for a discussion of Sinyavsky's treatment of Lenin.)

With such out-of-context quotations, Eremin tried to make a case for the moral delinquency, not covered by criminal law, of the two writers. To make a case for criminal delinquency, Eremin asserted

---

* *The Trial Begins*, pp. 26–27.
† *Fantastic Stories*, p. 210.
‡ *On Socialist Realism*, p. 92.

that Sinyavsky and Daniel, by their works, had engaged in psychological warfare against the Soviet Union, helping those who stir up the flames of international tension. They were, hence, not just morally depraved, but agents of international imperialism, to whom, he said—anticipating the court's findings—"no leniency can be shown."

Eremin's article—if that had been part of its intention—did nothing to allay disquiet in the West. It seemed almost incredible that the Soviet authorities would proceed to the trial of a case which had now been so hopelessly prejudiced. There were indeed signs of hesitation in the face of mounting protests.* *Pravda*, the party newspaper, said nothing. *Izvestia* tried to run a follow-up campaign of "massive indignation" in response to Eremin's article, but it could produce only three or four rather unconvincing expressions of outrage from provincial intellectuals. The classical orchestration was lacking.

On January 22, 1966, the *Literary Gazette* published a slightly more sophisticated, but no less prejudicial attack on the two writers by a literary critic, Zoya Kedrina (who was also to figure at the trial as a so-called public accuser, i.e., as a kind of "expert" witness for the prosecution). Like Eremin, she buttressed her argument with out-of-context quotations, and made great play with the passage from Daniel-Arzhak (pages 17–18) which she construed as an unambiguous call for terrorism against the Soviet regime, calling Daniel-Arzhak a Fascist who advocates a "program of bloody wars and *putsches*, a program of liberation from Communism by terror."

The rest of Kedrina's article was concerned not with proving moral or criminal delinquency (except for a new charge of anti-Semitism against Sinyavsky—this was backed up by attributing to the author anti-Semitic remarks put into the mouths of anti-Semitic characters), but with demonstrating that the two authors were no good anyway. Their work was described as primitive and boring, and Sinyavsky in particular was dismissed as a fourth-rate hack whose work was heavily influenced by certain prerevolutionary pornographers. She also taxed

---

* One of the most powerful appeals to the Soviet Government was a letter, signed by 49 of the leading writers of Europe and the United States, in the London *Times* of January 31, 1966.

him with plagiarizing Kafka, Saltykov and Sologub. There is no need to take issue with Madame Kedrina on the literary merit of Tertz, but it should be noted that she attacked him in a way which was clearly calculated to alienate the sympathies of Soviet writers who know Sinyavsky as a critic of distinction but have no access to his works published abroad under his pseudonym. The language of her attack was offensive and she described both writers as heirs of Smerdyakov, one of the vilest creations in all of Russian literature.

THE TRIAL

The trial opened on February 10, 1966, and went on for four days. There were several unusual features about it and in one respect it was unprecedented, namely, it was the first time in the history of the Soviet Union that writers had been put on trial *for what they had written.* Many Soviet writers have been imprisoned, banished, executed or driven into silence, but never before after a trial in which the principal evidence against them was their literary work. The poet Gumilev was shot for allegedly taking part in a counterrevolutionary conspiracy. Boris Pilnyak was denounced for publishing a work abroad in the late twenties, but he was not tried, and when he eventually was arrested and disappeared in 1937, no charges were ever specified. Isaac Babel was arrested in 1939, not apparently for anything he had written—he had published scarcely anything for a number of years—but for presumably nonliterary reasons which were never revealed. Akhmatova and Zoshchenko were denounced in 1946 for writing in an anti-Soviet spirit, but they were never tried or subjected to any administrative sanctions apart from expulsion from the Union of Soviet Writers. Boris Pasternak, who published *Doctor Zhivago* abroad as a deliberate act of defiance, was attacked and hounded, and called a pig and a renegade, but he was not the object of criminal proceedings. In the most recent case of the trial of a writer, that of Joseph Brodsky in Leningrad, the charge was "parasitism" and the actual content of Brodsky's work was not used in evidence against him.

The second unusual feature of the trial was that the accused did not plead guilty. This evidently took the prosecution by surprise and may partly explain the very maladroit handling of the trial. According to Tass,§ the two had admitted their guilt during the preliminary investigation, which lasted five months, but they withdrew this confession of guilt in court. Of course this would never have happened under Stalin, since people were never brought to open trial until the authorities were absolutely certain that there would be no departure from the script prepared in advance. It has been suggested that the plea of "not guilty" on this occasion is evidence of a general improvement in the administration of Soviet justice. One could find better instances to illustrate an improvement in the Soviet judicial system, but this is a special case and proves nothing, except that Sinyavsky and Daniel perhaps hoodwinked their interrogators in order to get as open a trial as possible.

The best that can be said of the proceedings is that—no doubt because of their unexpected defiance—the accused were able to have their say and defend themselves with arguments of their own choosing. In purely technical terms, however, the arrangements for the trial were grossly unfair to them: none of the written statements for the defense, including one by the well-known writer Konstantin Paustovsky, were admitted in evidence, and only one defense witness was allowed. The prosecution subpoenaed a number of friends and acquaintances of the two men. All of them had clearly been interrogated before the trial and were expected to play their part by giving incriminating evidence in court. To their credit they said no more than could not be denied, and behaved in a way which was entirely to the advantage of the defendants. Even the prosecution's two star witnesses, Remezov and Khmelnitsky, who had turned state's evidence, were rather unhelpful. However cooperative they may have been before the trial, they were clearly not happy about playing the roles assigned to them in court. It is a tribute to the growing strength of liberal opinion in the Soviet Union that they were more afraid of public contempt than of possible reprisals for not playing the parts expected of them.

The Soviet press is unaccustomed to reporting trials at which the defendants plead "not guilty," and in which there is something

---

§ See *Pravda*, February 11, 1966.

approaching an unrehearsed argument between them and the prosecution. *Pravda, Izvestia* and the *Literary Gazette* reported the trial as though it had been a judicial and moral triumph for the prosecution. The reports were written in the classical style of the Russian satirical *feuilleton,* and the guilt of the two men was assumed before the court had reached a decision. They were spoken of with heavy sarcasm or ludicrously exaggerated indignation, and presented as cowardly felons who squirmed helplessly under the withering attack and the iron logic of the prosecution. From these heavily biased reports it was impossible for Soviet readers to gain any real idea of how the case was actually conducted. There can be few instances in modern history where a country's judicial system has been so ill served by its press.

THE AFTERMATH

There is no need to describe in detail the foreign reaction to the trial. The following will suffice as an example of comparatively restrained comment:

The Soviet press attacks on the accused before the trial assumed their guilt. So did the Tass versions of what went on in the court. Since no full and objective version of the proceedings of the trial has appeared, outside opinion cannot form a proper judgment on the proceedings. The court has found the accused guilty, but the full evidence for the prosecution and defense which led the court to this conclusion has not been made public. Justice should not only be done but should be seen to be done. Unfortunately, this cannot be said in the case of this trial.

This was said by the general secretary of the British Communist Party, John Gollan.[‡]

Even Louis Aragon, who has never before in public deviated from his unswerving loyalty to Moscow, could not contain himself, and after a consultation with the head of the French Communist Party, Waldeck-Rochet, issued a statement, which was prominently printed in *Humanité,* condemning the conduct of trial. PEN expressed "shock and horror." The Swedish Nobel Prize committee sent a

---

‡ *Daily Worker,* February 15, 1966.

telegram to President Podgorny urging clemency. There has rarely been such unanimity, cutting across political boundaries, in the expression of international concern at the outcome of a trial.

What of reaction inside the Soviet Union? Official response to foreign criticism was muted. There was no direct reference to the protests of foreign Communist and left-wing circles, but *Pravda* (February 22, 1966) spoke vaguely of "some progressive figures" in the West having been misled into thinking that Sinyavsky and Daniel had been tried for their writings, whereas in fact they had been tried for "crimes against the Soviet regime and its Revolution." They were not punished for the "critical spirit" of their writing, but for "slander." *Pravda* was also insistent that the trial had been fair, the proceedings correct and the verdict just: "The careful and objective conduct of the case was a graphic proof of the democratic nature of the Soviet regime. It would be strange if the courts were expected to display a 'liberal approach' to the enemy's ideological scouts who were caught red-handed." The use of the word "ideological" here is interesting. It is tantamount to saying that Sinyavsky and Daniel were tried and sentenced for "ideological" deviation, or, to put it in other terms, for heresy.

There is evidence that the immediate reaction to the trial even among the sort of members of the establishment who are licensed to consort with foreigners was much the same as in foreign Communist circles—one of embarrassment and regret that the matter was handled in this way. The foreign editor of the London *Sunday Times*, Frank Giles, who was in Moscow during Prime Minister Wilson's three-day visit in February, 1966, reported:

No one I talked to approved of what the two writers had done—publishing abroad under assumed names, but many of more liberal tendencies regretted the trial and the harsh sentences. It could have been handled so much better, said one middle-aged intellectual, they could have been attacked in the newspapers for their twofacedness and then left to languish in natural disgrace.§

This view probably reflected wiser counsels that must have been urged in official circles, among the judiciary and even perhaps a

---

§ *Sunday Times* (London), February 27, 1966.

section of the police, during the five months in which the matter was under preliminary investigation. More liberal officials must have pointed out that the virtually closed trial of the two men, preceded by a campaign of defamation in the press, would antagonize public opinion both at home and abroad, and once more bring Soviet justice into disrepute.

It is clear from the extraordinary documents reproduced in this volume (pages 233–301) that the two condemned writers enjoy widespread sympathy in Soviet intellectual circles. In the past, as in the case of Pasternak when he was being hounded because of his acceptance of the Nobel Prize in 1959, the only practical way in which liberal public opinion could demonstrate moral support was by keeping silence and refusing to join in officially organized campaigns of denunciation. Since then, however, the Soviet intelligentsia has become more articulate and more conscious of its strength as a body. The case of Sinyavsky and Daniel has provoked it to an unprecedented show of solidarity. Almost as important and significant as the writing and circulation of protest letters is the failure of the authorities to elicit positive support among writers and intellectuals for the action against Sinyavsky and Daniel. The first collective expression of "indignation" to appear after the trial was not impressive: six Uzbek writers sent a telegram, couched in pathetically stereotyped Russian, to Izvestia (February 23), saying among other things: "We have greeted with satisfaction the news that the traitors have been brought before a people's court and received their deserts." There was only a brief and anonymous statement of approval of the sentence, in strikingly hackneyed language, in the form of an open letter to Literary Gazette (February 22) from the "Secretariat of the Board of the Union of Writers." The only other signed collective letter which the authorities were able to organize came not from fellow writers but from a group of eighteen professors and teachers of the Philological Faculty of Moscow University, where Sinyavsky was once a student.* This, however, provoked a remarkable counterreaction by Moscow University students, who walked out of a class given by one of the professors after he admitted that he had signed the letter

---

* Literary Gazette, February 15, 1966.

voluntarily.† Very few intellectuals of note showed any inclination to risk moral isolation by joining their voices to those of Eremin, Kedrina and Arkadi Vasilyev, a little-known novelist who had also appeared at the trial as a "public accuser." The actress E. Gogoleva expressed her approval of the verdict in a letter to *Evening Moscow* (February 15), and the editor of one of the literary newspapers, K. Pozdnyayev personally endorsed it.§ One other expression of approval by a minor figure deserves to be put on record. In June, 1966, the literary journal *Oktyabr* reported that the two "renegades" had been attacked by several speakers at a plenary session of the Union of Writers of the R.S.F.S.R., and that the poet S. V. Smirnov had read out the following verses which he had composed immediately after the announcement of the verdict:

> I can positively say
> —It's plain as plain could be—
> That the notion of "Fifth Column"
> Is still topical today,
> And when such creatures stink,
> Appealing to the country's foes,
> Weaken not nor wither,
> Dear dictatorship of ours! . . .

The only writer of stature who lent his support to the authorities was Mikhail Sholokhov. At the 23rd Party Congress he attacked not only the two "renegades" but, even more savagely, those Soviet intellectuals who had tried to intervene on their behalf:

I belong to those writers who, like all Soviet people, are proud to be a small part of a great and noble nation . . . we call our Soviet Motherland our mother. We are all members of one great family. How then are we to react to the behavior of traitors who have raised their hands against everything we hold most dear? The Russian proverb notes bitterly that "there's a black sheep in every family." But there are different kinds of black sheep. I think everybody understands that there is nothing more blasphemous and disgusting than to tell lies about one's mother, to insult her, to raise one's hand against her. . . . I am ashamed for those who have told lies about our Motherland and bespattered with mud everything that is most bright for us. They are immoral. I am ashamed for

---

† *New York Times,* June 27, 1966.
§ *Literaturnaya Rossia,* February 18, 1966.

those who have tried and are trying to defend them, whatever their motive for defending them may be. I am doubly ashamed for those who offer to stand surety for the condemned renegades. Some people, using phrases about humanism, moan about the severity of the sentence. I see here delegates from the party organization of our dear Soviet Army. What would they have done if traitors had appeared in one of their units? Nobody knows better than our soldiers that humanism is not slobbering softheartedness. . . . If these scoundrels with their black consciences had been caught in the memorable twenties, when people were tried not on the basis of closely defined articles of the Criminal Code, but "in accordance with revolutionary justice," then, my goodness, they would have got something quite different, these turncoats! But now, if you please, people talk about the sentence being too harsh.*

Lidia Chukovskaya points out in her reply to this speech (see page 286) that by expressing himself in these terms Sholokhov was not only setting himself apart from the majority of Soviet writers, but also deliberately flouting the best traditions of Russian literature.

What was tragic about this trial is not only that the two men were tried and sentenced for heresy, sacrilege and blasphemy, but that the trend toward an improvement in the administration of justice, the frequently expressed desire to do away with "distortions of justice" as part of Stalin's legacy—all this has received a severe setback. Sinyavsky's and Daniel's trial could have been a test case to show that "socialist legality" had really been established, that the earnest debate among Soviet jurists in recent years about the need to see that due legal procedures were observed really counted for something. Once, however, these good intentions were put to the test in a political trial, we find that, just as in Stalin's time, reason of state prevailed over the rule of law. It was decided beforehand that an example had to be made of the two writers, and an example was made—the law was set at nought in a flagrant fashion. This is what has shocked—and frightened—the Soviet public.

One of the letters of protest (see page 248) refers to an article which appeared in December, 1964, in *Izvestia*—the same paper that almost a year later was to open the public campaign against Sinyavsky and Daniel with the scurrilous article by Eremin. This was a long, authoritative article called "On Socialist Justice" by none other than

---

* *Pravda*, April 2, 1966.

the President of the Supreme Court of the U.S.S.R., A. Gorkin. It criticized as "throwbacks to the past" continuing instances in which a man's guilt is decided on beforehand: "Until the court has had its say, until the court has come to its final decision, a defendant cannot be regarded as guilty and cannot be called a criminal, however weighty and convincing the evidence against him may be." Gorkin went on to attack the widespread practice of presumption of guilt by the police and the people who conduct the preliminary investigation. In particular he sharply criticized, as being in blatant contradiction with the fundamentals of Soviet law, the practice of newspapers prejudicing court cases:

Sometimes articles appear in the press, in which persons are pronounced guilty before their cases have been heard in court, and the question of their punishment is predetermined. It is possible and necessary to criticize in the press deficiencies in the workings of the courts, but to anticipate the court's verdict and thereby to exercise pressure on it means not to combat mistakes in the administration of justice but to aid and abet them.*

Many Russians also doubted whether it was necessary once more to discredit before the whole world the operation of Soviet justice in a case involving heresy and sacrilege. This doubt even found expression in the Soviet press in an item which can only be read as an oblique, Aesopian comment on the handling of the case. Whether by accident or design, *Komsomolskaya Pravda* published prominently in its issue of February 12, on a different page from its report on the closing stages of the Sinyavsky-Daniel trial, an apparently innocuous feature article on a letter written by Pushkin to Nicholas I in 1828. The authenticity of this letter had just been established and it had caused something of a sensation, according to *Komsomolskaya Pravda's* correspondent, among Pushkin scholars.

In 1818 Pushkin had written and distributed anonymously a long poem called *The Gabrieliad*. This is a blasphemous epic in which Lucifer and the archangel Gabriel compete for the favors of the Virgin Mary, with the result that there is some question as to the paternity of Jesus Christ. The "ideology," very strictly guarded, of

---

* A. Gorkin, "O sotsialisticheskom pravosudii," *Izvestia*, December 2, 1964.

Russia under the Czars was *pravoslavie*, the Russian Orthodox religion. Sinyavsky's mildly impious references to Lenin clearly pale before Pushkin's horrendous blasphemy. In 1828 a government commission was set up to investigate the authorship of the poem, which was widely attributed to Pushkin, who at first denied that he had anything to do with it. Nicholas I then invited Pushkin to communicate with him personally, by-passing the commission. Pushkin wrote the following letter, which was passed on to Nicholas:

On being interrogated by the Government, I did not regard myself bound to admit to a prank as shameful as it was criminal. . . . But now, being asked directly by my Sovereign I hereby state that the *Gabrieliad* was written by me in 1818. I throw myself on the mercy and generosity of my Sovereign. Your imperial majesty's humble servant: Alexander Pushkin, 1828.

On a written inquiry from the commission as to how they should proceed and whether they should continue to interrogate Pushkin, Nicholas scribbled this *characteristic* (this is the word used by the correspondent of *Komsomolskaya Pravda*) remark: "*I know all about this case and regard it as closed.*"†

CONCLUSION

The official Soviet stand on the case of Sinyavsky and Daniel appears to be quite intransigent. On April 19, 1966, it was reported in the press that the general secretary of International PEN, Mr. David Carver, had left Moscow after being firmly rebuffed in an attempt to seek clemency for the two men. On the same day, the secretary of the European Writers' Community, Giancarlo Vigorelli, also left Moscow after a week of vain efforts on behalf of the two writers. Vigorelli had been authorized by the Community to discuss with the Union of Soviet Writers the question of whether, in view of the harsh verdicts on Sinyavsky and Daniel, conditions still existed for the sort of dialogue between East and West which is one of the major aims of

---

† Somebody in the editorial offices of the London *Daily Worker* saw the point, since this excursion into Russian literary history was published side by side with its Moscow correspondent's report on the verdict in the trial of Sinyavsky and Daniel.

the European Writers' Community. Tass, the official Soviet news agency, blandly announced that the purpose of Mr. Carver's visit had been to deliver to the Union of Soviet Writers an invitation to send observers to an international PEN congress which was held in New York in June, 1966; at the same time it was said that Vigorelli's visit and his exchange of views with Soviet writers had created a situation in which it was possible to resume "joint activities in a spirit of trust." No mention was made of the true purpose of Carver's and Vigorelli's fruitless mission to Moscow.

The two writers are serving their sentences in Potma, in the Mordvinian "autonomous republic," where there is known to be a large forced labor camp (camps are now known as "colonies" in order to achieve a verbal dissociation with the institution as it existed in the "period of the cult of personality"). This is the same area in which Olga Ivanskaya, the friend of Boris Pasternak and the prototype of Lara in *Doctor Zhivago*, was held for four years on charges trumped up by the KGB after Pasternak's death in 1960. They have joined there a number of other, lesser known, silent witnesses to the fact that the literary vocation is still considerably more hazardous in Russia under the Soviet regime than it was under the Czarist regime.

The Soviet authorities have stubbornly refused to listen to the voices of reason coming even from their staunch friends abroad. The atmosphere at the 23rd Party Congress, which took place in April, 1966, was decidedly anti-intellectual, and it seems fairly obvious that the new post-Khrushchev leaders, even if they have inner doubts about the wisdom of staging shameful spectacles such as the Sinyavsky-Daniel trial, have nevertheless for the time being decided on a policy of appeasing the more conservative and even Stalinist elements in the country. It should be noted, however, that they did not capitulate to these elements by granting the "rehabilitation" of Stalin, which seemed a threatening possibility in the few weeks preceding the opening of the Congress. To some extent this may have been due to the pressure of the intellectuals who are beginning to feel that they may have some bargaining power. Just before the opening of the Congress some of them, including the physicists Peter Kapitsa, Igor Tamm, the ballet dancer Maya Plisetskaya and even the former Ambassador to Britain, Ivan Maisky, are reported to have sent a letter to the First Secretary of the Soviet Communist Party, Leonid Brezhnev, warning against the consequences of "any step toward the rehabilitation" of Stalin.‡ There is, hence, in the country still some kind of "balance of forces" between those who want a return to the past and those who wish to achieve liberal reforms which, by giving greater independence to the judiciary and curbing the powers of the security authorities, would make more difficult such a clear mockery of justice as the trial of Sinyavsky and Daniel.

Liberal opinion inside Russia has so far been powerless to affect the outcome of this particular case, but it has not lost its voice. The journal *Novy Mir*, which published both Sinyavsky and Daniel, continues so far to appear under the same editor, Alexander Tvardovsky, who, although he has not been re-elected as a member of the party's Central Committee at the recent Congress, nevertheless persists in his constant plea for "truthful writing." In an editorial in the *Novy Mir* of March, 1966, which went on sale in Moscow just after the Party Congress ended, Tvardovsky wrote that such writing was in the higher interest of Communism and that it was important to see "reality as it is, in all its complexity, in its real contradictions and development." He warned that "when this reality is simplified or schematized, then art ceases to be art." The same issue of *Novy Mir* contained a tribute by Tvardovsky to the great Russian poetess Anna Akhmatova, who died on March 5, 1966. She had been a constant victim of persecution. Her ex-husband, the poet Gumilev, was shot in 1921, her son was arrested in 1937, and in 1946 she herself was violently attacked by Stalin's cultural lieutenant, Andrei Zhdanov, who described her as "half-nun and half-whore." In his obituary article Tvardovsky wrote, evidently referring to Zhdanov's remarks:

To be silent about these attacks before the fresh grave of the poet would be sinful, for the literary and living fate of Akhmatova was not easy. She went through all these tests with a dignity that can only inspire respect. . . . What about the attacks themselves? Life has long since turned them aside, and indeed these attacks inspired among readers a reaction that was not calculated by the critics—as happens with any unproved and unobjective criticism.

---

‡ See *New York Times*, March 21, 1966.

The outside observer has at the moment the impression of a leadership torn between powerful conflicting trends and attempting to placate, or at least not to antagonize, violently opposed groups in Soviet society, if not within the party itself. It is probable that the affair of Sinyavsky and Daniel—there were indications of this at the 23rd Party Congress—is a focal point of this violent clash of "progressive" and "conservative" opinion. Through the masterly defense which they conducted on their own behalf, Sinyavsky and Daniel forced the Soviet state into the strange position of being the first in the world to put literature as such on trial. It is as though one of the more unpleasant characters in a satire by Saltykov-Shchedrin, reincarnated in the person of Counselor of Justice (Third Class) O. P. Tyomushkin, had come to life in order to condemn and pronounce judgment on the whole of Russian literature.

I. THE TRIAL

Session of February 10, 1966

Reading of the Indictment

THE TRIAL OPENS on February 10 at 10 A.M. in Moscow Oblast [Province]§ Court, in a small hall seating 150–160 persons. The Supreme Court of the R.S.F.S.R.* under the chairmanship of L. N. Smirnov, president of the court, and N. A. Chechina and P. V. Sokolov, people's assessors, hear the case of A. D. Sinyavsky and Y. M. Daniel, accused under Section 1 of Article 70 of the Criminal Code of the Russian Republic, which says:

Agitation or propaganda carried out with the purpose of subverting or weakening the Soviet regime or in order to commit particularly dangerous

---

§ Explanatory words and phrases in square brackets have been supplied by the translator.

* The R.S.F.S.R. (Russian Soviet Federal Socialist Republic) is the largest of the "Republics" constituting the U.S.S.R. It is the Republic predominantly inhabited by ethnic Russians (see the remark made by the judge on p. 97 about the defendants being on trial before the court of the Russian Federation). The only higher judicial authority in the Soviet Union is the Supreme Court of the U.S.S.R. It is noteworthy that, evidently in order to mislead sympathizers of the accused, as well as representatives of the foreign press, the case was heard not in the building of the Supreme Court of the R.S.F.S.R., but was transferred to the premises of the Moscow Province Court. "People's assessors" (narodnye zasedateli) are persons elected to fulfill functions theoretically similar to those of the jury in a Western court, except that they are entitled to intervene in the proceedings in the same way as the judge. "Public accusers" (obshchestvennye obviniteli) are persons appointed by the professional organization to which the accused belong (though Daniel was not a member of the Union of Soviet Writers), and their function, at least in this instance, was to assist the prosecution more or less in the capacity of "expert" witnesses.

crimes against the state, the dissemination for the said purposes of slanderous inventions defamatory to the Soviet political and social system, as well as the dissemination or production or harboring for the said purposes of literature of similar content, are punishable by imprisonment for a period of from six months to seven years and with exile from two to five years, or without exile, or by exile from two to five years.

The prosecution is led by O. P. Tyomushkin, assistant of the Public Prosecutor and State Counselor of Justice (Third Class), and by A. Vasilyev and Z. Kedrina, public accusers nominated by the Union of Soviet Writers.

The accused are defended by E. M. Kogan and M. M. Kisenishsky, retained by the families of the accused.

The audience consists almost entirely of men. Entry is by special invitation cards only—a different color being used for each court session—and they are checked twice, once at the entrance to the building and again at the foot of the stairway leading to the courtroom, this time against identity cards. Policemen and court attendants are everywhere—on the street, in the courtyard, in the waiting room. The window shades in the hall are drawn; the courtroom is lit by fluorescent lighting. Window shades, walls and furniture are painted yellow. It is crowded and hot.

The accused are led in. They look what is evidently their usual selves, with no traces of the five-month detention under investigation. Sinyavsky is thin, short, with a reddish, unkempt beard, and wearing a snow-white nylon shirt under a black woolen sweater with a round collar. He looks like a gnome, or rather like a good-natured goblin. Daniel is tall, with dark, slightly thinning hair, a large strong mouth, nervous lips; he is dressed in a cowboy shirt and a worn jacket.

Behind each accused is an unarmed guard.

The prosecutor and counsel for the defense enter.

The court usher says "Please stand," and, after a short interval, adds loudly, with stress on the first word, "The court is in session."†

The members of the court enter. First Chechina, a thin woman wearing glasses, dressed in a plain dark suit; behind her, Smirnov, a

---

† "The court is in session" (Sud idyot) is the traditional cry of the court usher as the judge and other members of the court enter the courtroom. The phrase can also mean "The trial begins," which is the title of the first novel by Sinyavsky to be published in the West.

big man of fifty-eight, who walks with his head thrust forward in a bull-like manner, and has the purposeful look of one who is accustomed to exercise authority. Finally Sokolov, a well-built, good-looking man of forty, markedly precise in manner, with a military bearing, a narrow face, hollow temples, and the kind of shadows under his eyes that are usually associated in cheap literature with high living or with drug addiction.

All three mount the dais on which stand a table and three chairs; the middle chair is slightly higher than the others, and each is embossed with the coat of arms of the U.S.S.R.

Smirnov has scarcely reached the last step leading to the top of the dais when he says in a businesslike voice, without turning his head, "You may sit."

Then follow the usual procedural questions—whether the accused have any objections to the composition of the court, etc. There are no objections.

Counsel makes a number of requests to the court: to summon Duvakin, Yakobson and Voronel as witnesses; to obtain from the Lenin Library all foreign-press articles on Abram Tertz and Nikolai Arzhak; to admit as evidence written testimonials by K. G. Paustovsky, V. V. Ivanov and L. Z. Kopelev‡ about the works of Tertz and Arzhak.

The court leaves the room to confer, then returns (the usher again says "Please stand" and "The court is in session"). Smirnov an-

---

‡ Paustovsky (born in 1892) is one of the best prose writers of the older generation. In the years since Stalin's death he has played a notable and courageous part in the "liberal" movement in Russia. His autobiography has recently been published in America and England.

V. D. Duvakin was the only defense witness to be called (for his evidence see p. 150). He is an assistant professor (dotsent) of Moscow University, an authority on the work of the Soviet poet Vladimir Mayakovsky. After the trial there was an attempt to dismiss Duvakin from his post, but this was apparently abandoned as the result of strong protests by some of his colleagues (see p. 300). A. A. Yakobson, a poet and translator connected with the Moscow publishing house Soviet Writer, is a friend of Daniel whose evidence for the defense was not admitted. For his statement about the case see p. 252. Nothing is known of Voronel, and his name does not appear anywhere else in the trial documents. V. V. Ivanov (apparently the son of the well-known Soviet writer Vsevolod Ivanov) is a prominent linguist. For his statement see p. 263.

L. Z. Kopelev (born 1912) is a literary critic who specializes in Western European literature, particularly German. He has written essays on Samuel Beckett, Thomas Mann, Hemingway, Brecht and Kafka.

nounces the court's decisions: (1) to call Duvakin as a witness; (2) to defer the question of calling Yakobson and Voronel; (3) articles on Tertz and Arzhak to be obtained from the Lenin Library; (4) testimonials by Ivanov, Kopelev and Paustovsky not to be admitted as evidence.

On the last point, Smirnov explains that the question before the court is not the literary merits or shortcomings of the works of the defendants, but acts punishable by law. Therefore their literary merits are irrelevant to the case.

It is announced that certain witnesses and experts are present—Kostomarov, Dymshits,* Prokhorov and others. Two experts, Vinogradov† and Krasnov, have not appeared. The judge acquaints the experts with their rights, and asks the prosecutor, counsel and accused whether they agree to proceed in the absence of two of the experts. All reply in the affirmative. The judge also announces that expert evidence on psychology, handwriting and literature has been called for.

The clerk of the court then reads out the indictment accusing Sinyavsky and Daniel of having committed crimes under Section 1 of Article 70 of the Criminal Code of the R.S.F.S.R.

Briefly the charges are as follows:

The writings of a so-called Soviet literary underground have been widely distributed in the United States, France, Britain and other capitalist countries. Imperialist reaction is on the watch for means of ideological subversion to discredit the Soviet people, their government, the Communist Party of the U.S.S.R. and its policies. For this purpose, use is being made of slanderous anti-Soviet works of underground writers that are passed off by hostile propaganda as truthful accounts about life in the Soviet Union. Such works include the novels The Trial Begins and Lyubimov and the article On Socialist Realism by Abram Tertz, and the works This Is Moscow Speaking, "Hands," "Atonement" and "The Man from Minap" by Nikolai Arzhak. The state security organs have established that Sinyavsky concealed his identity behind the pseudonym Abram Tertz and Daniel behind that of Nikolai Arzhak.

The accused were arrested in September, 1965.

---

* Alexander Dymshits: the literary critic associated with the journal Oktyabr.
† Vinogradov: V. V. Vinogradov, the eminent linguist and literary scholar.

The investigation showed that Sinyavsky and Daniel, having adopted a position hostile to the Soviet state on a number of questions, started sending their writings abroad in 1956.

In the novel *The Trial Begins*, Sinyavsky, under the guise of criticism of the cult of personality,§ ridicules the Soviet system and the principles of Marxism-Leninism. Maliciously slandering Marxist theory and the future of human society, he writes: (Quotation. Here and subsequently, it was not possible to note down quotations from the writings of Daniel and Sinyavsky.)

In 1956 Sinyavsky wrote the essay *On Socialist Realism*, in which he tried to revise Marxist principles from an anti-Soviet point of view. This essay was directed against the guiding role of the Soviet Communist Party in Soviet culture. The author calls Communism a "new religion," treats all aspects of the life of Soviet society from a slanderous point of view as doing "violence to the personality," and dismisses all the achievements of Soviet literature as being based allegedly on "theological Marxist ideology."*

In 1956 Sinyavsky showed this essay to Daniel.

Sinyavsky sent his writings abroad through Peltier-Zamoyska, daughter of a former French naval attaché in Moscow.

In December, 1956, he gave Zamoyska the novel *The Trial Begins* and the essay *On Socialist Realism* and, at the same time, told her the pseudonym under which he wanted to see these things published abroad. Later he sent the last part of the essay to Zamoyska through Remezov,† who was traveling to France.

Bourgeois propaganda started to promote Sinyavsky's writings actively abroad. In the last few years, for example, *The Trial Begins* has been published in twenty-four languages in various countries by different anti-Soviet publishers. On one edition was printed the

---

§ "Cult of personality" (*kult lichnosti*) is the official euphemism for the adulation of Stalin which grew in intensity during the period when he was in complete personal control of the party and government machinery: roughly from 1929 until his death on March 5, 1953.

* The indictment here confuses the word "teleological" with "theological." See p. 9 of Introduction and p. 109 of transcript.

† Andrei Remezov is, or was, a research assistant in the Moscow Library of Foreign Literature. Under the pseudonym "Ivanov," he published abroad a play called *Is There Life on Mars?* and an essay "American Pangs of the Russian Conscience" (the latter was published in English in *Encounter*, June, 1964). For his examination in court see page 131.

slogan of an anti-Soviet organization that calls for the liquidation of the Soviet Communist Party. In 1959, 1960 and 1962, the novel was published by a Polish émigré agency† and broadcast over Radio Liberty, which prefaced the broadcast with an anti-Soviet introduction and described the story as "a revelation about life in the Soviet Union."

Daniel, who shared Sinyavsky's anti-Soviet views, approved of his writings and of his sending them abroad, and, for his part, gave Sinyavsky the story "Hands" to read. This story, written in 1956–57, contains malicious attacks on the Soviet system and the Soviet regime and calls for retribution for the violence that the Soviet regime has allegedly done to the people.

In the autumn of 1957, Daniel used the same channel, through Zamoyska, to send his story abroad. Being aware of the anti-Soviet character of his writings and trying to conceal his identity, he chose the pseudonym Nikolai Arzhak.

The story "Hands" was printed in Paris in the Polish-language magazine Kultura, 1961, No. 9.

In 1961 Sinyavsky wrote the novel Lyubimov, which is directed against socialism. He depicts socialist society as contrary to the nature of man, as a profanation. The Soviet system is portrayed as poverty-stricken and undermined by drunkenness, and the people as a herd that is apathetic about politics. The story contains aspersions on V.I. Lenin. Sinyavsky showed the story to Daniel and, in the autumn of 1963, gave it to Zamoyska for publication abroad. Enemies of the Soviet state duly appreciated the anti-Soviet character of this work; it was broadcast by Radio Liberty and the bourgeois press was delirious about its anti-Soviet character (quotations).

Daniel wrote the story This Is Moscow Speaking, which contains attacks on Communism and the Soviet Government. The story asserts in slanderous fashion that August 10, 1960, was supposedly proclaimed by the Presidium of the Supreme Soviet of the U.S.S.R. to be "Public Murder Day." The story calls for a settling of accounts

---

† "A Polish émigré agency" refers to the Paris-based magazine Kultura mentioned later. Radio Liberty is a station which broadcasts from Munich in the various languages of the Soviet Union (mainly in Russian, but also in other languages, such as Ukrainian and Georgian). It is staffed by refugees from the Soviet Union.

with the country's leaders, and other true sons of the people. (Indignation in the courtroom.)

In Daniel's story "The Man from Minap," Soviet people are depicted as idiots and monsters. Daniel gave these manuscripts in 1961 to Sinyavsky, who promptly sent them to Zamoyska in Paris. The story *This Is Moscow Speaking* was published by several publishers, including Pantheon Books in 1961, and in 1963 "The Man from Minap" was published in the United States by B. Filippov.§

Sinyavsky helped not only Daniel to publish his writings abroad, but also Remezov, whose works appeared in France under the pseudonym A. Ivanov and are being used for anti-Soviet propaganda. (Daniel smiles.)

In 1963 Daniel wrote the story "Atonement," in which he depicts Soviet society as being in a state of moral and political decay. The story suggests that the entire Soviet people is to blame for the cult of personality, that "our prisons are within us," that "the government is unable to give us our freedom," that "we sent ourselves to prison."

Daniel gave this story to Zamoyska in the autumn of 1963. The White émigré Filippov called Arzhak a "spiritual heir of Dostoyevsky."

The publishers who printed the works of Tertz and Arzhak set aside royalties for them.

Sinyavsky and Daniel circulated their anti-Soviet manuscripts and books among their acquaintances. Between 1956 and 1965, Sinyavsky showed his writings to Remezov, Dokukina,* the Kishilovs† and others, as well as to his wife. Daniel, between 1956 and 1963, showed his works to his wife, Garbuzenko, Azbel, Makarova and others.‡ His writings were also read and "appreciated" by Sinyavsky.

---

§ Boris Filippov is a Russian émigré resident in the United States who has published most of the work of Sinyavsky-Tertz and Daniel-Arzhak in the original Russian. These editions were published in Washington, D.C., and they have prefaces by Filippov.

* Dokukina is referred to further on in the transcript as a person who hid some of Sinyavsky's manuscripts (see p. 116). According to *Izvestia* of February 13, 1966, on hearing of Sinyavsky's arrest, she took these manuscripts to her *dacha* and burnt them. For her interrogation see p. 136.

† N. Kishilov is an artist with a French wife, Anne Carrive, who is mentioned below, p. 51. See p. 246 for a letter signed by Kishilov.

‡ Yakov Lazarevich Garbuzenko is the headmaster of a secondary school. For his examination by the court see p. 138. Nothing is known about Azbel and Makarova, who are apparently acquaintances of Sinyavsky and Daniel.

During the investigation Sinyavsky admitted that he had written under the name of Abram Tertz and sent these writings abroad, also that he gave them to several people to read and helped Daniel send his writings abroad. However Sinyavsky denied that his writings were anti-Soviet in character or that he helped Remezov.

But his hostile attitude toward the Soviet regime is confirmed in the manuscript, "An Essay in Self-Analysis," which was found during the search of his home. Although he knew that his works were being used to harm the Soviet regime, he took no steps against such use of them. During the investigation Remezov testified that Sinyavsky holds anti-Soviet views. His criminal activity was also borne out by Daniel's testimony.

Sinyavsky's guilt is further proved by the testimony of witnesses—Petrov,§ Dokukina, Kishilova, Remezov—by a confrontation with Remezov, expert analysis of vocabulary and style, an examination of typescripts and handwriting, actual copies of books published abroad, the manuscript of the article titled "An Essay in Self-Analysis," the writings of Remezov published abroad, correspondence with Zamoyska and other written evidence in the record.

Daniel admitted that he had written under the pseudonym Nikolai Arzhak and sent abroad the works titled *This Is Moscow Speaking*, "Hands," "Atonement" and "The Man from Minap," and circulated these writings among acquaintances. He denied that his writings were anti-Soviet in character, but conceded that he had caused a certain amount of harm to the Soviet regime insofar as his writings contained statements that could be interpreted as being explicitly anti-Soviet.

His guilt is further proved by the testimony of Sinyavsky, of the witnesses Garbuzenko, Khazanov and Khmelnitsky,† material evidence, and documents.

On the basis of the foregoing, the state accuses:

Sinyavsky, Andrei Donatovich, born October 8, 1925, Russian, not a member of the party, native of Moscow, father of a young son,

---

§ Alexander Petrov, an engraver. Like other friends and acquaintances of the defendants he was subpoenaed by the prosecution. See p. 149.

† Yuri Khazanov is a writer of children's stories. Sergei Khmelnitsky is an acquaintance of Daniel who appears to have played an ambiguous role. See pp. 48–49 and also the note by the author of the transcript on p. 144.

member of the Union of Soviet Writers, senior research fellow of the Institute of World Literature of the Academy of Sciences of the U.S.S.R., resident of Moscow, Khlebny Pereulok 9, Apartment 9, of having adopted a hostile position on several aspects of the policy of the Soviet Communist Party and the Soviet Government, of writing and sending abroad the stories *The Trial Begins* and *Lyubimov* and the essay *On Socialist Realism*, which contain slanderous statements maligning the Soviet system and are used by reactionary propaganda against the Soviet state; of circulating these works among acquaintances; of sending the writings of Daniel-Arzhak abroad; of having had a part in the dispatch from the U.S.S.R. to France of the writings of Remezov-Ivanov, i.e., of having committed crimes punishable under Section 1 of Article 70 of the Criminal Code of the R.S.F.S.R.

Daniel, Yuli Markovich, born November 15, 1925, Jewish,[‡] not a member of the party, father of a fourteen-year-old son, resident in Moscow, Lenin Prospect 85, Apartment 3, of having adopted a hostile position on several aspects of the policy of the Soviet Communist Party and the Soviet Government, of writing and sending abroad anti-Soviet works that malign the Soviet political and social system and are being used by reactionaries in the struggle against the U.S.S.R.; of circulating his works among acquaintances, i.e., of having committed crimes punishable under Section 1 of Article 70 of the Criminal Code of the R.S.F.S.R.

The indictment is dated Moscow, January 27, 1966.

Next, the order for the committal of Sinyavsky and Daniel to trial, dated February 4, 1966, is read out. The court then agrees to a request from a joint meeting of the secretariats of the Union of Soviet Writers[§] and the Union of Writers of the R.S.F.S.R. on

---

[‡] In this context the description of the defendant as Jewish is quite "neutral," and no significance should be read into it. Every Soviet citizen has his "nationality" (ethnic origin) recorded in his "passport" (identity card), and it was as "normal" for Daniel to be described in the indictment as "Jewish" as it was for Sinyavsky to be described as "Russian."

[§] The Union of Soviet Writers, founded in 1932, is the organization to which most professional Soviet writers find it almost essential to belong. Expulsion from it leads to loss of material and other privileges. Each of the component republics of the U.S.S.R., including the R.S.F.S.R., has its "Writers' Union," affiliated with and subordinate to the All-Union one.

February 3, 1966, to admit two Union members, A. Vasilyev* and Z. Kedrina,† to the trial as public accusers, and orders the continued detention of the defendants.

> JUDGE: Defendant Sinyavsky, do you plead guilty to the charges, in full or in part?
>
> SINYAVSKY: No, I do not, either in full or in part.
>
> JUDGE: Defendant Daniel, do you plead guilty to the charges, in full or in part?
>
> DANIEL: No, I do not, either in full or in part.

The prosecutor asks the court to adopt the following procedure: examination of Daniel, examination of Sinyavsky, followed by evidence of witnesses and experts in the order listed in the indictment.

Sinyavsky asks that he be examined first since he is listed first in the indictment. Both counsel for the defense second the request.

The judge (after brief consultation with the two assessors) upholds the prosecution's objection to this request.

The session resumes at 1:20 P.M. after a short recess.

---

* A Soviet writer, born in 1907, who has at one stage in his career worked as a police interrogator (*sledovatel*). He writes satirical novels and sketches. One of his recent novels *Monday Is a Bad Day*, according to the *Short Literary Encyclopedia* (*Kratkaya Literaturnaya Entsiklopedia*, Moscow, 1962), "unmasks parasites and black-marketeers."

† See p. 220.

Examination of Yuli Daniel

JUDGE: We will now proceed to the examination of Daniel.

PROSECUTOR: What was the nature of your literary activity in the U.S.S.R.?

DANIEL: I worked as a translator and wrote articles. The Children's Publishing House printed a story of mine called "Escape," but it was never put on sale.

JUDGE: Your story is part of the evidence. (*He holds up the book.*)

PROSECUTOR: In other words, as a poet-translator and writer you worked under your own name in the U.S.S.R.?

DANIEL: Yes.

PROSECUTOR: And you did not use any pseudonyms?

DANIEL: No.

PROSECUTOR: Which of your works were written under a pseudonym and when?

DANIEL: Works are not written under a pseudonym; they are published under a pseudonym.

PROSECUTOR: All right, then, what was published under a pseudonym?

DANIEL: Under a pseudonym I published "Hands," *This Is Moscow Speaking*, "The Man from Minap" and "Atonement."

PROSECUTOR: And have they been published?

DANIEL: Yes.

PROSECUTOR: These works are in Volume 9 of the record. Will the court please examine them.

JUDGE: The court certifies that the works named by Daniel were published under the pseudonym Nikolai Arzhak. (*He holds up the books.*)

PROSECUTOR: Daniel, are these the works you mentioned?

DANIEL: Yes.

PROSECUTOR: When and where were they written?

DANIEL: "Hands" was written sometime between 1956 and 1958. I don't remember exactly; *This Is Moscow Speaking* in 1960–61; "The Man from Minap" in 1961; and "Atonement" in 1963.

PROSECUTOR: Did you write these works yourself or did anyone help you?

DANIEL: I wrote them myself.

PROSECUTOR: Did anyone suggest to you the plot of any of these writings?

DANIEL: No, but the idea for *This Is Moscow Speaking* was not mine.

PROSECUTOR: Who suggested it? Tell us.

DANIEL: It was suggested by my onetime friend Khmelnitsky.

PROSECUTOR: Did you later speak with Khmelnitsky about writing up this idea?

DANIEL: Yes, twice. The first time was in 1962. In the presence of many witnesses he asked me whether I had already written a story with the idea he suggested. I cut him off.

PROSECUTOR: Oh, so you cut him off? In other words, you realized that he had to be cut off, that it would be undesirable to reveal your pseudonym?

DANIEL: Yes, because by this time the story had already been printed abroad. The second time we talked about it was when Khmelnitsky, who had heard someone say that the story was being broadcast by a foreign radio station, exclaimed, again in the presence of witnesses, "But that's our story, Daniel's and mine!"

PROSECUTOR: Which radio station was it?

DANIEL: I don't know.

PROSECUTOR: Wasn't there mention of the fact that this was Radio Liberty?

DANIEL: No, this was not mentioned.

PROSECUTOR: It was Radio Liberty, and the date of the broadcast is given in the record. Daniel, to which of your acquaintances, when, where, and in what form did you show your manuscripts and books?

DANIEL: I generally read out loud to them from my manuscripts. I read to our wives, mine and Sinyavsky's; I read to Sinyavsky. As far as other people are concerned, I don't remember exactly when I read to them. I read to Garbuzenko, but don't remember when—not before 1962. Then I read something else to him in '63 or '64. After 1963 I read something to Azbel, I don't remember exactly what, because I was reading a lot at that time—it may have been in the autumn of 1962, in Kharkov, or maybe it was "Atonement" a year later. Khazanov, too, knew about this story, but I had not lent it to him, or read it to him. I showed it to someone else in '64 or '65. In the summer of 1965 I read everything I had written to my friend Makarova.

The judge reads out the script of a Radio Liberty broadcast in which a reading of Daniel's work is prefaced by anti-Soviet comments.

PROSECUTOR: Was this the broadcast mentioned in your conversation with Khmelnitsky?

DANIEL: I don't know whether it was this one.

PROSECUTOR: Why did you cut Khmelnitsky off when he started talking in front of other people? Wasn't it because you were afraid of something?

DANIEL: Of course.

PROSECUTOR: Tell us, Daniel, what did your acquaintances and members of your family think from a political point of view of what you gave them to read?

DANIEL: Garbuzenko was the only one to say that he would not have published such a thing abroad because it might be wrongly interpreted and used by enemies of our country. The others talked only about the literary side of it.

PROSECUTOR: Which of your acquaintances was it who said "This is terrible" about something he had read?

DANIEL: I don't remember.

PROSECUTOR: Wasn't it Azbel?

DANIEL: No.

PROSECUTOR: During the preliminary investigation Garbuzenko stated that he had told you these writings could be used by our enemies for propaganda purposes. What was your reaction to this warning?

DANIEL: I did not attach any importance to it. I was interested in his literary judgment of my work.

PROSECUTOR: Why didn't you attach any importance to it?

DANIEL: Because I don't think my writings are in any way anti-Soviet.

PROSECUTOR: If you saw nothing anti-Soviet in your writings, why didn't you take them to a Soviet publisher?

DANIEL: I knew very well that Soviet editors would not publish anything on such controversial topics. My writings have a political tinge, and they would not have been printed on political grounds. What I mean is that editors and publishers have their own political considerations.

PROSECUTOR: In other words, Daniel, you knew there was something in your writings that stood in the way of their publication in the Soviet Union?

DANIEL: (irritated): I am simply talking about the practice of our publishers, who are afraid to print anything on a controversial topic.

PROSECUTOR: Yet you took your story "Escape" to a Soviet publisher? Daniel, did you send your writings abroad by legal means?

DANIEL: No, by illegal means.

PROSECUTOR: Who helped you send them abroad?

DANIEL: Helène Peltier-Zamoyska. I can't say I know her very well, but I asked her to offer these manuscripts for publication and she agreed.

PROSECUTOR: What do you think, Daniel: Is it ethical for a Soviet citizen to send abroad through a foreigner things that, to use your own expression, have a political tinge?

DANIEL: No, I would not call it ethical.

PROSECUTOR: Tell us, who is this Zamoyska?

DANIEL: She is a specialist on Russian literature, she is studying Leonid Andreyev,§ loves Russia and (*smiling*) is simply a nice woman. (*Laughter in the courtroom.*)

PROSECUTOR: You identified her during the investigation?

DANIEL: Yes, I recognized her from a photograph that was shown to me.

PROSECUTOR: Will the court please examine the documents showing that Zamoyska has been in the U.S.S.R.

The judge confirms that these documents are in the record.

PROSECUTOR: In other words, you sent your writings abroad with the help of the daughter of a naval attaché?

DANIEL: I sent them through Zamoyska, and I had no interest in whose daughter she was.

PROSECUTOR: Daniel, who else helped you send your manuscripts abroad?

DANIEL: I don't know whether you can call it help, but I made use of a journey abroad in 1961 by an acquaintance, Anne Carrive.* I gave her the manuscripts of *This Is Moscow Speaking* and "The Man

---

§ A Russian writer (1871–1919) who emigrated after the October Revolution of 1917. He is best known in the West for his play *He Who Gets Slapped*.

* A French citizen married to Kishilov. From this and other passages in the transcript, it appears that Anne Carrive and her Soviet husband made several trips to Paris before the arrest of Sinyavsky and Daniel. According to Sinyavsky (p. 113), they were about to make another trip at the time of his arrest, but their exit permit was rescinded.

from Minap," wrapped in a parcel, and told her that it was a book for Zamoyska. She thought that it was simply a book and acted, so to speak, as a postman.

PROSECUTOR: And how did Sinyavsky help you?

DANIEL: As far as getting my work out was concerned, in no way.

PROSECUTOR: In what way did he help then?

DANIEL: I had been looking for ways of sending manuscripts abroad. I already knew Helène Peltier, to whom Khmelnitsky had introduced me. I asked Sinyavsky to help me to get to know her better.

PROSECUTOR: You knew that Sinyavsky was using Peltier to publish his writings abroad?

DANIEL: No, at that time I didn't know it yet.

PROSECUTOR: When did you find out?

DANIEL: Later, after my own manuscripts had been sent off.

PROSECUTOR: Aren't you trying to play down Sinyavsky's role? In the investigation you stated that you knew. Here is what you said: "At first I didn't want to implicate Sinyavsky and gave incorrect evidence. Now I have decided to tell the truth. I did give the manuscripts to Sinyavsky, but I don't know how he transmitted them." Daniel, why are you now going back on that evidence?

DANIEL: I am not going back on it; I am denying it completely.

PROSECUTOR: Daniel, when were you lying, during the investigation or in what you have just said—

JUDGE: I would request you not to use such words.

DANIEL: I gave the package to Anne Carrive when Sinyavsky was out of the room. He knew nothing about it and had nothing to do with it.

PROSECUTOR: From December 14, 1965, onward you said that "Previously I did not want all the responsibility to fall on Sinyavsky and that was why I gave incorrect evidence. . . ." (*The prosecutor reads Daniel's evidence revealing that Sinyavsky had transmitted Daniel's manuscripts.*)

DANIEL: This statement does not correspond to the facts. At that time I did not remember exactly how things were, but now I do.

PROSECUTOR: Did you give this evidence voluntarily during the investigation?

DANIEL: Yes.

The prosecutor reads Daniel's evidence of January 13, 1966, saying that he gave the manuscripts to Sinyavsky, but did not know how or when they were sent abroad.

PROSECUTOR: Daniel, why are you now changing your evidence?

DANIEL: My evidence is confused and the record contains various statements of mine made at different times. I am not a machine, I am only human, I can't remember everything exactly, especially something that happened five years ago.

PROSECUTOR: In the investigation you first denied that you were Arzhak, then you tried to push the time of writing of your works as far into the past as possible. But you must remember through whom you sent out your manuscripts. Through Sinyavsky or through Anne Carrive? After all, that is no minor detail.

DANIEL: Through Anne Carrive. I remembered this clearly only after the investigation had been completed.

PROSECUTOR: Did you interest yourself in what happened to the things you sent out? Did you see them in their published form?

DANIEL: Yes, I knew that three things had been published. Peltier brought them to me. But I don't remember where they were given to me. I never saw "Atonement" in book form.

PROSECUTOR: Do you confirm your previous evidence that Zamoyska gave you these books in Sinyavsky's apartment?

DANIEL: I don't remember. It's possible.

PROSECUTOR: Did you know which publishers were printing your books, and with what sort of introductions?

DANIEL: No, I didn't know.

The prosecutor asks the court to examine letters from the "Progress" Publishing House [in Moscow] listing the editions of Arzhak's writings.

The judge reads out the information about where and when these writings were published.

PROSECUTOR: Did you receive royalties for these books?

DANIEL: No.

PROSECUTOR: What royalties were set aside for you, and how? What do you know about royalties?

DANIEL: I haven't got the slightest idea how much. All I knew was that they existed.

PROSECUTOR: Did you speak with Zamoyska about royalties?

DANIEL: Yes. She said that royalties were being set aside, that they were large, but I don't know exactly how much they come to.

PROSECUTOR: Did you talk with her about Sinyavsky's royalties?

DANIEL: No.

PROSECUTOR: And now, Daniel, will you explain the ideology of *This Is Moscow Speaking?*

DANIEL: For me there is a difference between content and ideology. First, I want to tell how and why this story was written. The idea was suggested by a friend. I was attracted by the notion that in describing an imaginary Public Murder Day I could shed light on the psychology and behavior of people. The plot itself, a Public Murder Day, was what gave this particular story its political coloring. I must mention my own political position, leaving aside the literary aim I had set myself. In 1960–61, when I was writing this story, I—and not only I, but any person who thought seriously about the situation in our country —was convinced that a new cult of personality was about to be established. Stalin had not been dead all that long. We all remembered well what were called "violations of socialist legality." And again I saw all the symptoms: there was again one man who knew everything, again one person was being exalted, again one person was dictating his will to agricultural experts, artists, diplomats and writers. Again we saw one single name in the newspapers and on posters, and every utterance of this person, however crude or trivial, was again being held up to us as a revelation, as the quintessence of wisdom. . . .

JUDGE: And so, in fear of a restoration of the cult of personality in our country, you decided to turn to the publishers Harper & Row in Washington?†

DANIEL: I am not talking now about why I sent the story abroad, but about why I wrote it.

JUDGE: Go ahead.

DANIEL: Well, seeing all this happen and remembering the horrors of the purges and violations of legality under Stalin, I concluded—and I am a pessimist by nature —that the terrible days of Stalin's cult could come back. And, as you may recall, in those days things happened that were far more terrible than anything in my story. Remember the mass purges, the deportation and annihilation of entire peoples.‡ What I wrote was child's play by comparison. . . .

---

† In the transcript this appears as "Herner i Bro," which is clearly a garbled form of "Harper & Row." (In Russian the letters "n" and "p" are very similar in appearance.) Harper & Row published the paperback edition of *Dissonant Voices in Soviet Literature* (edited by Patricia Blake and myself), which was originally published in hard cover by Pantheon Books in 1962. This anthology includes an English translation of Daniel-Arzhak's *This Is Moscow Speaking*. The judge, or the person who made the transcript, presumably transfers Harper & Row to Washington because he imagines that, as in most countries, the main publishing houses are located in the capital city.

‡ This refers to the deportation toward the end of World War II, on charges of alleged collaboration with the Germans, of the Kalmyks, the Crimean Tartars, the Chechens and Ingush, and some other small Caucasian peoples. Since Stalin's death, all these peoples, with the exception of the Crimean Tartars, have been allowed to return to their original homelands from exile in Central Asia and Siberia. Daniel may also have had in mind the decimation of the population of the Baltic States and other border regions by mass deportations in the immediate postwar years.

JUDGE: I understand, of course, that the author's narrative and words spoken by his characters are two different things. But here is what you wrote in *This Is Moscow Speaking*. (*He quotes the conversation with Volodya Margulis, including the passage, "But, do they expect to gain from this Decree?" etc.*) *

DANIEL: You are quite right in saying that the attitude of the author is not always identical with that of his characters. And the hero of my story objects to the words you have quoted. He says, "We must stand up for the Soviet regime." So the passage you have just read is quite clear.

JUDGE: Is that the same hero who fires his tommy gun "from the hip"?§

DANIEL: That's right. And I'll explain this too. The idea of the story is, briefly, that a human being should remain a human being, no matter in what circumstances he may find himself, no matter under what pressure and from what quarter. He should remain true to himself, to himself alone, and have nothing to do with anything that his conscience rejects, that goes against his human instinct. . . . Now about this passage with the words "from the hip." The indictment describes it as a call to settle accounts with the party leaders and the government. It is true that my hero is speaking about the leaders; he mentions them because he remembers the mass persecutions and feels that those who are guilty should bear responsibility. But at this point the indictment breaks off the quotation. The book does not stop there, nor even does this particular soliloquy of my hero stop there. He recalls scenes of killing and slaughter that he saw in the war. And this mental image fills him with revulsion. The

* *Dissonant Voices*, p. 289.
§ For the whole of this key passage see Introduction, pp. 17–18.

indictment obviously gives a tendentious interpretation to this passage. After all, the same hero says
further on: "I want to kill no one." How can any
reader then say this character wants to kill? It should
be clear to everyone that he does not.

JUDGE: But you are by-passing the main point. Your hero is
allowed to kill by decree of the Soviet Government.
In other words, we have a bad government, and a
good character who does not want to kill anyone
except the government?

DANIEL: That does not follow from the story. The hero says
"no one." No one means no one.

JUDGE: But you do have such a decree in the story?

DANIEL: Yes.

PROSECUTOR: I would like to ask Daniel to read the epigraph to
Chapter 4.

JUDGE: I don't see any need for reading unprintable language in this courtroom.

PROSECUTOR: I still would like permission to read the epigraph,
with cuts, without the bad language.*

JUDGE: Go ahead, but without the bad language.

PROSECUTOR: (*reading*): "I hate them so much I have spasms, I
scream, I tremble. Oh, if only all these——could be
collected and destroyed at once!" Well, Daniel, how
do you explain this epigraph?

DANIEL: It's an epigraph to the hero's thoughts. . . .
(*Laughter in the courtroom. Daniel looks around
nervously.*)

PROSECUTOR: Who is it that you hate so? Who do you want to
destroy?

DANIEL: Who are you talking to? To me or to my hero, or to
someone else?

PROSECUTOR: Who is your positive hero?† Who expresses your
point of view in the story?

---

* The "bad language" omitted is the Russian word for "whores." (The quotation is on p. 277 of *Dissonant Voices*.)
† In the language of Soviet literary criticism the characters (referred to as

DANIEL: I have already told you once before in our preliminary talk that the story has no entirely positive hero and that there doesn't have to be one.

PROSECUTOR: We had no preliminary talk. But who expresses the author's point of view? Where does it come in?

DANIEL: The characters do convey the author's attitudes, but only in part. No single character is identical with the author. Maybe it's bad literature, but it is literature, and it doesn't divide everything into black and white.

PROSECUTOR: I would like to read out the findings of Glavlit[‡] about Arzhak's story: "*This Is Moscow Speaking* is a monstrous lampoon." . . . (*There follows an assessment of the story that agrees completely with the indictment, except that the Glavlit report finds that the story also has an element of anti-Semitism.*) Do you agree with this assessment, Daniel?

DANIEL: Certainly not. The report says that I express my ideas through "the mouths of my characters." That is a naïve accusation, to put it mildly. That way you can accuse any Soviet writer of being anti-Soviet.

"heroes") of novels and plays, etc., are divided into "positive" and "negative." It is implicit in the official doctrine of "socialist realism" that "positive" heroes should set a good example in their public and private lives, and that they should triumph over the "negative" characters, at least morally. In the last years of Stalin's life the rigid enforcement of this requirement resulted in a standard plot in which an inevitable "happy ending" was preceded by a "conflict" between the "negative" and "positive" characters.

‡ "Glavlit," a portmanteau word derived from: "*glavnoye upravlenie po delam literatury i izdatelstv*" (Chief Directorate on Matters of Literature and Publishing Houses), is the Soviet censorship agency originally set up by decree of the Council of People's Commissars in 1922. It is rarely referred to in public, but all works appearing in print in the Soviet Union have to be submitted to it. In recent years (precisely when is not known) it has been restyled as the "Chief Directorate for the Protection of Military and State Secrets in the Press" (*glavnoye upravlenie po okhrane voyennykh i gosudarstvennykh tain v pechati*— see the entry on "Glavlit" in *Slovar sokrashchenii russkogo yazyka* [Dictionary of Abbreviations in the Russian Language], Moscow, 1963). Judging from this evidence provided at the trial, however, it would seem that Glavlit must have retained, or had restored to it, its functions as an agency for the censorship of literature.

Just take the White Guards in the works of
Lavrenev, Sholokhov, Leonov—§

PROSECUTOR: (interrupting): Have the Western press comparisons of you with Dostoyevsky gone to your head so
much that you now compare yourself with leading
Soviet writers?

DANIEL: I am not comparing myself with anyone. All I mean
is that it is not what characters say but the author's
own attitude toward what they say that is important.

PROSECUTOR: In the preliminary investigation didn't you say you
were in partial agreement with the Glavlit findings?

DANIEL: That is true, but only with the bare facts as given
there.

PROSECUTOR: (reading from the Glavlit report): "In the author's
view, the Soviet people blindly follow the party
leadership." How would you judge your story in the
light of this?

DANIEL: I didn't mean to say anything so harsh. To some
extent I agree with the idea that the political initiative of the masses . . . I don't believe in it very
much. I consider the masses politically passive.

PROSECUTOR: In other words, if a "Public Murder Day" were
proclaimed, you would expect everyone simply to
rush off to kill as they were told?

DANIEL: No, I don't say that in the story. The "Public
Murder Day" is a literary device, chosen as a way of
studying people's reactions.

JUDGE: There is something I want to clear up. Just imagine
a communal apartment where Ivanova is having a
quarrel with Sidorova.* If Ivanova were to write that

---

§ Boris Lavrenev (1891–1959), Mikhail Sholokhov (born 1905), and Leonid
Leonov (born 1899) are "classical" Soviet writers who had White Guardist
characters in novels dealing with the Civil War. The portrayal of "counterrevolutionaries" in Soviet literature in the first years after the Revolution (e.g., in
Leonov's Badgers, 1925) was often remarkably detached. The hero of Sholokhov's And Quiet Flows the Don, Grigori Melekhov, actually serves the White
Guardist cause for considerable periods during the Civil War.

* Sidorova and Ivanova are common Russian surnames in the feminine form.

there is a certain lady who is making life difficult for another lady, then it would be an innuendo, a figure of speech. But if she were to write that Sidorova was throwing garbage into her soup, then we would have something like a libel, slander or something else subject to legal proceedings. You were, after all, writing about the Soviet Government, not about ancient Babylon, but about a specific government that proclaimed a "Public Murder Day," and you name the date—August 10, 1960. Is that a device or outright slander?

DANIEL: Let me just use your example. If Ivanova were to write that Sidorova literally flies about on a broomstick or turns herself into an animal, that would be a literary device, not slander. I took an obviously fantastic situation.

JUDGE: But here is what B. Filippov wrote: "Can we say that what Arzhak describes is all that far removed from reality?"† So, you see, Daniel, it is not just a literary device, is it?

DANIEL: It is a literary device.

PROSECUTOR: Daniel, do you deny that the "Public Murder Day" supposedly proclaimed by the Soviet Government is in fact slander?

DANIEL: I hold that slander is something you can make people believe, at least theoretically. (*Laughter in the courtroom.*)

JUDGE: I want to clear this up. (*Reading from the law code:*) "Slander is the spreading of information known to be false and defamatory." That is the legal side of it.

DANIEL: What about imaginary situations, then?

JUDGE: I will go back to my example. If Ivanova were to assert that Sidorova did something that Sidorova did

A communal apartment is a fairly standard kind of dwelling in Soviet cities in which the inhabitants share certain facilities like the kitchen and the bathroom.

† The passage quoted is from Filippov's preface to the Russian edition of *This Is Moscow Speaking* published by him in Washington, D.C.

not in fact do, then lawyers would call such a statement slander.

PROSECUTOR: You have slandered ordinary Soviet people. Just look how Soviet people supposedly react to the proclamation of "Public Murder Day." (*He reads excerpts.**) These are supposed to be educated people. How can that be anything but slander? Take your conversation with Margulis—

DANIEL: (*interrupting*): That's not my conversation, it's my hero talking.

PROSECUTOR: But isn't that slander on the Soviet people?

DANIEL: In that case Mayakovsky's *Bathhouse* and *Bedbug*† would also be slander on the Soviet people. Didn't Mayakovsky slander Pierre Skripkin?

PROSECUTOR: Let's not talk about that. Just show me a single Soviet person in your story who seems like a real Soviet person. Just look at the picture you give of our intellectuals!

DANIEL: You talk about Soviet intellectuals as if they were all worthy of admiration.

PROSECUTOR: Just show me one person who is portrayed in a good light. (*He reads excerpt.*) Isn't that slander on the Soviet people, on the Soviet Government?

DANIEL: Even the statutes of the Writers Union don't require writers to write only about noble, intelligent and good people. Why should I be obliged to write about good people in a work of satire? Satirists from Aristophanes to Gogol—§

---

* *Dissonant Voices*, p. 266.

† Famous plays written by Mayakovsky in the last years of his life, toward the end of the NEP (New Economic Policy) period. Both are virulent satires on bureaucracy and the general corruption of revolutionary purity by careerism and greed, etc. Both plays were severely criticized at the time of their appearance (1928 and 1929) as "distortions" of Soviet reality. Pierre Skripkin is a former worker in *The Bedbug* who goes "bourgeois" and adopts the classy name "Pierre," instead of the common-sounding Russian equivalent.

§ Nikolai Gogol (1809–1852): famous Russian novelist and playwright, author of the picaresque novel *Dead Souls* and the play *The Inspector General*, both of them written in a sharply satirical spirit about life in Russia under Nicholas I.

PROSECUTOR: Your head has been turned!

DANIEL: May I make a statement? I am a writer. I cannot avoid referring to the history of literature, to the experience of other writers. That does not mean I put myself on a par with them. I don't, either as regards wisdom or talent. I wish the prosecutor would stop saying that I do.

PROSECUTOR: In your story you mention *Izvestia* and *Literature and Life*, you mention the writers Bezymensky and Mikhalkov.* You slander the entire Soviet press, all Soviet writers. What is it if not slander on the Soviet press?

DANIEL: No, it is not slander on the Soviet press. I was alluding to individual writers, timeservers. It is a parody of the hackneyed style, the clichés that we often find in our papers.

PROSECUTOR: I expected that answer, and I am going back to the passage about *Izvestia*. It says that "as usual, the paper printed an editorial calling for observance of 'Public Murder Day,'" etc. As usual! Isn't that slander on the entire Soviet press?

DANIEL: It's a gibe at the style of newspaper articles.

PROSECUTOR: Now, at last, you are speaking with your real voice.

JUDGE: There is no need for remarks that do not advance the case.

DANIEL: I always speak with my real voice.

PROSECUTOR: You write that the people are anti-Semitic and just waiting to start a pogrom. You compare its mood

---

* See pp. 269 and 270 of *Dissonant Voices*. *Izvestia* is the second most important newspaper (after *Pravda*) in the Soviet Union and is nominally the mouthpiece of the government, as opposed to *Pravda*, which is the party organ. *Literature and Life* (*Literatura i zhizn*) is a now defunct literary newspaper of a markedly reactionary trend. (It published scurrilous attacks on Evtushenko for his poem *Babi Yar* dealing with anti-Semitism.)

Alexander Bezymensky (born 1898) and Sergei Mikhalkov (born 1913) are Soviet poets well known for their political adaptability. Both of them are adept at turning out verse at short notice to suit any occasion.

	with what led to Babi Yar.† But there the killers were Fascists. Isn't it blasphemous to compare our entire people with the Fascists?
DANIEL:	It does not follow from the passage that the entire Soviet people is anti-Semitic; all that follows is that a few individuals are so inclined. I was talking about certain people, without mentioning names, who might want to settle private accounts; I said there might be a few examples of such scum. Nothing more than this can be read into the text.
PROSECUTOR:	A few individuals or the entire people—we will see right away. (*He reads a passage describing how Georgians killed Armenians, Armenians killed Georgians, and in Central Asia everyone killed Russians.*)‡ Isn't that slander on the entire Soviet people?
DANIEL:	No. It is not slander on the entire Soviet people.
PROSECUTOR:	And you say that all this happens under the direction of the Central Committee. Isn't that slander?
DANIEL:	You keep forgetting that the starting point for all this is an imaginary situation, not something that actually happened. (*Laughter in courtroom.*)

The prosecutor reads from a commentary by the émigré, Filippov, describing the Arzhak work as anti-Soviet.

PROSECUTOR:	What do you have to say about that?
DANIEL:	I suggest you ask Filippov for an explanation. I am not responsible for what he writes.
PROSECUTOR:	It was you who turned to Filippov rather than to Soviet publishers.
DANIEL:	I never wrote to Filippov or to anyone else, and I never knew where my work would be printed.

---

† A ravine in Kiev where the Germans massacred thousands of Jews in 1941. In his famous poem Evgeny Evtushenko complained that no monument had been put up there. The prosecutor's reference is to a passage on p. 273 of *Dissonant Voices*.

‡ The passage in question is on pp. 302–303 of *Dissonant Voices*. See also p. 16 of Introduction for discussion of this passage.

JUDGE: But it was Filippov who published it.

DANIEL: I learned this only in 1963.

PROSECUTOR: But you knew that anti-Soviet circles were broadcasting your writings over the radio.

DANIEL: You have no grounds at all for that statement.

Recess. The session is resumed at 3:30.

PROSECUTOR: Here is what you wrote, Daniel. (*He reads a passage from* This Is Moscow Speaking *about a circular from the Central Committee on "Public Murder Day."*)§

At this moment, the lights go out in the courtroom. Someone shouts excitedly, "Lev Nikolayevich [*the judge*], what shall we do about the lights?" The judge's displeased voice: "I am a judge, not an electrician." The lights go on again.

PROSECUTOR: Isn't that malicious slander on the Ukrainian people?

DANIEL: I have already said what slander is. It is something that is credible. And the situation I depict is not credible. And if you can't believe it, it's not slander, it's fantasy. But I want to repeat that everything I wrote would be possible if the personality cult were to be restored. If it were to return, anything could happen. I feel nothing is impossible if the state is under the control of one man.

PROSECUTOR: What has the personality cult got to do with it? You are talking about the Soviet Union of 1960. Here on pages 50 and 51 of the story your hero comes to the Lenin Mausoleum [on Red Square] and someone tries to strangle him, but the only thing that upsets the sentry on duty is a spot of dirt on his boot.° This scene is narrated by the author. And the madman

---

§ The passage is on p. 303 of *Dissonant* Voices.

* In *Dissonant* Voices this scene occurs on pp. 296–297. The prosecutor's reference is to the pages in the Russian edition published by Filippov.

who attacks the hero cries out: "I am doing it by order of the Motherland!" What is this if not defamatory?

DANIEL: I don't know about you, but I served in the army and I know that a sentry on duty does not have the right to leave his post. There is nothing defamatory here.

PROSECUTOR: It's defamatory in the sense that all this takes place in front of the Mausoleum, that a Soviet sentry is worried only about mud on his boot.

DANIEL: There is nothing defamatory about this. If the sentry had left his post, he would have been court-martialed, and rightly so. Please read the two or three sentences before that passage.

The judge reads the same passage.

DANIEL: I asked you to read what went before, not to repeat the same passage. All right, I'll summarize it myself. Just before this the hero exclaims: "Stop! He did not want it, he who was the first to be laid to rest within these marble walls." Lenin was opposed to murder, terror and persecution.[†]

The judge reads a lengthier extract.

PROSECUTOR: In the preliminary investigation you agreed that the whole idea of the story, as noted in the Glavlit report, was that the people of the U.S.S.R. are so cowed that they would not balk even at the most outrageous measures. Do you now confirm that statement?

DANIEL: I have to repeat again that the story dealt with what *could* happen if the personality cult were to be restored.

---

† *Dissonant Voices*, p. 297.

PROSECUTOR: (*reading the conversation between Kartsev and Svetlana,† to the effect that the entire people were frightened*): How about this? Doesn't it confirm Glavlit's findings that you have slandered the entire people and the government?

DANIEL: I repeat again that the story deals with what could happen if the personality cult were revived. After all, in 1961 there was a real threat that this might happen.

PROSECUTOR: You're slandering again, Sinyavsky.

DANIEL: (*half-bowing*): My name is Daniel.

JUDGE: [*addressing the prosecutor*]: There is no need for comment of that kind. The purpose of the examination is to establish the facts; it is up to the court to pronounce judgment on them.

PROSECUTOR: During your interrogation on January 13 you admitted that the story contains passages that could be construed as anti-Soviet. Do you confirm this evidence?

DANIEL: Yes.

The judge reads Daniel's evidence about the passages that could be construed as anti-Soviet.

JUDGE: Do you confirm this evidence?

DANIEL: Yes, I do.

PROSECUTOR: Your writings "The Man from Minap," "Hands," and "Atonement" are also anti-Soviet in character. (*He reads from the Glavlit report:*) "All these works are, from an ideological and political point of view, typical samples of anti-Soviet writing for anti-Communist purposes." . . . The idea of "Atonement" is that the entire Soviet people is to blame for the personality cult, that the people do not believe in the party's cause. The political message of the

---

† *Dissonant Voices*, p. 305.

story is contained in the ravings at the end, such as "Comrades, they're still persecuting us," "You can't run away from yourself," "Our prisons are within us," etc. The story "Hands" contains malicious attacks on the Chekists[†] and depicts party policies as anti-Communist. "The Man from Minap" portrays a Moscow Institute of Scientific Profanation;[§] it is a crude libel, making fun of our morals and certain scientific ideas. Do you agree with the Glavlit report, Daniel?

DANIEL: Certainly not.

PROSECUTOR: But in the preliminary investigation you took a different view of these writings. (*He reads excerpts from the interrogation of December 23, 1965, where Daniel admitted that Chapter 6 of "The Man from Minap" contained lines that could be interpreted as an attack on the Soviet Government.*) Do you confirm this?

DANIEL: Yes, I confirm that these lines could be so interpreted.

PROSECUTOR: (*reads another passage*): And these lines, could they be construed as anti-Soviet?

DANIEL: They could be, but they aren't. (*Laughter in the courtroom.*)

PROSECUTOR: Daniel, what prompted you to write slanderous anti-Soviet works maligning the political system of the U.S.S.R.?

[†] Members of the Cheka, abbreviation of "*chrezvychainaya kommissiya po borbe s kontrrevolyutsiei i sabotazhem* (Extraordinary Commission for the Struggle against Counterrevolution and Sabotage), set up in December, 1917, as the special police force to defend the Revolution. It was later renamed GPU, OGPU, NKVD, MVD, etc., and had responsibility for internal security and the "suppression" of "enemies of the people." It is currently called KGB (*komitet gosudarstvennoi bezopasnosti*—Committee of State Security). The original terms "Cheka" and "Chekist" are still used in Soviet rhetoric as a romantic reminder of the past.

[§] Minap (*Moskovsky institut nauchnoi profanatsii,* abbreviated as MINAP) is the mock title of the scientific institute in "The Man from Minap" which exploits the extraordinary sexual powers of the story's hero. See p. 19 of Introduction.

DANIEL: I refuse to reply to a question posed in that form.

PROSECUTOR: What prompted you to write these works?

DANIEL: *And Quiet Flows the Don* was also once denounced as anti-Soviet.* (*Unrest and laughter in the courtroom.*) There's a difference between "is" and "could be." . . .

JUDGE: This is no literary debate, and we don't need digressions into the history of literature.

DANIEL: I insist on my right to draw literary analogies. I am being accused of a political crime, and I am defending myself by drawing analogies.

JUDGE: You compare "The Man from Minap" with *And Quiet Flows the Don.* That is not very modest of you.

DANIEL: I am not comparing myself with anyone.

PROSECUTOR: Why did you write works that could be interpreted as anti-Soviet?

DANIEL: Are you asking about them all or about any one in particular?

PROSECUTOR: You can tell us about any one of them.

DANIEL: I'll talk about "Hands." I know I don't have the right to put questions to the court. But can the prosecution point to a single sentence, a single word, a single syllable that could be interpreted as anti-Soviet? This story is a literary version of an actual event that was recounted to me. There is nothing in the story to justify the charges against me. The indictment contradicts itself when it talks about this story. The indictment contends that the Soviet regime has never used force. But such a point of view is not scientific, it is not Marxist, it is not Leninist. According to Lenin, revolution is coercion, and the state is coercive, and [in a revolutionary

---

* Sholokhov's classic was indeed attacked by some Soviet critics when the first part appeared in 1928.

state there is] coercion of the minority by the majority. The indictment charges that I wrote: "The Soviet regime used violence against the Soviet people." There is nothing along these lines in the story, which is about the execution of counterrevolutionaries. There is nothing in the story to suggest that this calls for retribution. It cannot be interpreted as in the indictment. Now, about "The Man from Minap." I don't like this story; it is poorly written, crude, and in bad taste, but it contains nothing anti-Soviet. It is a satire, a caricature, an extravaganza; all this is in the tradition of satiric writing. Why is the portrayal of ten bad persons passed off by the prosecution as a portrayal of the whole of Soviet society? The characters of a satirical work are always negative, and the positive hero is always a conventional figure in such writings. There is no basis for saying that the story is directed against the morals and ethics of Soviet society. Why did I write it? Among my friends there are many scientists, and one of them told me about the fuss over Bashyan and Lepeshinskaya† (I don't equate these two names) and that such sensational affairs have done harm to our science. The story dealt with that scandal and not with the branch of science in question. Glavlit evidently feels I should have glorified the events that I satirize.

---

† Olga Lepeshinskaya (1871–1963) was a Soviet biologist who, like Lysenko, became notorious in the last years of Stalin's life for her attacks on genetics and strident advocacy of her own dubious theories. In 1950 she received the Stalin prize for what was claimed to be "a great discovery in biology." This consisted in a claim that there were noncellular forms of life. One of her most active supporters was G. M. Boshyan (misspelled Bashyan in the transcript). One aspect of Stalin's rule was the ease with which bogus scientists were able to gain control of scientific institutions by denouncing, often on political grounds, those who disagreed with them. Many Soviet scientists went to concentration camps during this period. Daniel's "The Man from Minap" is to some extent a satire on the "profanation" of science under Stalin, the consequences of which have still not been overcome.

The prosecutor and Daniel have a long argument about the "scientific theories" mentioned in the Glavlit report.

The judge reads a passage from the report describing the story as a libel on "certain scientific theories."

JUDGE: Daniel, were you attacking Bashyan in this story?

DANIEL: No, I was attacking the practice of making sensational publicity about scientific discoveries.

JUDGE: And if that is the main point of the story, why does your character Volodya think about Karl Marx and Klara Zetkin at such an inappropriate time and in such a situation?[‡]

DANIEL: That can be explained by the haste with which the story was written (*Disapproving murmur and coarse laughter in the courtroom.*)

JUDGE: Your story "Hands" is about the distant past. Why did you send this story abroad instead of, say, "Escape"?

DANIEL: I wanted what I had written to be printed. I am convinced that there is nothing anti-Soviet in my works. But I know that our editors and publishers think that there are certain forbidden themes which should not be dealt with in literature. There are a number of topics on which writers do not write, or publishers do not publish them. The subject of "Hands" is a taboo one which is passed over in silence. It is about a kind of work which is bloody and difficult, but necessary. The hero of the story is a worker who later serves in the Cheka. And because of this work his hands tremble. (*Summarizes the story.*)

JUDGE: But why did you send this one abroad first?

DANIEL: Because I could assume that this story would not be published here: it is about a forbidden subject that has not been dealt with in our literature since the 1930's. . . .

---

‡ See pp. 18–19 of Introduction.

JUDGE: But why this, and not "Escape" or some translations? It is written in a gruesome style. (*Reads a
passage.*) But that's not the point. Why was the
subject of the shooting of the priests so important to
you at this time? Why did you have to bring the
subject up again at this time? The *émigrés* made a
lot of fuss about Tikhon.§ Does this have anything
to do with literature?

DANIEL: But the hero does not know why he is executing
people.

JUDGE: (*reads a passage, then says*): It is obvious that they
would love to publish this abroad.

DANIEL: I had no political purpose when I wrote this story.
(*Laughter in the courtroom.*)

PROSECUTOR: Let us assume that you did not understand the
political implications of the story. Why, in that case,
did you send it abroad under a pseudonym and by
illegal means?

DANIEL: I sent it out to be published; that was an adequate
reason for me. If I had been a physician or an
engineer, I would have published it under my own
name. But I am a translator. Getting work for a
translator of my class depends on good relations with
publishing houses. If it had become known that I
was being published abroad, I would have lost my
translation work. When I gave these things to
Peltier, I did not know where, when and in what
country they would be published. The final stage of
any literary work is publication. You can interpret
this as you wish—as vanity or as excessive pride. But

§ Tikhon was the first Patriarch of the Russian Orthodox Church after the
October Revolution of 1917, when the Patriarchate, which had been abolished by
Peter the Great, was restored as part of a move to separate State and Church.
Tikhon soon fell foul of the Soviet authorities, was placed under house arrest and
died in 1925. Many priests (like those executed in Daniel's story) suffered
because of their support of him. After his death the Soviet authorities did not
permit the appointment of a new patriarch until 1943, when Stalin made
temporary peace with the Church as part of his wartime concessions to Russian
national feeling.

if I had been a physician or engineer, I would not have used a pseudonym. I have already said that it was unethical.

PROSECUTOR: You wanted to be published. But didn't you think about our enemies, about the fact that these writings could be used for anti-Soviet propaganda?

DANIEL: I did not think about it.

PROSECUTOR: And when did you start thinking about it?

DANIEL: After 1963 when I first saw two of my books, one with a foreword by Filippov. Then I realized what construction was being put on them. Despite my doubts, I sent one more manuscript abroad. But since 1963 I have written nothing more and sent nothing more abroad.

The prosecutor reads evidence of Garbuzenko at the preliminary investigation of October 25, 1965, to the effect that these manuscripts should not have been sent abroad since the mere fact of their publication abroad automatically made them anti-Soviet; reads the testimony of Khazanov, who was horrified at the possible consequences for Daniel's family, and who said that from a political point of view it was like thumbing one's nose behind somebody's back.

PROSECUTOR: Now why after all this, after Khazanov had expressed his horror, did you nevertheless send "Atonement" abroad?

DANIEL: Khazanov was horrified about what might happen to me.

PROSECUTOR: But didn't Garbuzenko tell you that these things automatically fell into the category of anti-Soviet works? This surely should have given you food for thought. And then take what you were saying about Khmelnitsky. As early as May, '62, Khmelnitsky said, in the presence of others, that this story had been broadcast by an anti-Soviet radio, and yet once again, for a third time, you sent something abroad. In

other words, you knew full well what you were
doing?

DANIEL: The mere fact of a radio broadcast doesn't mean
anything in particular. I didn't know what station it
was. It could have been broadcast from abroad by
stations which were not anti-Soviet. Garbuzenko
said that it might be regarded as anti-Soviet propaganda, not on the strength of its contents, but only
because of the fact of its publication abroad. As
regards Khazanov, he was in general frightened of
everything.

PROSECUTOR: What was the meaning of your words: "This might
cost us dearly"?

DANIEL: I realized that it was unethical.

The judge again quotes introduction to the Radio Liberty
broadcast.

PROSECUTOR: Well, all right, suppose you really didn't know what
sort of station it was, suppose you thought it was a
friendly station, and you paid no attention to what
your friends said to you. But then at last, at the
beginning of 1964, you received your works as published abroad and you read Filippov's introduction,
and now you see how you are being used. But you do
nothing about it—you make no protest or any attempt to prevent the publication of your next work.

DANIEL: Having decided that I would not write anything
more or send it abroad, I did not wish to give myself
away as the author of the earlier works. Any protest
would have given away my real name and I was
afraid to do that.

PROSECUTOR: But at other times you were braver. Sinyavsky told
you that it was dangerous to send your things
abroad.

DANIEL: You are misquoting his evidence.

The prosecutor reads evidence.

DANIEL: Yes, I'd forgotten. You are quoting correctly.

PROSECUTOR: But your courage failed you when it was a question of neutralizing the damage inflicted on your Motherland?

DANIEL: I turned out not to be all that brave. I had hoped that things would blow over. Moreover, I wasn't on my own, and a man's courage fails him when he thinks of his family. As regards the harm done to our country, I cannot think that a couple of books by us, or even a score, could inflict substantial damage upon a country like this.

JUDGE: You did, however, go from strength to strength. Your "Atonement" was published by a number of other firms. (*Laughter in the courtroom.*)

DANIEL: I never saw "Atonement" in its published form. I was not as brave as I had been at the beginning. I lost my courage because of the threat to my family. I think the damage to the country was not great.

PROSECUTOR: You wrote things which, upon your own admission, could be interpreted as anti-Soviet. You did this over a long period of time. You knew how these things were interpreted in the West. Let us hear how you yourself would describe your conduct.

DANIEL: I've always thought and I continue to think that my books were not anti-Soviet and that I put no anti-Soviet meaning into them, since I did not criticize or make fun of the basic principles of our life. I do not equate individuals with the social system as such, or the government with the state, or a certain period with the Soviet epoch as a whole. The state may exist for centuries but a government is often short-lived and frequently inglorious. As regards my attitude to their publication abroad, this is another matter—I regret it. Until my arrest I could only guess at the reaction to my works in the West. During the investigation I understood that my works had been interpreted there as being attacks not on individual persons but on the system, not as attacks on a certain period but as attacks on the cause as a whole. None of my things is anti-Soviet in its basic idea—you cannot say that it is anti-Soviet to suggest that a man should always remain human, even if he finds himself in a situation like that of the "Public Murder Day."

JUDGE: Even in the monstrous situation involving the Supreme Soviet of the U.S.S.R.?

DANIEL: Yes, and I do not regard that as anti-Soviet.

JUDGE: And you sent these literary figments of your imagination abroad?

DANIEL: That I regret.

JUDGE: Your inventions involve one political idea after another. (*Repeats passages already quoted in the indictment.*)

DANIEL: Our literature and press are silent about the things on which I write. But literature is entitled to deal with any period and any question. I feel that there should be no prohibited subjects in the life of society.

PROSECUTOR: But you took the year 1960. You thought up this decree! My question was straightforward. If you do not wish to describe your conduct in your own words, that is your business.

DANIEL: I do not regard myself as guilty on account of what I have written, but I regret that I published it abroad. I repeat that in 1961 the danger of the restoration of a cult of personality was real.

JUDGE: And did you get in touch with Filippov because of the cult of personality?

PROSECUTOR: These works have nothing to do with the period of the cult of personality!

DANIEL: I didn't get in touch with Filippov.

PROSECUTOR: I see. Tell me, Daniel, what do you know about the literary activities of Sinyavsky? Do you know his works?

DANIEL: I know all those works of his which have been published abroad. He read them to me in manuscript. I have seen the books *Lyubimov* and *Fantastic Stories*.

PROSECUTOR: Did you read Filippov's introduction?

DANIEL: No.

PROSECUTOR: How did you judge the works of Sinyavsky?

DANIEL: As literature.

PROSECUTOR: What about the political side?

DANIEL: I do not think that there is anything anti-Soviet in them.

PROSECUTOR: And have you read his essay *On Socialist Realism?*

DANIEL: I don't remember.

VASILYEV: (*public accuser*): Where did you take the pseudonym Arzhak from?*

DANIEL: I liked the sound of it.

VASILYEV: It's not taken from a song?

DANIEL: No. I don't know of any such song.

KISENISHSKY: (*Daniel's defense counsel*): Since when have you been engaged in literary work?

DANIEL: Since 1957.

KISENISHSKY: What is the number of your publications?

DANIEL: During this time about forty anthologies have appeared which include translations by me. (*Names some of them.*)

KISENISHSKY: When you began to write prose, what was your first work?

---

* In its report on the trial of February 2, 1966, *Izvestia* explained and commented on the pseudonyms of the two defendants as follows:

"It is said that in Smolensk dialect *arzhak* means 'bandit.' The name Abram Tertz is also not without interest. In the twenties an underworld song went the rounds in Odessa and one of the characters in it was 'Abrashka Tertz, the bandit from Odessa.' Perhaps this choice of pseudonyms by the two friends was not fortuitous, or perhaps it was just a coincidence. . . ."

DANIEL: My first thing was the story "Escape." I began it in 1952–53 and finished it in '57–'58.

KISENISHSKY: Tell us in chronological order when you wrote and sent your works abroad.

DANIEL: The story "Hands" was written between '56 and '58 and sent abroad in '60; *This Is Moscow Speaking* was written in '61 and sent abroad in the same year; "Atonement" was written and sent out in 1963.

KISENISHSKY: In the story "Hands" are there any passages which would show the work is not anti-Soviet?

DANIEL: Yes, there are. (*Quotes several passages.*)

KISENISHSKY: How did the story come to be called "Hands"?

DANIEL: At first it was called "An Event," and later "Hands." There are traces of this in the text.

KISENISHSKY: Are there any politically tactless passages in the story "The Man from Minap"?

DANIEL: Yes, there is, for example, the mention of Marx in a certain context, although there's nothing bad about Marx himself. (*Laughter in the courtroom. A voice: "He's lost all sense of shame!"*)

KISENISHSKY: And you were not putting a wider interpretation on this context?

DANIEL: (*laughs*): No, I just can't imagine how that could be done.

KISENISHSKY: Tell us how you got the idea for the story "Atonement."

DANIEL: In recent years we have often heard about people being exposed as slanderers whose denunciations landed innocent people in jail. I wanted to show a rather different situation—how a man must feel if he has been falsely accused of doing something as terrible as this. This was something that actually happened to somebody I knew well. That's how the idea of the story came to me. The indictment says that the underlying notion of the story is that everybody is to blame for the cult of personality and the mass persecutions. I agree with this interpretation, but not with the word "slanderous" used to describe the story. I feel that every member of society is responsible for what happens in society. And I make no exception for myself. I wrote that "everybody is to blame" because there has been no reply to the question of who is to blame. Nobody has ever publicly stated who was to blame for these crimes, and I will never believe that three men—Stalin, Beria and Ryumin†—could alone do such terrible things to the whole country. But nobody has yet replied to the question as to who is guilty.

KISENISHSKY: When did you last send a manuscript abroad and why did you stop sending them?

DANIEL: In 1963.

KISENISHSKY: Give us the main facts about your life.

DANIEL: I was born in 1925. I went straight from school to the front line; during the war I fought on the second Ukrainian and third Byelorussian fronts. After being severely wounded, I was demobilized and received a pension as a war invalid. In 1946 I entered Kharkov University, and then transferred to the Moscow Province Teachers Training College, from which I was graduated. Then I taught for two years at a school in Lyudinovo.‡ After that I taught for four years in Moscow.

SOKOLOV: (people's assessor): Obviously you must have foreseen the impact of the publication of your manuscripts. What did you think it would be?

DANIEL: If I had foreseen such an impact, I would not have sent my manuscripts abroad.

JUDGE: But you must have foreseen their political effect?

DANIEL: I did not think about how my works would be

---

† Beria was almost continually responsible for the Soviet security services (NKVD–MVD) from 1938 till his arrest and execution after Stalin's death in 1953. Ryumin was a Deputy Minister of State Security in the last months of Stalin's life. He was executed after Stalin's death, in July, 1954, as an accomplice in Beria's crimes.

‡ A town in Kaluga Province.

judged from a political point of view. I thought only in terms of how they would be judged from the point of view of their literary qualities or failings.

JUDGE: Then why did you have all these political details—that monstrous decree, the execution of a priest because of Tikhon, and the Institute of Scientific Profanation?

DANIEL: In *This Is Moscow Speaking* all these details are part and parcel of the fantastic plot of the story.

JUDGE: All the people in it are moral degenerates—surely this has a political purpose, and has nothing to do with the plot. Why, for what reason, did you have all this? Wasn't it in order to create a certain impression?

DANIEL: It was not part of my intention to depict good people. The colors are laid on rather thick in my story, but I was not trying to portray good people. I was showing how bad people might behave in an imaginary situation.

JUDGE: In the situation resulting from that decree of the Supreme Soviet!

DANIEL: I've already said that I would regard any excesses as possible if the cult of personality were to return.

JUDGE: During the preliminary investigation you gave different explanations of your works.

DANIEL: These concerned matters of detail which had no importance for the basic idea.

SOKOLOV: Did Zamoyska understand why you sent her the manuscripts through Carrive?

DANIEL: Of course she understood—there had been a precedent for this.

SOKOLOV: Why didn't you want Sinyavsky to see the parcel?

DANIEL: I thought that Sinyavsky might take a poor view of it, since he was against bringing Carrive into all this.

JUDGE: That's not logical. He sent things out, so why should he prevent you doing the same?

DANIEL: He wouldn't have wanted to see Carrive brought into the business.

JUDGE: Now just note the word you have used—"brought in." That means something bad, doesn't it? It means you felt it was a bad business.

DANIEL: But why? After all, one talks about bringing people into the . . . collective. (*Laughter in the courtroom.*)

PROSECUTOR: You say that you didn't think about politics. But what about this sentence here, for example, in your story *This Is Moscow Speaking:* "Anyway, to tell the truth, to be printed abroad, by anti-Soviet publishers is not so good"? What are we to make of this?

DANIEL: It means exactly what it says—it's not very nice. I repeat once more that I've already said what I think about the ethical side of the matter.

JUDGE: Are there any points which you would like to make to the court?

DANIEL: Yes. The prosecution constantly equates the author with his characters. This is particularly impermissible if the characters in question, to put it mildly, are not quite right in the head. For instance in "Atonement" the main character has gone out of his mind and it is he who shouts: "Our prisons are within us!"

JUDGE: (*interrupts*): He only goes mad a page further on.

DANIEL: No. On the next page he is already in a mental hospital. Another thing—quotations are always given without any reference to the state of the characters who utter them. One has gone out of his mind, another is an alcoholic.

JUDGE: All your intellectuals are drunkards.

DANIEL: I beg you, in the first place, not to quote out of context, and, in the second place, to take account of the condition of the characters. And if I have overdone things here and there, this should not be put down to my being anti-Soviet, but to my lack of literary skill. (*Laughter in the courtroom.*)

Examination of Andrei Sinyavsky

JUDGE: Let us now proceed to the examination of Sinyavsky.

This happens at approximately six o'clock on February 10.

PROSECUTOR: Sinyavsky, where did you graduate, what degree do you have?

SINYAVSKY: I was graduated from Moscow University, I am a candidate of philological sciences.§

PROSECUTOR: Where did you work after that?

SINYAVSKY: I worked in the Institute of World Literature of the Academy of Sciences of the U.S.S.R.

PROSECUTOR: Have you ever published under a pseudonym?

SINYAVSKY: Yes, I have published nine works abroad under the pseudonym of Abram Tertz.

PROSECUTOR: Why did you choose this particular name?*

SINYAVSKY: I just happened to like it. I don't think that it can be explained in any rational way.

PROSECUTOR: Had you ever heard the pseudonym before?

SINYAVSKY: No, I hadn't.

---

§ "Philological sciences" is the term for literary and linguistic studies, etc. "Candidate" is approximately equivalent to the doctor's degree in the West.

* See note above on p. 76.

PROSECUTOR: What exactly has been published by you under this pseudonym?

SINYAVSKY: I have published *The Trial Begins*, *On Socialist Realism*, "The Icicle,"† a collection of *Fantastic Stories*, *Unguarded Thoughts*, *Lyubimov*.

PROSECUTOR: (*hands over to the court these works, giving their titles and dates of publication*): *Lyubimov* (1964–65), *The Trial Begins* (1960), *On Socialist Realism* (1959), *Fantastic Stories* (1960), *Unguarded Thoughts* (July 19, 1965, in the journal *New Leader*). . . . Sinyavsky, are these your works?

SINYAVSKY: Yes, they are mine.

PROSECUTOR: When did you write those three of them which figure in the charge?

SINYAVSKY: I wrote *The Trial Begins* and *On Socialist Realism* in '56; I wrote *Lyubimov* in '61–62.

PROSECUTOR: Where did you write them?

SINYAVSKY: In Moscow.

PROSECUTOR: Did anybody help you to write them, did anybody suggest the ideas or the plots?

SINYAVSKY: Nobody gave me any help.

PROSECUTOR: How did you get them abroad?

SINYAVSKY: I sent them out with the help of Zamoyska, whom I knew when we were students together at the university.

PROSECUTOR: Did you send your manuscripts illegally?

SINYAVSKY: I sent them out unofficially, but not illegally.

PROSECUTOR: How would you describe the manner in which you chose to send them?

SINYAVSKY: As "unofficial." I don't think it was illegal and I do not know the implication of this word in the juridical sense.

PROSECUTOR: Did anybody else help you?

SINYAVSKY: Yes, I sent out one page through Remezov. This was an addendum to my essay; it is concerned only with

---

† "The Icicle" was published as part of the collection of *Fantastic Stories*.

the question of the fantastic in art, and there's nothing in it about socialist realism or politics.[†]

PROSECUTOR: And he handed over this page?

SINYAVSKY: Evidently he did, since it was published.

PROSECUTOR: And is there anybody else who helped you?

SINYAVSKY: No.

PROSECUTOR: Did you ever send anything through Anne Carrive?

SINYAVSKY: No, I sent nothing through her.

PROSECUTOR: Who did send things through her?

SINYAVSKY: I sent nothing through her myself. If Daniel sent something through her, I have no knowledge of it.

PROSECUTOR: Did you recognize Zamoyska in the photograph?

SINYAVSKY: Yes.

PROSECUTOR: Did you give Zamoyska your manuscripts in type-script?

SINYAVSKY: Yes.

PROSECUTOR: Were they typed on an "Optima" typewriter?

SINYAVSKY: Yes.

PROSECUTOR: Where and when did you hand over *The Trial Begins, On Socialist Realism* and *Lyubimov?*

SINYAVSKY: *The Trial Begins* and *On Socialist Realism* at the end of 1956; *Fantastic Stories* in 1960; *Lyubimov* and *Unguarded Thoughts* in 1963.

PROSECUTOR: You always handed your works to Zamoyska on the eve of her departure from the Soviet Union. Why? As a precaution?

SINYAVSKY: I suppose so. I don't know what the reason was. It just happened that way. It was different on different occasions. I don't remember exactly.

PROSECUTOR: (*reads out evidence from preliminary investigation*): "I handed over my works, with no one present, in my apartment. She took them shortly before her departure." Was it just fortuitous that it was "shortly before her departure"?

[†] The gist of this addendum, giving Sinyavsky's literary credo, is quoted on pp. 10–11 of the Introduction.

SINYAVSKY: Whenever I gave her my manuscripts, I never made any conditions or requests. I don't know why it is that I handed them to her always on the eve of her departure.

PROSECUTOR: Wasn't Zamoyska afraid that she might be detained at the frontier?

SINYAVSKY: I cannot remember us talking about that.

PROSECUTOR: With whom did you acquaint your works?

SINYAVSKY: I read them aloud to various people—I am fond of reading aloud. This is over a ten-year period, and I cannot remember exactly to whom I read, and what. Daniel knows them all, except the essays. I don't remember whether I read the essays to him. I gave him the two books *Fantastic Stories* and *Lyubimov*. Remezov also knew these two books. I read everything to my wife. At the beginning of 1965 a lot of it was read by Petrov. At the end of '64 and the beginning of '65 Remezov saw and, I think, read these books, or perhaps only one of them. It is possible that earlier I read him an extract from *The Trial Begins*, but as regards my essay, I don't remember. I read my short stories to other people, and perhaps in the process of writing it, I read parts of *Lyubimov*, but I don't remember exactly. When I read out these things I generally didn't give the title, since it hadn't yet been settled, and I didn't always tell people that I was the author.

PROSECUTOR: On November 18, 1965, you said in your evidence that you had read to a group of people: to Petrov, to the Kishilovs, to Khmelnitsky, to the Menshutins, to the Sergeyevs, to the Gerchuks and to Golomshtok.§ Do you confirm this statement?

SINYAVSKY: Yes, but you are questioning me about three works, whereas during the investigation there were ques-

---

§ A. Menshutin collaborated with Sinyavsky on the book mentioned in the footnote on p. 3 of the Introduction. Golomshtok was co-author with Sinyavsky of a book on Picasso (see pp. 7–8 of Introduction).

tions about all my writings. But as regards these three, I read them perhaps to Daniel and Golomshtok, and parts of *Lyubimov* to my wife and to Petrov.

PROSECUTOR: During the investigation you named a number of French people as well—Claude Frioux, Michel Aucouturier and Alfreda Aucouturier.* Do you confirm that you read your work to them?

SINYAVSKY: They read it themselves. Yes, as far as I remember, I think they did. I told Frioux that these works were written by me, but the others learned this in some other way.

PROSECUTOR: When and from whom did you get the published versions of your works?

SINYAVSKY: Zamoyska brought me *Fantastic Stories* in 1963; and at the beginning of 1965 I got *Lyubimov* from Zamoyska through Anne Carrive, in a parcel of books. I saw *The Trial Begins* for the first time only when it had appeared together with other things in a collection.

PROSECUTOR: When did you learn that your works had been published abroad?

SINYAVSKY: I knew that the essay had been published, but I did not see it.

PROSECUTOR: And did you know what construction was being put on your works abroad?

SINYAVSKY: No.

PROSECUTOR: Do you know Daniel's works?

SINYAVSKY: He read them all out loud to me.

PROSECUTOR: Did he read them in manuscript or from the published versions?

SINYAVSKY: I do not look over people's shoulders while they are reading to me.

PROSECUTOR: But have you ever seen the published versions?

---

* Claude Frioux and Michel Aucouturier are French scholars of Russian literature, who spent some time in Russia as exchange students. Alfreda Aucouturier is the wife of Michel.

SINYAVSKY: Yes, I've held them in my hands.

PROSECUTOR: Give us the titles of his works.

SINYAVSKY: They have been mentioned here today so many times that even if I did not know them I should have learned their titles by heart.

PROSECUTOR: In what way did you help Daniel to get his manuscripts abroad?

SINYAVSKY: I'm not quite sure what sort of help I gave him. But I knew what was going on.

JUDGE: Did you send them out, or did Daniel do it himself? What are the facts of the matter?

SINYAVSKY: I would like to give a full reply to that. I knew that he was being published abroad, but I do not remember any case of his manuscripts passing through my hands. When the interrogator showed me any new evidence, I believed it implicitly, regarding Daniel's memory of the matter as better than mine. I remember all about my own manuscripts, but it was up to him to remember about his, and I trust him completely on this score.

PROSECUTOR: Where did Daniel and Zamoyska meet? At your home?

SINYAVSKY: They did sometimes meet in my home.

JUDGE: So in other words Daniel's manuscripts did pass through your hands?

SINYAVSKY: I don't remember exactly. It happened in the way he says.

JUDGE: Did he hand over his manuscripts in your presence?

SINYAVSKY: He may have done so. On one occasion. Perhaps he did, or perhaps he didn't.

PROSECUTOR: In your earlier testimony you said that you knew that Daniel was sending his manuscripts abroad. Is this correct?

SINYAVSKY: I just don't remember. Perhaps I did say that.

PROSECUTOR: During the investigation you admitted that you were the intermediary in the transmission of Daniel's manuscripts. Do you confirm this evidence?

SINYAVSKY: I do not confirm it. I was using the word loosely, not in the legal sense of the word. At that time I did not understand its meaning in law.

JUDGE: Daniel, you tell us how it all was.

Daniel repeats his evidence concerning Anne Carrive and the transmission of his manuscripts without Sinyavsky's knowledge.

JUDGE: Sinyavsky, do you confirm what Daniel says?

SINYAVSKY: I confirm everything except what I have not seen.

PROSECUTOR: Here is what you stated (I quote): "I admit that I got out Daniel's manuscripts through Anne Carrive." Why are you now saying something different?

SINYAVSKY: I don't remember the facts. During the investigation I agreed with Daniel's evidence.

PROSECUTOR: And did you give Daniel the published versions of his books?

SINYAVSKY: I don't remember. Perhaps I did, but perhaps I just saw them at Daniel's, who got them himself from Zamoyska.

PROSECUTOR: Daniel, how did your books get to you?

DANIEL: I don't remember.

Examination of Andrei Sinyavsky

(Continued) ⁝

JUDGE:	We will continue with the examination of Sinyavsky.
PROSECUTOR:	Sinyavsky, do you know Ivanov and his writings published abroad?
SINYAVSKY:	Yes, he is Remezov.† He read to me aloud from his *Is There Life on Mars?*—not all of it—and the article "American Pangs of the Russian Conscience," or it may have been sections from both; he also read parts of a play about a robot.
PROSECUTOR:	What did you think of these writings?
SINYAVSKY:	His style, with its highly polemical and partisan approach, is far removed from mine. I was less than enthusiastic.
PROSECUTOR:	And what did you think of their political angle?
SINYAVSKY:	I found them rather highly pitched on some ideological problems. *Is There Life on Mars?* is about 1953.* I don't really know his writings well enough to judge them from the political point of view.
PROSECUTOR:	Did you give him your writings to read?

---

† See note † on p. 41.
* The play is an allegory about the anti-Semitic campaign in the last months of Stalin's life.

SINYAVSKY: In 1964 I showed him those that were published abroad. Maybe I read them [in manuscript] to him, I am not sure.

PROSECUTOR: Remezov helped you send out the last part of the article *On Socialist Realism?*

SINYAVSKY: It was a short addendum to the article, not the final part.

PROSECUTOR: And you helped Remezov send out his writings?

SINYAVSKY: No.

PROSECUTOR: At your confrontation with him, Remezov said that, through Zamoyska, you helped him send four of his works abroad. Do you confirm this now?

SINYAVSKY: That's what Remezov said, but it is not true.

PROSECUTOR: Why would he not tell the truth?

SINYAVSKY: I wouldn't know. I knew that his friend Busseno[†] was handling his literary affairs.

PROSECUTOR: But at the confrontation he spoke quite categorically. What are your relations with Remezov?

SINYAVSKY: We were colleagues. We were childhood friends, but in the last ten or twelve years we have been just colleagues. I rather lost touch with him. We saw each other rarely.

PROSECUTOR: Is he hostile to you? Why should he tell falsehoods about you? He doesn't have any reasons, does he?

SINYAVSKY: Not before my arrest. I don't know why he started to slander me after my arrest. Remezov is a witness for the prosecution; he has stated in evidence that I hold anti-Soviet views. Maybe he is trying to strengthen his position by these references to me. The protocol drawn up during the investigation contains only Remezov's confession, and the references to me are purely speculative. He has no facts except for one conversation I had with him in 1951, after my father had been arrested, when I supposedly told Remezov that they should have arrested me,

---

† Busseno (spelling uncertain): apparently a French publisher. See the reference to him in Remezov's evidence, pp. 133–34.

since my father had always defended the Soviet point of view. But I remember that conversation, and that is not quite what I said. During the search, one of the MGB [secret police] people had said that I ought to be arrested together with my father. This staggered me, and I kept telling people that my father had always been a loyal Soviet citizen. Remezov is tendentious, he tries to give the impression that I share his views, and refers to me in such a way as to make it appear more convincing that every intellectual thinks as he does.

PROSECUTOR: These three works that figure in the charge represent, I suppose, your political views and convictions?

SINYAVSKY: They represent my position as a writer. In the essay *On Socialist Realism* I discuss my views on art in an informal way.

JUDGE: How about the first part of the essay? Is that also about art?

SINYAVSKY: In this essay, which deals with complex and confused questions of which there are many possible interpretations, I wanted to express my own point of view on socialist realism. There are various opinions on the subject. In the West it is often said that socialist realism is a fraud, an invention—

JUDGE: (*interrupting*): How about the first part?

SINYAVSKY: Excuse me, I want to answer in greater detail. I'll get to the first part—I'm not trying to avoid an answer. As I was saying, my view is that socialist realism is an organic phenomenon in our literature. But my interpretation differs from the commonly accepted one. To define the essence of socialist realism, I took as my starting point a more general frame of reference —that the concept of a purpose is central to our society and our literature. "Purpose" in Greek is "*telos*," hence my term "teleological." And the first part of the article is a general discussion of teleology.

I examine man as a teleological being; then I say
that there are periods—for example, ours—when
purpose is the crucial concept, and in this context I
touch on Marxism, not in the economic or social
sense, but in a moral context, in its aspect as an ideal
of universal happiness. This essay was not written
from the point of view of Marxism or of our theory
of socialist realism. I find it difficult to define my
approach; in general terms it is idealistic. I regard
Communism as the only goal that can be put forward by the modern mind; the West has been
unable to put forward anything like it. I use the
word "religious" in various senses—with reference to
the moral imperative and ironically, with reference,
for example, to the mystique of *The Short Course.**
I talk about our difficulties and contradictions in the
last few years under Stalin; I say that brutalities and
inhuman methods were used. But the Stalinist
period has its legitimate place in history and I don't
reject it. I reject the accusations of the Western
world about the brutalities; they resulted from
action against inertia. Western ideas about the
renunciation of force have no appeal to me. My
reply to liberal critics is: And what have all your
humane old dodderers achieved?

JUDGE: You mean to say that in this essay you welcome a
Communist society?

SINYAVSKY: What I say is that Communism is a supreme goal.
But the actual ways and means are not always in
keeping with the goal. They are similar, but not
identical. Once achieved, the goal is only a poor
likeness of what was envisioned at the beginning.

---

* *The Short Course of the History of the Communist Party of the Soviet
Union*, the authorship of which was ascribed to Stalin personally, and which was
regarded as holy writ from the time of its publication in 1938 until after Stalin's
death.

JUDGE: Here is what you wrote. (*He reads:* "Why do you laugh, scum . . . ?" *etc.*)‡

SINYAVSKY: You are reading a translation from a Polish translation. That was not a good version; it was tendentious.

The judge says there are a number of translations in the record.

SINYAVSKY: I can refer you to Field.§ In his article of July 19, 1965 [in the *New Leader*], he said that the translator distorted my essay, as one scholar affirmed after having read the original. The text was obviously rendered very freely; for this reason I can answer only for the general sense, not for the details.

JUDGE: The court finds no differences in the translations. Would you like me to call in a translator?

SINYAVSKY: No.

PROSECUTOR: So you defend socialist realism in your essay? (*He reads a passage to the effect that the very term contains a contradiction, that socialist means "religious," purposeful, in other words, unreal; that literature should reject a realism ill-suited to it if it wants to express the great and improbable meaning of our time.*) Is that how you defend socialist realism?

SINYAVSKY: I contrast socialist realism with the art of the nineteenth century. It is in socialist realist art that the purpose is crucial and the positive hero stands at the center of the stage, but in the nineteenth century it was the negative hero who predominated. I am against eclecticism, against mixing things that are incompatible. I am not against *The Cherry Orchard*;

---

‡ This is to be found on pp. 38–39 of the Pantheon edition of *On Socialist Realism*.

§ Andrew Field is a regular contributor to the *New Leader*. He has written several articles on the work of Abram Tertz. In the article referred to here he criticizes most of the existing English translations of Tertz.

I am against an unnatural union of The Cherry
Orchard with Mystery-Bouffe.*

JUDGE: Incidentally, about Chekhov. Here you write:
"There is one thing art does not tolerate: eclecticism. . . . But we all went to school, we read all
sorts of books and we knew all too well that there
were remarkable writers before us—Balzac,
Maupassant, Tolstoy, and there was another, what's
his name, Che——, Che——, Che——, oh, yes,
Chekhov. This was our undoing because we all
wanted to write like Chekhov." What's the meaning
of this "Che——, Che——, Che——, Chekhov?"

SINYAVSKY: It should be obvious that I am being ironical.
(*Someone in the courtroom shouts: "It's anti-
Soviet."*) You are just echoing the indictment and
the Glavlit report, where I am said to believe everything I reject.

JUDGE: We are not carrying on a literary debate; we are
concerned with matters of law. So you had better
deal with the first part of the essay which is more
relevant to the charges against you.

SINYAVSKY: I've been dealing with the literary aspect because the
prosecutor raised it.

PROSECUTOR: I brought this in because further on there are political attacks. For example, here on page 46 of the
essay you contrast Lenin with Stalin; you talk about
Communism as a religious system.‡ What has this
to do with socialist realism? What's all this about
Lenin? Why the comparison with Stalin?

SINYAVSKY: It has a bearing on the essay in that literature draws
its sustenance from the soil in which it is rooted.

---

* *Mystery-Bouffe* is the title of a mock mystery play written by Mayakovsky
and staged by Meyerhold in 1918 to glorify the October Revolution of 1917. It is
in a strident "futurist" style very different from the sort of nineteenth-century
realism represented by Chekhov's *Cherry Orchard*. For Sinyavsky's critique of
socialist realism see p. 9 of Introduction.
‡ See p. 92 of the Pantheon edition of *On Socialist Realism*.

The literature of the Stalin period was religious and mystical in character. Here I am talking about the religious-mystical cult that underlay the arts in the Stalin era.

PROSECUTOR: Please don't lecture us on literature. I ask you a simple, concrete question: Why did you portray Ilyich [Lenin] in such an unattractive way?

SINYAVSKY: I said that you cannot make a cult of Lenin. To me Lenin is a human being; there is nothing wrong about saying that.

JUDGE: What did you mean in this passage about the deification of Stalin? (*Reads excerpts.*)

SINYAVSKY: I am being ironical about making a cult of him. If Stalin had lived a little longer, it might well have come to this.

PROSECUTOR: Do these three works reflect your political views and convictions?

SINYAVSKY: I am not a political writer. No writer expresses his political views through his writings. An artistic work does not express political views. You wouldn't ask Pushkin or Gogol about their politics. (*Indignation in the courtroom.*) My works reflect my feelings about the world, not politics.

PROSECUTOR: I had a different impression. Take *The Trial Begins*. (*He reads the passage about fish embryos:*)† ". . . in accordance with Marxism . . ."

JUDGE: (*continuing the quotation*): ". . . Spiral development."

PROSECUTOR: Now tell us, what is all this about? Give us your view of this passage.

SINYAVSKY: Yes. This is a very cynical statement, an attempt to belittle the future, a sneer at Marxism. And it is said by the most negative character in the story, Karlinsky. He is a cynic. He is the one who says that socialism is free slavery. I show in the story that

---

† See pp. 11–12 of Introduction. (Pantheon edition, p. 32.)

Karlinsky is an amoral, worthless person. The author's attitude toward Karlinsky is perfectly clear. After the passage you read, the story goes on as follows. (*He quotes.*) You confuse the character with the author. If you take that approach, then we would identify Gorky with Klim Samgin, and Saltykov-Shchedrin with Yudushka Golovlev.†

JUDGE: Let's take something said by the author. "The filter below the toilet bowl"—what's that? The scene in the camp—isn't that the author speaking?§

SINYAVSKY: I'll explain the scene in the camp. The actual historical events in the story are strictly limited to the end of 1952 and the beginning of 1953, from the "Doctors' Plot"* to the death of Stalin. But a number of scenes only ostensibly refer to real events. This is a literary work, not a political document. (*Laughter in the courtroom.*) Please allow me to speak. One of my characters is a madman—

JUDGE: (*interrupting*): We are interested in another aspect of your work. You write about thought-readers and filters under toilets. In other words, someone made a decision about the installation of such devices. That's the sort of thing covered by Article 70—

---

† Klim Samgin is the "negative" hero of a long novel *The Life of Klim Samgin* (1925–36) by Maxim Gorky (1868–1936).

Mikhail Saltykov-Shchedrin (1826–1889) is a famous Russian satirist whose novel *The Golovlev Family* (1875–80) includes a portrait of one of the most evil figures in Russian fiction, Yudushka Golovlev. "Yudushka" is a diminitive of Judas.

§ This refers to a passage in *The Trial Begins* in which two secret police agents indulge in a daydream about setting up a system of filters in the sewers so as to enable the secret police to recover and reconstitute manuscripts that have been torn up and flushed down toilets. In the epilogue to *The Trial Begins* Sinyavsky prophetically describes how his fictitious author ends up in a labor camp because his work does not please the authorities. The relevant passages in the Pantheon edition of *The Trial Begins* are on p. 97 and p. 122.

* In December, 1952, a large group of Kremlin doctors, mostly Jewish, were arrested on charges of having conspired with the American and British intelligence services (through the Jewish international charity organization Joint) to murder Soviet leaders. They were said to have murdered Zhdanov in 1948. They were released after Stalin's death in March, 1953.

slander. Doesn't this malign our people, our society, our system?

SINYAVSKY: No. These events refer to a specific period, on the eve of Stalin's death. The characters in question are police agents. This is the time of the Doctors' Plot with its atmosphere of arrests and suspicion. The epilogue, written in the first person as though coming from the author, is dated 1956, the year when the story was completed. The "I" in the story is neither Sinyavsky nor Tertz; he is the fictitious author, whose mood is one of fear and exaltation. Kolyma† would be the logical end of the road for him. This is not reality, but something that appears to the author in his nightmares. There is no attempt here to depict the historical reality of the year 1956. (*Laughter in the courtroom.*) This is a literary device, the setting up of an imaginary situation.

JUDGE: But the abortion is real!‡ Why was that brought in?

SINYAVSKY: It is mentioned, but not shown. In literature there is the notion of conventions.

JUDGE: We'll talk about conventions later. You have depicted the Russian people as drunkards.

SINYAVSKY: I can give a detailed answer to that. (*Laughter in the courtroom.*)

JUDGE: All these "unguarded thoughts" of yours—is this the author speaking?

SINYAVSKY: Not entirely. (*Laughter in the courtroom.*)

JUDGE: Field writes that it is "self-flagellation in front of a mirror."§ Do you agree with that?

SINYAVSKY: Yes, up to a point.

---

† Region with gold fields in northeastern Siberia where there were many concentration camps in the Stalin period, and in the immediate post-Stalin years.

‡ See pp. 11–12 of Introduction.

§ In Field's essay in *The New Leader* of July 19, 1965, there is the phrase "ordeal by mirror," but this applies to works other than *Unguarded Thoughts*. In talking about the latter, Field at one point uses the expression "self-abasement." Evidently by some process of contamination the phrase "ordeal by mirror" has been associated with "self-abasement" to produce this phrase, which does not occur in Field's article.

JUDGE: *(reads passage about the Russian people from Un-guarded Thoughts,* then says):* Is this a lyrical digression? Why did you send out this lampoon? This is your people, the Russian people, which has made such sacrifices, which has borne such sacrifices in a terrible war, and suffered, and forged steel for victory, lost twenty million, but stood firm and has created a great culture. These are your "thieves and drunkards," are they? Don't forget that you are being tried by a court of the Russian Federation! *(Disturbance in the courtroom.)*

SINYAVSKY: I can give an answer as regards my attitude to the Russian people and as regards those interpretations to which my works lend themselves. I know that I shall gain nothing by baldly asserting that I love and know my people. Such words prove nothing and they would only seem to be an attempt at self-justification. But nobody can reproach me with partiality toward the West, of not loving the Russian people—I've even been called a Slavophile.† Even in the West my work has been interpreted in this way. What I value most of all in my fellow Russians is their inner spiritual freedom and what one might call their fantastic nature, which manifests itself both at the sublime level of the gift to the world of Dostoyevsky, in their art and songs, and also at a more humble, everyday level. But it does not seem to me that we have to praise the Russian people at every end and turn, even though I regard them as the greatest people on earth.

JUDGE: Did you have to send all this out to the West?

SINYAVSKY: I believe that failings are not simply a counterpart to good qualities—the two are closely interconnected. Drunkenness is another aspect of the spiritual qual-

---

* *New Leader*, July 19, 1965, p. 19.
† Term applied to those Russian thinkers in the nineteenth century who urged a return to purely native traditions, as opposed to the "Westernizers" who thought Russia's salvation lay in the adoption of Western ideas and institutions.

ity. This is what the passage is about. Even in these things (thievishness and drunkenness) not only the bad side of the Russian character comes out, but also its best side. You talk as if they used to think in the West that we were a sober people, but now that Tertz has slandered us, they have found out that we are a lot of drunkards! Another point I should like to make is that we Russians do not like to show off; we prefer to speak of ourselves in a self-deprecating way, rather than in an exalted manner. My words "not capable of creating their own culture" is a case in point; it is an example of how Russians talk about everything in a self-deprecating way. But an opposite view emerges from the whole of my writing—my belief in the capacity—(*Laughter in the court-room.*)

I talk about the nonacceptance of Western civilization. Russians tend to scorn Western comforts, they show indifference to their own ancient monuments; this, too, shows how the Russians set greater store by spiritual values. When I say that we are capable of astonishing the whole of Europe with a heresy, I am referring to the sublime heresy of Dostoyevsky.

JUDGE: "Beggars and thieves suspect in the eyes of other peoples." What is this if it is not a slander on the Russian people? I have myself checked the English translation with the original.

SINYAVSKY: (*Tries to reply.*)

JUDGE: (*interrupts*): Now here is your article about Evtushenko's poem "The Bratsk Hydroelectric Station." Here you stand up for the pyramid of Cheops.† You stood up for that, and you sent this

---

† In Evtushenko's poem there is a dialogue between the Bratsk Hydroelectric Station (representing the new, optimistic world of the Soviet Union) and an Egyptian pyramid (which represents the skeptical ancient world). In his article, originally submitted for publication in *Novy Mir* just before his arrest, Sinyavsky "stood up" for the Egyptian pyramid as a monolithic work of art inappropriately quoted by Evtushenko as a symbol of skepticism. The article never appeared

article about your own people to England?

SINYAVSKY: There are things in this article about the Russian people, I can point them out, if I am given a chance to refer to it.

JUDGE: (to the prosecutor): Continue your questioning.

PROSECUTOR: The views you expressed in *Unguarded Thoughts* are not accidental. We find them in your fiction as well. In *Lyubimov*, for instance, you write that we have no books and that when pickles[§] were turned into sausages, everybody rushed for them, and that only the dogs wouldn't eat them (pages 27 and 160). And this you say about our country where there has been such a great development of libraries! Is this also praise for the Russian people?

SINYAVSKY: Is that a rhetorical question? I can talk about *Lyubimov* as a whole. I am not clear about the way in which this examination is being conducted. Am I only being questioned about certain sentences? Am I expected to answer only "yes" or "no," or am I allowed to give detailed explanations?

JUDGE: You can reply to a concrete question in as detailed a fashion as you please, but you must not wander away from the question.

SINYAVSKY: *Lyubimov* is my last work. I invested this little backwoods town of Lyubimov with some of my favorite qualities of the marvelous and the fantastic. The people who walk around the town are phantoms who are liable to change their shape. It is pure invention. The basic idea is one of illusoriness, of invisibility. This is not a real town, it's a town existing only in my imagination. The novel is a lyrical one, not a political one. It is not a political satire, as is said by some people who even compare

---

in the Soviet Union and was first published in English translation in *Encounter*, April 1967. However, it was not, as the judge says (this whole passage looks as though it had been garbled in the transcript), "sent to England."

§ Actually, it was "red peppers." See p. 13 of Introduction.

my Lyubimov with Shchedrin's Glupov.* I cannot accept this comparison; if only people would read the title properly. Shchedrin's town Glupov is derived from the word "*glupy*" ["stupid"], but my Lyubimov is derived from the word for "love" ["*lyublyu, lyubit*"]. And my attitude to my town is kindly. I have there the words: "Good morning, my love, my Lyubimov." The town is a small piece of my native land, but it is nothing more than that; it is not a symbol for the Soviet Union as a whole, and there are no reasons for putting a wider interpretation on it. The inhabitants of this town put their dreams in place of reality. . . .

JUDGE: But Boris Filippov thinks that Lyubimov and the U.S.S.R. are one and the same thing: "The Soviet Union is reflected in Lyubimov as in a drop of water." This is Filippov's interpretation. Do you agree with him?

SINYAVSKY: No. There are other views—Field's, for example. The whole of Filippov's introduction is based on quotations from various authors—Mandelshtam, Zabolotsky, Slutsky.† These quotations are tacked onto Filippov's anti-Soviet views. His interpretation is quite arbitrary. One can see this where he says that there is something in the novel to the effect that the town of Lyubimov would be saved by a woman. There is nothing of the sort in the novel. And then it is absurd to say that the people living in Lyubimov are usurpers. Vasyuki§ wanted to become a new Moscow, but this didn't mean that the inhabitants were usurpers; they were

---

* See pp. 12–13 of Introduction.

† Soviet poets. Osip Mandelshtam died in a Soviet concentration camp, Nikolai Zabolotsky died in 1958, and Boris Slutsky (born 1919) is a well-known living poet who has come into prominence since Stalin's death.

§ Name of small town in *The Twelve Chairs* (Chap. 23) by Ilf and Petrov which aspires to become the capital of Russia.

patriots of their own town. Interpretations of this sort are an old trick.

The judge quotes Field on *The Trial Begins.*

SINYAVSKY: *The Trial Begins* is about Stalinism; it is more closely related to actual events than *Lyubimov*. My positive hero is the town of Lyubimov itself. And my laughter is kindly, not malicious. My attitude, as author, to Lenya Tikhomirov, who had once been a good man, is disapproving.

JUDGE: The lady who translated the novel[‡] writes that the name "Lenya" has associations with "Lenin," with "*len*" ["idleness"] and with Leshy [the spirit of the woods in Russian folklore]. Was she right in comparing Lenya Tikhomirov with Lenin?

SINYAVSKY: No. She is taking liberties here. She also says that my old Proferansov is Marx, and things like that.

JUDGE: But was she right in saying that you have a negative attitude to Lenin, that you cast a slur on his sacred name?

SINYAVSKY: I would like to say something about that. . . .

JUDGE: Was she right in saying this or not?

SINYAVSKY: No. I do not have a negative attitude to Lenin.

JUDGE: Well just listen to this. (*Quotes the passage in* Lyubimov *where Lenin bays at the moon.*[§] *Commotion in the courtroom.*)

Why do you have this? Is this supposed to be in the spirit of Joyce, Kafka, surrealism or something? Is this an expression of sympathy for the town of Lyubimov? Or for Lenin? Tell us more about this passage.

---

‡ Manya Harari, who wrote an introduction to her translation of *Lyubimov* (*The Makepeace Experiment*, Pantheon Books, New York, 1965). The reference is on p. 8.

§ See p. 22 of Introduction and p. 142 of *The Makepeace Experiment.*

SINYAVSKY: I regret that I brought in Lenin—that was tactless of me. The whole of this chapter is called "The Life of S. S. Proferansov in This World and the Next." The entire chapter consists of gibberish; it is based on a series of absurdities rather as in the children's song "Past the peasant rode the village . . ."‡ (*Commotion in the courtroom. Voice: "Why bring in a Soviet song?"*)

It is a deliberate farrago of nonsense, everything in it contradicts common sense, everything is topsy-turvy: "Proferansov was an astronomer, a Diogenes and philanthropist"; Nicholas I is confused with Nicholas II; the hero talks with Arina Rodionovna in the verse of Esenin*—everything is obviously made up and absurd. (*Commotion in the courtroom.*)

I was not trying to run down Lenin, but I regret that I introduced him into this gibberish together with a number of other names such as those of Pushkin, Esenin, Leo Tolstoy and Lavoisier. . . .

Recess for twenty minutes.

PROSECUTOR: That's not the only passage where you besmirch the bright name of Lenin. You have explained this passage. But here is another place, on page 110, in an author's footnote, where the walls have been papered over with money: "The money on the walls came briskly to life, the Celestial Emperors with their little beards . . ."† and so forth. What did you mean here? What is that for?

---

‡ A nonsense rhyme which is probably not specifically Soviet in origin.

* Arina Rodionovna was Pushkin's nurse, to whom he was indebted for his knowledge of popular Russian speech. Sergei Esenin was a Soviet poet, who committed suicide in 1925.

† See pp. 126–127 of *The Makepeace Experiment*. It is the translator's note that identifies the Emperors with Lenin, but since Lenin's profile does appear as a watermark on Soviet banknotes, this would seem to be a justified gloss.

SINYAVSKY: It is not said by the author. In *Lyubimov* the author does not speak in his own voice. And this passage is not about Lenin. It is a description of how the undercover agent Vitya Kochetov[‡] begins to have hallucinations.

PROSECUTOR: That's just not true. This is an author's footnote! Why do you deny it? (*Quotes passage containing the footnote.*)

SINYAVSKY: These are not footnotes as in a work of scholarship, but they are used by me in a fictional work as a device. This particular footnote conveys what is going on in the mind of Vitya Kochetov. I was not referring to Lenin, and you will not find his name here.

JUDGE: The room is papered over with money. And the money had Lenin's portrait on it. There is nobody else's portrait. And your words in the text are blasphemous.

SINYAVSKY: They are not about the money, nor are they about Lenin. The Emperors are not on the money, but belong to the motley pattern [on the wall].

PROSECUTOR: And this is how you describe the bright future to come (*quotes:* "*The town, like a patchwork quilt,*" *and so on, pages 77 and 78*[§]). About what future are you talking here?

SINYAVSKY: All this is said in connection with Lenya Tikhomirov of whom I, as author, disapprove. Because of his methods he does not evoke the author's sympathy. He is unable to change anything in the life around him, all he can do is to work on people by suggestion so that they think changes have taken place.

[‡] A caricature of the extreme right-wing editor of the Soviet literary monthly *Oktyabr*, the novelist Vsevolod Kochetov, who is also scathingly referred to in Daniel's *This Is Moscow Speaking*. See p. 17 of Introduction.

[§] This passage is on p. 85 of *The Makepeace Experiment*. It is a somewhat comic description of Lyubimov as "transformed" by Lenya Tikhomirov (Leonard Makepeace in the English translation). The prosecution is trying to make out that it is a parody of the "bright future" promised under Communism.

Tikhomirov calls on people to be happy. The whole of his activity is, if you like, voluntarist*—it is divorced from real life. The water in the river does not really change into champagne, but under the influence of Tikhomirov people think it does. Tikhomirov's actions have nothing in common with Marxism, and the picture of the future has nothing to do with Communism. The whole story is narrated by the characters in it, and all these characters speak in their own peculiar way. You must take account of this. Some of the characters use clichés and they become even more exaggerated as recorded by Saveli Kuzmich, an old man full of book learning, who tries to speak in a scholarly way and whose style is stilted and high-flown. Fun is being made of the speakers, not of what they say. There are many examples in literature of the use of parodied newspaper language, and there is nothing political about this device. Just think of Mayakovsky's *Bathhouse* and *Bedbug*.

JUDGE: And who are you making fun of in the scene about the money? And what about this bit where it says that we shall "outstrip [Holland]"?†

SINYAVSKY: I'm making fun of Lenya Tikhomirov.

JUDGE: And what about "the little beards"? And Lenin's well-known words about a "universal breathing space"? (*Quotes Lyubimov.*)‡ What is the author making fun of here? This is not the same as in *The Bathhouse.*

SINYAVSKY: I'm making fun of Lenya Tikhomirov, who talks in clichés and always thinks "on a world scale."

PROSECUTOR: And who are you making fun of here? (*Quotes.*)

---

* See pp. 13–14 of Introduction.
† This refers to an allusion in *The Makepeace Experiment*, p. 102, to the Soviet slogan about overtaking the West.
‡ *The Makepeace Experiment*, p. 102.

SINYAVSKY: Saveli Kuzmich Proferansov. I should point out that sometimes he moves away from Lenya and at other times he comes back to him. . . .

PROSECUTOR: You are trying to move away from the point!

SINYAVSKY: I'm not making fun of Communism, but of Proferansov.

PROSECUTOR: And what about this: "They have planes, but we have nothing except our naked imagination. . . ."[‡] Into whose face are you sticking this bloody hyperbole?

SINYAVSKY: This is a description of a concrete situation—an air raid on the town of Lyubimov. And Lenya Tikhomirov averts the danger by using his extraordinary mental powers.

JUDGE: Field interprets that differently. And here you have the scene of a conference in the provincial party committee, and the secretary, Comrade O, says: "And we don't want any consequences of the cult of personality."[*] Doesn't this express the author's attitude either? Is this a metaphor, a hyperbole? Is this something said just by Comrade O?

SINYAVSKY: In the person of Comrade O, the secretary of the provincial party committee, there is a hint of certain features of Khrushchev, but it was not my intention to criticize him or his activity—I just borrowed certain of Khrushchev's mannerisms—the way in which he got worked up during his speeches and used crude language.

PROSECUTOR: Let's go back to your essay *On Socialist Realism*. Let's take your political views. What did you have in mind when you wrote: "To do away with prisons, we built new prisons. . . .[§] We defiled not only our bodies, but our souls"? What has this got to do with socialist realism?

[‡] This refers to an attempt, described in Chapter 6 (p. 150) of *The Makepeace Experiment*, to "reconquer" Lyubimov by means of airpower.

[*] *The Makepeace Experiment*, p. 73.

[§] See p. 38 of Pantheon edition of *On Socialist Realism*.

SINYAVSKY: I was talking about purposes, about difficulties and contradictions, about inhuman methods under Stalin. But even these I don't reject. (*He quotes a passage.*) I even justify such methods. I said: "What did you do, you humane old dodderers?" and "How nice it is to drink tea with jam." I was referring to the Western liberals.

PROSECUTOR: I wouldn't say you justify them. Here is what you write: "In the name of the ultimate goal, we resorted to methods used by our enemies. . . . We introduced torture and epaulettes[†] . . . we placed a new Czar on the empty throne. . . . It seemed at times as if for the sake of a complete victory of Communism all we had to do was to give up the idea of Communism."[*] How are we to understand this?

SINYAVSKY: We glorified the old Russia, we put a new Czar, Stalin, on the throne. As I said before, you must bear in mind that I was referring to the Stalinist era.

PROSECUTOR: And here is how you compare the West with us: "How can a believer possibly wish freedom from his God?" What are we to make of this?

SINYAVSKY: Western democracy is based on "freedom of the individual," "freedom of competition," etc. In the West they talk about freedom of choice. I am being ironical about his. The Lord God is not a parliament. For a religious person, the question of freedom does not arise. For a theologically minded person there can be no "freedom of choice." I say all this with reference to Soviet writers, for whom there is no question of any freedom of choice. Either you believe or, if not (*he looks at the prisoner's dock*), you go to jail.

---

† Reference to Stalin's reintroduction of epaulettes for officers during World War II.

* *On Socialist Realism*, p. 38.

JUDGE: "Such a writer welcomes directives from above with delight."[†] What does that mean? Is that your political credo?

SINYAVSKY: This is obvious irony. And it's quite clear at whose expense.

JUDGE: There we have it. This is exactly what Article 70 is about. You say, "directives of the party and the government." This is not a literary device, is it? It's a plain statement.

SINYAVSKY: That's how things were under Stalin.

JUDGE: What has Stalin got to do with it? Times have changed.

SINYAVSKY: And who was the greatest authority on linguistics and economics and music? Wasn't it Stalin? Isn't it clear what I was talking about?

JUDGE: Do you think reactionary publishers would have printed your books so beautifully if there had been nothing anti-Soviet in them? Just look at this paper, just look at this book jacket. . . . Incidentally, here is an edition of the essay and the story *The Trial Begins*. Two-thirds of the book jacket is black and only one-third red. Is this meant to show that dark aspects predominate in the Soviet Union? Would you have been so highly rated if this was not anti-Soviet propaganda?[‡]

SINYAVSKY: I did not order the jacket. And opinions vary. "Tertz is no anti-Communist"; "American readers would be mistaken if they regarded Tertz as an enemy of Communist society"—that is what Milosz wrote.[§]

---

† *Ibid.*, p. 42.

‡ The judge's point about the color of the jacket of *The Trial Begins* is mysterious. It is true that about one-third of the cover of the American edition (Pantheon) is red, but the rest of the jacket is predominantly white, with a patch of gray. (The British edition [Collins] is green and white.) However, the Pantheon edition of *On Socialist Realism* has an almost entirely black jacket, and if one were to put it side by side with *The Trial Begins* one would get an effect similar to that described by the judge.

§ Czeslaw Milosz, eminent Polish émigré poet and critic, author of *The Captive Mind*, wrote the introduction to the Pantheon edition of *On Socialist Realism*.

JUDGE: Tarsis was proclaimed a new Dostoyevsky over there. Field makes you into a new Schopenhauer. Soon they'll be comparing you with Shakespeare.

SINYAVSKY: Citizen Chairman, we are not talking about Dostoyevsky, but about politics. I want to quote you a passage from *On Socialist Realism* to show you what the author thinks about politics: "If the monarchy or Western democracy were to return, which is one and the same thing, we would start a revolution again."†

JUDGE: (*to prosecutor after short pause*): Continue with your questions.

PROSECUTOR: In this essay, too, you have slurred the bright name of Lenin. This is what you write: "Mayakovsky soon realized what things cannot be made fun of. He could no more permit himself to make fun of Lenin, than Derzhavin could permit himself to sneer at the Empress."‡ How do you explain this?

SINYAVSKY: This passage is about stylistic peculiarities. The classicism of the twentieth century echoes the classicism of the eighteenth century. The disease of the nineteenth century was irony. The young Mayakovsky made fun of things, but then he stopped. Mayakovsky was confronted by limits to what could be made fun of. But in the nineteenth century there were no such limits. Derzhavin represents classicism,* and I am comparing his classicism with that of the twentieth century.

PROSECUTOR: You also have a dig at Pushkin. "By the hand of the depraved and bashful Tatyana¶ Pushkin wrote indecent verse."

SINYAVSKY: Pushkin was an ironical writer.

---

† See p. 80 of *On Socialist Realism*.
‡ See p. 75 of *On Socialist Realism*.
* See p. 10 of Introduction.
¶ Heroine of Pushkin's epic poem *Evgeni Onegin*. In the Pantheon edition (p. 75), this sentence reads, more plausibly: "Pushkin . . . addressed indecent verses even to the chaste and modest Tatyana."

The prosecutor reads out the findings of Glavlit on the essay *On Socialist Realism* which describes it as an attempt to examine the concept from a revisionist point of view and declares that the article is full of anti-Soviet propaganda, is against Communism and the guiding role of the party, and alleges that Russians do not have freedom of speech and creative activity.

PROSECUTOR: Do you agree with this conclusion?

SINYAVSKY: No. This report is based on a distortion of the text. (*Quotes from his essay.*) Instead of "teleological" the report has "theological." It leaves out passages which would not support its case. I did not say "we sacrificed martyrs," but "martyrs sacrificed themselves."§

JUDGE: Let's have this quotation in full. (*Quotes.*) One must quote in full.

SINYAVSKY: I am talking about Glavlit's report. Here are examples of distortions. (*Quotes.*)

JUDGE: Give the rest of this quotation. (*He quotes.*) What you say about Gorky‡ here is not very sympathetic to him. One must quote accurately.

SINYAVSKY: I am talking about distortions in the Glavlit findings. Here is another example of how Glavlit attributes to me the opposite of what I actually say. I have: "Many people say such and such. But Mayakovsky showed this to be false." But Glavlit writes: "Sinyavsky says such and such."*

JUDGE: Let's have the rest of this passage. (*Quotes the wider context.*)

PROSECUTOR: Sinyavsky, now if Glavlit had quoted the passage as it has just been quoted by the president of the court, would you agree with their conclusions?

---

§ See p. 36 of *On Socialist Realism.*

‡ There are several references to Gorky in *On Socialist Realism.* See, for example, pp. 47 and 49 of the Pantheon edition. It is difficult to say which one the judge is quoting, but none of them seem all that "unsympathetic."

* This probably refers to p. 88 of *On Socialist Realism.*

SINYAVSKY: No, I would still not agree with them.

The judge quotes even wider context.

SINYAVSKY: I've already explained that. Socialist realism is incompatible with the literature of the nineteenth century.

PROSECUTOR: When did you write the manuscript of an article entitled "Taking a Reading,"* which was found during a search of your home?

SINYAVSKY: It is also called "Essay in Self-Analysis."

JUDGE: It's the same thing.

SINYAVSKY: This is an incomplete rough draft, a fragment of an article that I never finished. The first section was written in 1953–54, another section in 1960. The indictment says it expresses the "essence of my views." I hold that a part of a rough draft cannot express the essence of a writer's views. I never showed it or read it to anyone. Not even to Daniel.

The prosecutor is about to read a passage.

JUDGE: This manuscript does not figure in the charge against Sinyavsky. It throws light on his personality and nothing more. I should explain that manuscripts and diaries cannot be used as the basis of charges if they have not been circulated.

PROSECUTOR: You write here about Lenin's enormous brain, about his "hypertrophy of the reason," and that when an autopsy was made his brain turned out to be eaten away with sclerosis.§ Doesn't this link up with what you write about Lenin in your [other] works?

SINYAVSKY: No, it doesn't. In *Lyubimov* Lenin appears in a deliberately nonsensical sequence, in a situation that

---

* In Russian, *Tochka Otscheta*.

§ This and the following reference are to Sinyavsky's "Essay in Self-Analysis," which was confiscated at the time of his arrest, and of which no copy is so far available in the West.

does not, I think, show him in his proper light. But these reflections of mine refer to 1937. (*Commotion in the courtroom.*)

The judge quotes comparison of Lenin with Stalin.

SINYAVSKY: It was easier for people with a petty-bourgeois mentality to understand Stalin. About Lenin I speak with respect. (*Laughter in the courtroom.*)

The judge quotes passage which says that Lenin is inexplicable to people with a petty-bourgeois mentality.

SINYAVSKY: Stalin was possessed. People with a petty-bourgeois mentality cannot rise to the level of Lenin.

PROSECUTOR: Doesn't it follow from what you say that the year 1937 was foreshadowed by Lenin? You say, for instance: "Stalin made Lenin's metaphors come true."

SINYAVSKY: I am talking here about metaphors. If we were to make them come true, then it would be the end of the world. We say, for instance, "Shadows fall," or "The heavens fall," and so on and so forth. If this were to happpen in actual fact, then the world would be struck by catastrophe. When Lenin spoke about the enemies of our ideology, he used metaphors. Stalin put these metaphors into effect, and we had the horrors of the year 1937. Stalin twisted metaphors inside out. But Lenin is no more responsible for Stalin than language is responsible for the literal putting into effect of metaphors.

JUDGE: But according to you the whole business begins with Lenin. (*Quotes.*)

PROSECUTOR: You write: "The bloodletting was still to come!"

SINYAVSKY: I am held responsible for every word. I would like to point out to the court that this is a rough draft. During the search of my apartment other manuscripts, notes and rough drafts were taken away, and if such rough drafts are now to be quoted in evidence, then I should like to refer to the marginal notes I made on the writings of the émigré Bunin, where I scribbled: "wild reactionary rubbish." So you can see that the question of what represents my true views is debatable.

JUDGE: The articles asked for by the defense on the works of Abram Tertz have been brought from the Lenin Library. Some of the materials requested are not available in the library.

Recess.

Session of February 11, 1966, 3:30 P.M.

Examination of Andrei Sinyavsky

(Continued)

PROSECUTOR: Did you receive royalties for your writings and what do you know about the amount?

SINYAVSKY: I did not write out of material interest, I wasn't trying to make money either in my work here or in publishing over there. A few years ago Zamoyska jokingly called me a millionaire. But what this means now, after the monetary reform in France, I don't know.

PROSECUTOR: Does that mean you're not a millionaire any longer?

SINYAVSKY: I don't know.

PROSECUTOR: Did you make any use of your royalties?

SINYAVSKY: The last time Zamoyska was here, I asked her to use my royalties for a subscription to a French journal on art. I don't know whether it comes out of my royalties, but I have been getting the magazine regularly since January, 1965. I sent Soviet magazines and books in return. In addition, I asked the Kishilovs, who were going to France, to buy me some books. But this idea never got beyond talk, since I was arrested and the Kishilovs' visa† was canceled.

---

† Their Soviet exit visa.

PROSECUTOR: And you wanted to pay off your debt to Kishilov from your money abroad. Isn't that what you told him?

SINYAVSKY: I don't remember such a conversation. I was told during the investigation that there is a tape recording of such a conversation, but I think it more likely that they recorded a discussion about money I had with my wife.[†]

PROSECUTOR: You mean the tape recorder that Kishilov was planning to buy for himself in France?

SINYAVSKY: I am talking about the tape recorder that was used to take down my conversations. . . .

PROSECUTOR: (interrupts): Why didn't you try to publish your things in the U.S.S.R.?

SINYAVSKY: As a literary critic, I had a pretty good idea of the prevalent tastes and standards in our literature. On a number of important points they did not coincide with my tastes as a writer. My literary work differs substantially from what is acceptable here. I don't mean in politics, but in artistic attitudes. Even the six pieces for which I am not being charged could not be printed here, at least not now. I know the publishing business here and that is why I never submitted my things to our publishers. As the critic Andrei Sinyavsky, who appeared in our press, and as the writer Abram Tertz, who was being printed abroad, I was, of course, aware of the difference between my two identities. But I never held that this difference was fundamental, that it was a case of split personality. That is why I don't consider myself a double-dealer and hypocrite.

PROSECUTOR: Why did you send abroad the three things for which you are being charged?

SINYAVSKY: I told you: because they could not be published here.

[†] This refers to microphones hidden in the Sinyavskys' apartment by the KGB.

PROSECUTOR: I can't blame our publishers.

SINYAVSKY: I thought the court was interested in—

JUDGE: (*Interrupts.*) No. Why did you send out these particular writings, and why did you conceal your name?

SINYAVSKY: I concealed my name in the publication of all nine works, including the six for which I am not being charged, and not just the three that are supposedly anti-Soviet. As a literary critic, I tried to write about authors who were close to me as a man and as a writer. I wrote about Mayakovsky, Pasternak, Khlebnikov, Babel.§ It seems to me that some of them influenced my writings as Abram Tertz. I don't consider my work as a Soviet critic either as a mask or as a subterfuge, nor just as a means of making a living. It is my life's vocation. That is why my work was never easy; it involved a lot of problems, which could not always be overcome. My favorite writings, those about Babel and Pasternak, were held up by the publishers for seven or eight years, even though they had been commissioned.

PROSECUTOR: But you didn't try to send these articles abroad?

SINYAVSKY: No, they were eventually printed here. Altogether, in the last two or three years, I have found it possible to express my own views. The study of literature for me was not a mask, it is my life's work, and there was always a close relationship between my work as a critic and my work as a writer. But I knew that if they were so reluctant to publish my articles on literature, then the chances of my fiction's being published were even slighter. But I didn't think this would always be so. My writings are complex and strange, and I did not regard them as

---

§ Velemir Khlebnikov (1885–1922), a futurist poet known for his extreme linguistic experimentalism. Isaac Babel (1894–41), famous Soviet short story writer, author of "Red Cavalry." He was arrested in 1939 and died in a concentration camp.

intended for the mass reader. In my own mind I never regarded my publications abroad as a means of establishing contact with a reading public. It was just a way of preserving them for the few people who, maybe, sometime, might find something of interest in these writings. This is literature for myself and for a few others, wherever they may live or in whatever age. I actually say this in one of my works.*

PROSECUTOR: Were you ever shown how you were published, and in how many copies, and what sort of a public your publishers are aiming at?

SINYAVSKY: I can only talk for myself and of my own attitude. In one of my things there is a passage which reads: "Only an eccentric enthusiast could put words together like this." I was very little interested in the number of editions and copies in which my works appeared.

PROSECUTOR: But I understood you to say that you sent your works abroad not because they were anti-Soviet but because you wished to see them published?

SINYAVSKY: Published in the sense of preserved.

PROSECUTOR: Why did you keep your manuscripts at Dokukina's and not in your own home?

SINYAVSKY: You're jumping to conclusions, as with the question of my pseudonym. The indictment treats this as a proof of my guilt, saying that I understood the anti-Soviet nature of my things and adopted a pseudonym because I realized I was writing anti-Soviet propaganda. But a pseudonym is not an underground code name, and every author has a right to use one as he pleases. I adopted a pseudonym, just as

---

* His short story "The Icicle" begins with an "author's note" saying: "I write this story as a castaway tells of his distress. Sitting on a piece of wreckage or stranded on a desert island, he throws a bottle with a letter into the stormy sea in the hope that the waves and the wind will bring it to people who will read it and learn the truth long after its poor author is dead." (*Fantastic Stories*, Pantheon edition, p. 35.)

I kept things at Dokukina's, as a precaution—I kept
everything there, including the things that are not
"anti-Soviet." I took account of the possibility that
my works, even though they weren't anti-Soviet,
might be the object of some kind of sanctions,
although I had no particular idea as to what form
such measures might take. I was apprehensive that
this could happen even to those of my writings
which could not be interpreted as anti-Soviet. We
all remember the measures taken against Zoshchenko and Akhmatova in 1946.[†] Perhaps I was a
little more anxious than other people, but when my
father was arrested in 1951, my diaries were taken
away. This is the psychological reason for my caution. I even hid things in connection with which I
am not being charged.

JUDGE: What have Zoshchenko and Akhmatova got to do
with it? Those were different times, but you still go
on hiding things.

SINYAVSKY: It was mainly other things I hid, not the three things
[which figure in the charge].

JUDGE: Your first works are *The Trial Begins* and the essay
on socialist realism. They sell in the West in vast
editions.[‡] This has nothing to do with their literary
side. There's that disgusting scene of intercourse
with a corpse, for instance.[§] If something like that
were to happen in real life, it would be dealt with
under the relevant articles [of the Criminal Code].
But such acts are not anti-Soviet. These two works
are another matter; you deliberately calculated that

[†] Mikhail Zoshchenko (1895–1958) and Anna Akhmatova (1889–1966) were
the main victims of a campaign launched against "erring" writers by the party in
1946.

[‡] The sales of Tertz's work in the West have been by no means as large as the
judge suggests.

[§] An illusion to a scene involving necrophilia in "The Icicle," one of the
stories in the collection *Fantastic Stories*.

they would be published and attract attention to you.

SINYAVSKY: The necrophilia scene is a flash-back to the past, to the fourteenth century.

JUDGE: Here is what you write about the fears of Proferansov [a character in Lyubimov]: "If I'm called to account by dread judges"—these thoughts of Samson Samsonovich, do they reflect your own fears and anxieties?

SINYAVSKY: This is said not by Samson Samsonovich but by Saveli Kuzmich [a descendant of the other Proferansov], and these are not my thoughts.

JUDGE: But all the same, when you sent your work out you were concerned with protecting yourself and taking precautions?

SINYAVSKY: Earlier, during the preliminary investigation, all the works of Abram Tertz were described as anti-Soviet. Now only three are described as anti-Soviet. My interrogators read everything very carefully. It appears that the political characterization of a literary work is a tricky business, if one and the same work is sometimes found to be anti-Soviet and sometimes not. I beg the court to go into this matter as carefully as possible, so as to avoid mistakes.

JUDGE: But your essay [on socialist realism] has little to do with literature. This is not literature, and the court will pay particular attention to the first part of it.

SINYAVSKY: No, this essay is not literature. The problem is approached from a philosophical and psychological angle. This happens all the time among people interested in literature. I touch on the concept of "purpose." It is usual in a literary study to look first at the general background. There is nothing, therefore, sinister about this.

PROSECUTOR: Sinyavsky, now tell the court, when did it become clear to you that your works were being exploited by bourgeois propaganda?

SINYAVSKY: I'm still not completely clear about this.

PROSECUTOR: When did you see the book with Filippov's introduction?

SINYAVSKY: In 1965, a few months before my arrest. In the indictment it says that "I knew, but did nothing to prevent," etc. But until 1965 my information was of a different order. What the indictment says is based on mere suspicion. That I knew, but took no preventive measures [to stop any more of my works being published at all] is simple guesswork on the part of the investigative authorities. I had received two books in published form: *Fantastic Stories* (1961, without a preface) and *Lyubimov* (1965, with a preface by Filippov). Now what facts did I actually know? I knew, for example, that Frioux, a French Communist, had read *The Trial Begins* and had found nothing anti-Soviet in it. Incidentally, Frioux was recently mentioned by Simonov in *Pravda* as a friend of our poetry.* Further, Zamoyska had told me that they wanted to publish Tertz in Czechoslovakia and Hungary. I saw an announcement in *Lettres Françaises*† about the publication of Tertz's works. For me this was a sign that progressive circles in the West did not regard my works as anti-Soviet. I thought Filippov's article was something exceptional. I still have no full picture about Western reaction to my works, but I have a strong impression that bourgeois propaganda indulges in wishful thinking. The epithet "anti-Soviet" is often used in the West for sensational purposes. I have no confidence in the objectivity of the investigative authorities—they have included in the indictment

---

* This was an article about a recent collection of Russian verse, *La poésie Russe*, Paris, 1965, edited by Elsa Triolet, the wife of the prominent French Communist poet, Louis Aragon. Some of Frioux's translations appeared in this volume. Konstantin Simonov is the well-known Soviet novelist and poet.

† A French Communist literary magazine.

materials about my arrest and comments on my works published in the bourgeois press after my arrest (*Time* of October 19, 1965, Washington *Post* of November 20, 1964), and these materials are produced as objective proof of my anti-Soviet activities. In the West they have published stories that I am from an Old Believer family, that I was a very close friend of Pasternak, etc. Goodness knows what else they may have written about me there. There must be objective ways of judging foreign reaction to my works. On November 30, 1965, I asked the investigative authorities to allow me to obtain through my French friends a complete set of all the reviews and other material on Abram Tertz. I suggested that this should be done by whatever way they might think would be the most tactful, for example, through my Communist friends. This request was turned down. Even so, even in the materials tendentiously selected by my interrogators, I found different judgments of my work, for instance those of Milosz and Field. Why did the investigative authorities select only such material as was in support of the prosecution? Why did they set more store by Filippov than by Field? I am still not sure that all the material on my work has been gathered together in its entirety. I know that some reviewers describe me as nothing more than an "unorthodox Soviet writer." This comes closer to my own estimate of my work. I pointed to these comments, rather than to the blatantly sensational anti-Communist articles which the prosecution refers to in support of its case.

JUDGE: Only the court can decide whether you have written any anti-Soviet works; as regards the reviews, they are only evidence as to who is exploiting your work and in what way. Radio Liberty, for instance, did three broadcasts on *Lyubimov*. Did they do it just for fun, or what?

SINYAVSKY: But what about the announcement in *Lettres Françaises?*

JUDGE: That was simply a commercial advertisement, not a recommendation to read your work. There is a certain Mark Slonim, a Swiss professor.§ In 1964 he wrote about Tertz (I quote): "For Tertz the Soviet Union is a madhouse."

SINYAVSKY: Slonim is talking here about things which do not figure in the charge against me.

JUDGE: If even these things are regarded as anti-Soviet, then this applies even more to those works in connection with which you are being charged. TSOPE* stamped a slogan on a book by Tertz. What do you think they did it for, just for fun?

SINYAVSKY: This slogan, which was printed on the book by Lord knows who, has now been mentioned three times. I am not saying that my works are in the spirit of socialist realism. You couldn't print a slogan like that on Fadeyev.† But I could quite conceive of a TSOPE slogan being printed on Zoshchenko, or Akhmatova's *Requiem*,‡ on *One Day in the Life of Ivan Denisovich*,¶ or on Babel.

JUDGE: (*quotes remark by Field on Tertz's treatment of socialist realism, then says*): And him you regard as objective, don't you?

---

§ Well-known Russian critic and scholar, author of a number of books on Soviet literature, now resident in Switzerland. (But he is not "Swiss.")

* An organization of postwar refugees from the Soviet Union which publishes a literary journal *Mosty* (*Bridges*).

† Alexander Fadeyev (1901–1956), Soviet novelist, leading exponent of "socialist realism" (e.g., in his novel *The Young Guard*, 1946, which he republished in a revised form in 1951 to meet party criticism of it) and onetime general secretary of the Union of Soviet Writers. He committed suicide after Khrushchev's revelations about Stalin at the 20th Party Congress in 1956.

‡ A long poem, not yet published in the Soviet Union, but available in émigré editions (it has been translated into English by Robert Lowell: see *Atlantic Monthly* for October, 1964), in which Akhmatova talks of her personal ordeal and that of the Russian people.

¶ Novel by Alexander Solzhenitsyn which caused a great stir when it was published in Moscow, in the journal *Novy Mir*, in 1962. It was the first Soviet work to describe life in the concentration camps under Stalin. See p. 5 of Introduction.

SINYAVSKY: What Milosz says about my essay on socialist realism is more accurate. I refer to Field because I have very little material at my disposal. But I try not to repeat the same passage three times over, as the prosecution does.

JUDGE: Do you really think your essay on socialist realism isn't covered by Article 70 of the Criminal Code? (Quotes:) "So that there should be no more prisons, we built new prisons; so that not one drop of blood should be shed, we killed and killed and killed." What connection does this have with the study of literature?

SINYAVSKY: I've already given my answer about this passage.

JUDGE: I see. (Quotes, reading more of the same passage.) And is this what you would call a literary comment? The court can only go on what you have written. Why were these two works the first to be sent abroad? Was it just accidental? It wasn't just some innocuous story or other that went out first, but The Trial Begins and On Socialist Realism, isn't that right? What was the reason for this? This has nothing to do with what Field says.

SINYAVSKY: I didn't start talking about Field on my own initiative.

JUDGE: Now, you have conducted a seminar on Soviet poetry and you probably talked about Mayakovsky and his epic poem on Lenin. You talked to the students about Lenin as seen by Mayakovsky. And then you have him [Lenin, in Lyubimov] baying at the moon! For this alone the enemies of our country would confer any title you like on you. And it's these two things which are being sold in the West in such large editions. You, a Soviet man of letters, a candidate of philological sciences, a senior research fellow [of the Gorky Institute of World Literature]! Do you understand what you've done?! Now Daniel—he fought in the war, he was wounded, but you had a very easy war. . . .

SINYAVSKY: That wasn't my fault.

JUDGE: I'm not saying it was. You were just lucky. But the people fought, went through a great ordeal, and made steel, and here you go and write things like this about them. You should understand that what concerns the court is that by sending your works abroad you did harm to the state and to your people.

SINYAVSKY: I can only say what I have already said about my attitude to the Russian people.

JUDGE: We have to size up your acts and your own attitude toward them. Take this passage about the Russian people being drunkards. You wrote that in 1964, it was published in 1965. Did you understand what you were doing? That this is a slander on the Russian people?

SINYAVSKY: It's not slander.

PROSECUTOR: When did you first learn that your works were being used abroad for anti-Soviet purposes?

SINYAVSKY: I saw Filippov's article in 1965.

PROSECUTOR: In the journal *Foreign Literature* No. 1, 1962, there is an article by Ryurikov in which he writes about the anti-Soviet writings of Abram Tertz.* (Quotes.) And yet after this article your *Lyubimov* appears. In other words, you knew what people thought of your work, but you nevertheless carried on as before, didn't you?

SINYAVSKY: I only read Ryurikov's article during the preliminary investigation.

PROSECUTOR: Do you mean to tell the court that you had not read Ryurikov's article?

SINYAVSKY: Well, you see I don't follow the journals very closely. (*Laughter in the courtroom.*)

PROSECUTOR: How could you take two different lines simultaneously, publishing articles in the Soviet press from the

---

* Boris Ryurikov, a Soviet critic of orthodox views. In his article he asserted that Abram Tertz was in fact an émigré and not a writer living in the Soviet Union.

point of view of socialist realism, telling other Soviet writers—in particular Sofronov and Bergolts[†]—their business, while at the same time publishing in the West works of a completely different character under the name "Abram Tertz"?

SINYAVSKY: I do not regard my works as anti-Soviet. As regards Sofronov, I've written about him both here and abroad.[‡] My attitude toward him finds its fullest expression in *Lyubimov*.

PROSECUTOR: Let me remind you about your articles [in the Soviet press]. In *Novy Mir*, No. 2 for 1962, you reproached one of our poets for not depicting our life vividly enough. But you are pretty vivid in your own works!

SINYAVSKY: In my articles [in the Soviet press] I was giving not only my own views but also the views of the editors who commissioned these articles from me. (*Laughter in the courtroom.*)

It's only during the last two or three years that I've been able to give fuller expression to my own views. But this has scarcely brought me any laurels— I have been attacked and quite a lot was done to stop me publishing what I wanted to.

PROSECUTOR: In *Novy Mir* you wrote about Sofronov and criticized him. How are we to reconcile this with your anti-Soviet works?

SINYAVSKY: I do not regard as anti-Soviet my works published abroad. And I do not think they differ basically from what I have published here.

PROSECUTOR: In *Novy Mir*, No. 12, 1964, you wrote about the Soviet writer Shevtsov, accusing him of defamation.[§] (*Laughter in the courtroom.*)

[†] Anatoli Sofronov: mediocre Soviet poet and playwright of conservative views. Unfavorably reviewed by Sinyavsky in *Novy Mir* for August, 1959.

Olga Bergolts: Soviet poetess. Sinyavsky's article about her work in *Novy Mir* for May, 1960, is favorable to her. Perhaps the prosecutor doesn't realize this. For Sinyavsky's campaign against "influential yes-men," see pp. 6–7 of Introduction.

[‡] There are satirical references to him and Kochetov in *The Makepeace Experiment*.

[§] See p. 7 of Introduction.

How does this fit in with the defamatory anti-Soviet idea of your story *The Trial Begins?* What is the connection between these two things published in different places?

SINYAVSKY: The idea of my story is not defamatory, and there is no connection between the two.

JUDGE: In *The Trial Begins* you write that in 1956 you land up in Kolyma. Isn't that defamatory?

SINYAVSKY: I've already explained that it isn't. *The Trial Begins* is set in the time of the Stalin cult.

JUDGE: And the epilogue to the story—isn't that defamatory either?

SINYAVSKY: No.

PROSECUTOR: As Abram Tertz you mocked at the name of Lenin, but in *Novy Mir*, No. 5, 1960, in an article about Olga Bergolts, you wrote differently about Lenin. What are we to make of this?

SINYAVSKY: Those sentences in *Lyubimov* do not express my attitude to Lenin. I can tell you what my attitude to Lenin is.

JUDGE: You've already told us in your works.

PROSECUTOR: Sinyavsky, let us hear how you would describe your behavior yourself. How do you, a senior research worker who achieved his position in this country, went to school in this country—how do you yourself view the fact that you sent your anti-Soviet works abroad?

SINYAVSKY: I do not agree with that description of my works and so I cannot reply to the question.

VASILYEV: Who was the draft of "Taking a Reading" meant for?

SINYAVSKY: This is the draft of an article which didn't work out. It was written for nobody in particular, just for myself.

VASILYEV: Did you often go to the Lenin Library?

SINYAVSKY: Yes.

VASILYEV: How many files did you have? One or two? One for works written for the Soviet press and another for manuscripts to be sent abroad?

SINYAVSKY: That is a thinly disguised sneer, and I shall not answer the question.

JUDGE: There is no sneer here. The question is: Where did you keep those manuscripts intended for the Soviet press, and where did you keep those intended for publication abroad?

SINYAVSKY: I did not have special files for either type of manuscript.

JUDGE: You kept manuscripts at Dokukina's. In other words, you kept your manuscripts in two places?

SINYAVSKY: As regards Dokukina I've already given my reply.

VASILYEV: Where does the name Arzhak come from?*

SINYAVSKY: I don't know.

VASILYEV: During the preliminary investigation you stated that the name was taken from a song.

SINYAVSKY: Read out my evidence.

JUDGE: (reads): "If I am not mistaken, it is from a song . . ."

SINYAVSKY: I don't know.

VASILYEV: What were the things that you got from Zamoyska?

SINYAVSKY: I received presents from French friends and I gave them presents in return. I don't see anything wrong about this.

VASILYEV: During the investigation you stated that you received two jackets, two sweaters, a nylon shirt and something else.

SINYAVSKY: That's right. Read a little further—it also says what I gave them.

VASILYEV: I'm interested in what you got. (*Murmur of approval in the courtroom.*)

SINYAVSKY: What you're trying to say is that I sold my country for these rags?

---

* This is probably a mistake in the transcript, since Arzhak was Daniel's pseudonym.

The judge reads record of interrogation.

SINYAVSKY: Please read the parts about the presents which I gave to Zamoyska and the others.

VASILYEV: You said that you saw two of your books in published form, and Zamoyska said that you were a millionaire. How come so much money for two books?

SINYAVSKY: I only knew that I was being published.

VASILYEV: (to Daniel): Did it ever occur to you to write to your publishers and ask them to stop printing you?

DANIEL: I've already given my answer to that question. I could only have done that by revealing my identity. I've already explained that.

VASILYEV: But you did consider it?

DANIEL: I did consider it, but I didn't write to them.

VASILYEV: Why didn't you send them a letter?

DANIEL: I didn't know how to do it. And then I didn't write letters which would come in handy if I were arrested.

JUDGE: Surely the point is that things were going better and better. It was like a chain reaction. First one small book comes out, and then a de luxe edition. Why should you have written a letter?

DANIEL: I've already said that a letter would not have stopped my foreign publishers. Now as regards the point that the mere fact of my being published abroad speaks against me. I've seen the anthology *Dissonant Voices*† which came out in London. I am published there together with Grin, Shklovsky, Chukovsky and others. I am no more to blame for being printed there than Zoshchenko, Babel and all the others.

JUDGE: There is a difference here. All the others had already been published in this country.

---

† See note to p. 55 on this volume, which was first published in America, and only about two years later in England.

DANIEL: The only difference is that I was published under a pseudonym.

JUDGE: But no, all the rest were published here,‡ but Arzhak wasn't! The others are honest writers who never sent anything abroad. That's the difference!

DANIEL: It only confirms my argument that the mere fact of publication by a bourgeois publisher is not in itself evidence of the anti-Soviet nature of the work. The publishers interpret works as they please.

VASILYEV: Do you know about the prosecution of his French publishers by the Soviet writer Kuznetsov?§

DANIEL: No I don't know about it.

Recess for fifteen minutes.

KOGAN: (*Sinyavsky's defense counsel*): Sinyavsky, the prosecution regards three of your works, but not the others, as anti-Soviet. What is your own subjective attitude toward your works? Did you yourself set particular store by some of them? And what had you in mind when you sent your works abroad?

SINYAVSKY: I had only one thing in mind in sending all my works abroad: that they should be published. I had no political aims, I was guided only by my literary interests and my needs as a creative writer. I do not see any radical differences between any of my works from a political point of view.

KOGAN: Your essay *On Socialist Realism* was not published

---

‡ This is not true of Boris Pilnyak, who sent the manuscript of his short novel *Mahogany* (excerpted in *Dissonant Voices*) to Berlin, where it was published in Russian by an émigré firm in 1929. The novel has still not been published in the Soviet Union. See p. 24 of Introduction.

§ Anatoli Kuznetsov (born 1929) in 1960 successfully sued a publisher in Lyons for an allegedly distorted translation of his novel *Continuation of a Legend* (1957), and the addition of "anti-Soviet" comments. Under French law an author enjoys protection of this kind even if his country of origin is not party to the Berne copyright convention, as the Soviet Union is not. In April, 1966, a Lyons court of appeal confirmed the decision of the lower court, awarded costs to Kuznetsov, and ordered the confiscation of the translation.

abroad in Russian, though from the political point of view this is the most controversial of your works. Yet no *émigré* publishers seized on it. How do you explain this?

SINYAVSKY: I don't know why one thing was published in one place, and something else in another. I just don't know why. Zamoyska told me that one *émigré* firm offered to publish it, but that she had turned them down. At the very outset I asked Zamoyska not to give my works to reactionary publishers—I should not have liked that.

KOGAN: What do you think of the opinion expressed in the indictment that in *Lyubimov* you had recourse to mysticism in order to cover up your anti-Soviet views?

SINYAVSKY: I don't agree with it. My work is full of fantasy. It seems that by "mysticism" they mean my interest in the outlandish and the fantastic.

KOGAN: You sent out *On Socialist Realism* in 1956. In 1958 you sent out an additional page. You evidently attached some importance to this page. Why did you send it out?

SINYAVSKY: I wanted to give my own literary creed.

KOGAN: Was it just an additional page, or was it the conclusion of the essay?

SINYAVSKY: Yes, it was the conclusion.

KOGAN: What was the point of this page?

SINYAVSKY: As a writer I am drawn to "fantastic realism" with its hyperbole and outlandishness. I mention Gogol, Chagall, Hoffmann, and Mayakovsky, some of whose works I would define as "fantastic realism."

The judge reads out this page.

SINYAVSKY: Yes, that is my program.

KOGAN: Do you think it is correct to call this "mysticism"?

SINYAVSKY: No, it isn't; it is just my special way of perceiving reality. As regards *Lyubimov* it is difficult to define its exact logical meaning in a legal sense, since a literary image is always complex. Even for me, as the author of the work, it is difficult to answer the question as to the meaning of this, that or the other. I do not think that a literary text can be analyzed in legal terms, since it is impossible to define a literary work with the precision required in law. Even so it is easier for me, as the author, than it is for others to make sense of my own works. My works are complicated and prolix, and even I would find it difficult to pin down their meaning. In my final plea I shall touch on the literary side of the question, leaving the legal aspect to my defense counsel. The court is interested in the political aspect, but I want to explain my work from a literary point of view and defend it as literature.

SOKOLOV: Did you talk with Daniel about the possibility of owning up?

SINYAVSKY: That is not accurate. I did not regard my works as anti-Soviet, and therefore there was nothing to own up to. But it did occur to me that it would be better to lead one existence rather than two—although I do not regard these two existences as incompatible.

SOKOLOV: Did you discuss this with Daniel?

SINYAVSKY: We did have a talk about it before our arrest, but it was only by-the-by, and I attached no importance to it.

SOKOLOV: Didn't you talk with Daniel about denying your authorship [of the works of Tertz and Arzhak]?

SINYAVSKY: No, but we did say that we shouldn't reveal our names.

Examination of the Witnesses

Examination of the Witness Remezov

(Remezov, Andrei, candidate of philological sciences,
research assistant in the Library of Foreign Literature) †

PROSECUTOR: You have published abroad? Which works have you published abroad, and under what name? (*Remezov names the works published abroad under the pseudonym Ivanov: Is There Life on Mars? and others.*)

PROSECUTOR: How did you get your works out?

REMEZOV: Through Sinyavsky.

PROSECUTOR: Did Sinyavsky know what was in your works?

REMEZOV: I read one thing out to him—*Is There Life on Mars?*

PROSECUTOR: Why did you decide to publish your works abroad?

REMEZOV: I decided on this before 1953,* but saw no possibility of doing so then. I knew that I could not publish them in the Soviet press because the things I was writing about—things which were later recognized as anti-Soviet—were at the time regarded as all right. For this reason what I wrote about them would also have qualified as anti-Soviet. I understood already then that our literature was dominated

---

† This and subsequent notes by the witnesses are by the anonymous author of the transcript.
* I.e., before Stalin's death.

by the barefaced lie; this was so under Stalin, and later under Khrushchev. The fact that it was still impossible to speak out against this led me once again to the idea of publishing my work abroad. When mistakes and crimes are being committed and one is not able to come out openly against them but is forced to be enthusiastic about them, then one has to speak one's mind abroad.

Remezov goes on to say that he already felt in his student days that lies and insincerity reigned supreme, that real literature was under strong attack and in effect being destroyed. He saw that he was not the only one to understand this, and that the other students felt as he did, though none of them dared come out and say it openly. Both he and his fellow students of the humanities were forced to become hypocrites, to lead a double life, in which some things were said aloud but others couldn't be said to anybody, except perhaps to close friends. It was this that had driven him to publish his works abroad.

PROSECUTOR: Why did you approach Sinyavsky in this matter?
REMEZOV: I knew that he had published an essay abroad and, since I wanted to do the same, I asked him to help me.
PROSECUTOR: Did you know by what means he got his works out?
REMEZOV: No. I just assumed that he had some friends, but I knew nothing.
PROSECUTOR: Did he acquaint you with his works?
REMEZOV: I read "The Icicle," *Lyubimov* and the essay [*On Socialist Realism*].
PROSECUTOR: What do you think of them?
JUDGE: That is of no interest to the court.

Prosecutor asks Sinyavsky why his evidence conflicts with Remezov's about the way in which the latter's works were sent out of the country.

Sinyavsky says that he did *not* pass on Remezov's work and he stands by his own version.

Prosecutor asks Sinyavsky whether Remezov has any reason to malign him.

Sinyavsky says that he doesn't know. He thinks that Remezov had no reason to do so, at least not until his arrest.

Prosecutor questions Remezov about Sinyavsky's views.

REMEZOV: I can only guess at them. I do not know his views. In my evidence during the preliminary investigation I mentioned the incident of the arrest of Sinyavsky's father, when Sinyavsky said that he couldn't understand why they had arrested his father and it would have made more sense if they'd arrested him. I mentioned this incident in my evidence only for the light it threw on the evolution of my own views. This was what I thought myself and I could only assume that Sinyavsky shared my views.

Prosecutor reads the evidence Remezov had given during the preliminary investigation and asks Remezov whether he stands by it.

REMEZOV: I have explained that the whole system of teaching in the Arts Faculties meant that we had to learn lies by rote in order not to be expelled. We resorted— and at the moment I am talking about myself—to mimicry or we made deals with our conscience.

PROSECUTOR: And did you start this sort of talk again after 1956?

REMEZOV: I don't remember. Perhaps we did. The generation of our fathers tried to make excuses for everything, but we were critical.

KOGAN: Why don't you tell the court that your works were printed by your friend the publisher Busseno? How did you establish contact with him?

REMEZOV: I established contact with him while I was in France in 1958. We agreed that if I could get any of my work to him he would publish it.

KOGAN: When were the manuscripts got out to him?

REMEZOV: The first—*Is There Life on Mars?*—was written in 1958–59. The other two in '63.

KOGAN: Is that the truth?

REMEZOV: Yes.

KOGAN: How did Busseno take your proposal?

REMEZOV: He agreed.

KOGAN: In what circumstances, and when, did you get to know him and make your agreement with him?

REMEZOV: In 1960 or '61.‡

KOGAN: But you say you sent manuscripts to him in '59?

REMEZOV: The first manuscript I simply gave to Sinyavsky.

KOGAN: You said in the preliminary investigation that you sent all four manuscripts to Busseno. And you have just repeated this here in court. Did you know Zamoyska yourself?

REMEZOV: I saw her at Sinyavsky's.

KOGAN: You're not telling lies about Sinyavsky?

REMEZOV: No.

KOGAN: In what connection and when were you summoned to the KGB?

REMEZOV: I was summoned as a witness in the Sinyavsky case, on December 6, 1965.

KOGAN: Did you know that Sinyavsky had mentioned you in his evidence?

REMEZOV: No.

KOGAN: When did you give evidence that you are Ivanov?

REMEZOV: On the ninth of December.

KOGAN: Had you seen Sinyavsky's evidence at this time?

REMEZOV: I was shown four lines which said that I knew what he was doing.

JUDGE: What were your feelings about Sinyavsky after you were called to the KGB? What did you think of his

‡ This contradicts Remezov's earlier reply that he met Busseno in 1958. Perhaps he means they made their agreement in 1960 or 1961. Kogan is trying to establish, in order to show that Sinyavsky was not guilty of being his intermediary, that Remezov had an independent contact with a foreign publisher.

behavior? Did his evidence give you the idea of putting the blame on him?

REMEZOV: No.

JUDGE: You did send out your manuscripts through Sinyavsky?

REMEZOV: Yes.

JUDGE: Is that the truth?

REMEZOV: Yes.

KOGAN: You have no real facts about Sinyavsky's opinions?

REMEZOV: No.

JUDGE: You knew the works that Sinyavsky published here in our press, and you knew the works he published abroad?

REMEZOV: Yes.

Judge reads evidence given by Remezov during the preliminary investigation: "I got used to a double life. I realized I was a candidate for prison. This wasn't true of me alone, but probably of Sinyavsky as well."

JUDGE: You deduced this from your knowledge of the truth about Sinyavsky's life. Isn't that so?

REMEZOV: I can only guess about Sinyavsky by analogy with myself.

Sinyavsky asks the witness to give more details about his relations with Zamoyska. How often had he seen her, had he ever talked to her on his own?

REMEZOV: Yes. I saw her at Sinyavsky's. I talked to her, but our conversations were on neutral themes.

Daniel asks Remezov whether he is perhaps confusing the facts. He might have handed the manuscripts over at Sinyavsky's flat, but not through Sinyavsky.

REMEZOV: No. I gave them to Sinyavsky himself. (*Voice in court:* "*He's frightened for his skin. The witness has a noose around his neck.*")

JUDGE: Next witness.

Examination of the Witness Dokukina

(Dokukina, Elena)

PROSECUTOR: How long have you known Sinyavsky?

DOKUKINA: Since 1946.

PROSECUTOR: On what terms are you?

DOKUKINA: On good ones.

PROSECUTOR: Did Sinyavsky ever ask you to keep some manuscripts for him?

DOKUKINA: That's not an exact way of putting it. He once brought me a few papers and asked whether he could leave them with me.

PROSECUTOR: When was this?

DOKUKINA: I don't remember exactly, since I attached no importance to it. About five years ago.

PROSECUTOR: What was his request to you when he left the manuscripts?

DOKUKINA: He didn't make any requests. He asked me whether he could leave them with me.

JUDGE: Do you know why he asked you this? Didn't it seem odd to you that a man with an apartment in Moscow, in the center of the city, should suddenly ask you to keep some manuscripts for him?

DOKUKINA: No, I didn't think it was odd. I thought it must be some personal papers he didn't want to be seen by anybody, or by other members of the household.

JUDGE: Did you never wonder what was in these papers?

DOKUKINA: No. Sometimes he took some of them away and brought new ones, but I attached no importance to this.

JUDGE: How did these papers come to be in your friend's *dacha?*

DOKUKINA: After Sinyavsky's arrest I took them to the *dacha* where I lived, and burned them. I suppose I was guided . . . well, by an instinct of self-preservation.

JUDGE: But why did you do that? Suppose there had been something very patriotic in them, which might have helped Sinyavsky?

DOKUKINA: I was sorry afterward. It was an impulsive act.

JUDGE: But did you read them before burning them?

DOKUKINA: No, but I had a look, and I can say what was there. I think there were summaries of works of Soviet literature—I saw something about socialist realism—they were private notes. They were private notes and I didn't want to look at them.

JUDGE: You mean you really didn't read them? Not even a few lines?

DOKUKINA: Well, perhaps I did read a few lines.

JUDGE: You must have read a little more. You're an educated person and you can't just have read a few lines and not been interested in what came next.

DOKUKINA: Well, I've already said that I did read a little, that I looked through them.

PROSECUTOR: What else was there, apart from the essay?

DOKUKINA: I . . . even if it could be proved what the papers were, I can't confirm it, I can't say anything, because they didn't have the author's name on them. I read one of the stories, though, the story "Pkhentz."

KOGAN: How would you describe Sinyavsky's outlook as a human being?

DOKUKINA: I have known him for twenty years. In the whole of this time I have never come across anything to find fault with in his character. He is kind, intelligent, hard-working and has a great sense of purpose. As far as I know, his views on literature . . . well, he loved everything which is generally recognized to be the best. He never said anything counterrevolutionary, I never even heard him say anything in anger. He talked just like anybody else in our circles. I can say nothing about Sinyavsky's religious views. In answering questions about this, during the preliminary investigation, I said and I can repeat it now: "I think it's possible that Sinyavsky believes in God, but in a kind of philosophical sense."

VASILYEV: When you read the story "Pkhentz," did you like it?

DOKUKINA: No, I didn't. I don't see why everybody should like the same things.

VASILYEV: So, you just picked out this one story, "Pkhentz"— that's the only thing you read?

DOKUKINA: Yes.

JUDGE: Next witness.

Examination of the Witness Garbuzenko

(Garbuzenko, Yakov Lazarevich, member of the party, headmaster of a secondary school)

PROSECUTOR: Do you know Daniel?

GARBUZENKO: Yes.

PROSECUTOR: What are your relations?

GARBUZENKO: I knew him as a fellow student at the University. We were on friendly terms.

PROSECUTOR: Do you know Sinyavsky?

GARBUZENKO: I know him, but not so well.

PROSECUTOR: What are the relations between them—between Sinyavsky and Daniel?

GARBUZENKO: They are good friends.

PROSECUTOR: Do you know of the works which Daniel sent abroad?

GARBUZENKO: Yes, I do.

PROSECUTOR: When and where did you get to know them?

GARBUZENKO: In Daniel's apartment. I don't remember exactly when. At first I didn't know that they were being published abroad, but then he told me that one of his works would appear in a foreign country.

PROSECUTOR: What was your reaction to this?

GARBUZENKO: I took a poor view of the fact of his publishing it, and I told him so.

PROSECUTOR: And did you see the books in their published form?

GARBUZENKO: Yes, I saw *This Is Moscow Speaking* in 1964.

PROSECUTOR: You said during the investigation that you did not approve of the basic theme of *This Is Moscow Speaking*.

GARBUZENKO: Before I knew about its publication abroad, I discussed it with Daniel only from the literary point of view.

JUDGE: (*reads from record of preliminary investigation*): "When I read it in typescript I did not approve of its basic theme, but we only talked about its literary quality. I thought it was a first attempt. I advised him to write for publication here."

GARBUZENKO: I didn't tell him I disapproved of the idea, I kept that to myself. I didn't like it, but I didn't say anything to him.

JUDGE: As a member of the party what do you think of it?

GARBUZENKO: It frightened me. But it's a fantasy.

JUDGE: The author slanders the Supreme Soviet. This, you think, is an innocent fantasy?

GARBUZENKO: But there were no murders. Nobody was killed. (*Laughter in the court.*)

JUDGE: Do you regard it as in order for a Soviet writer to come out with a work in which the basic idea is a decree of the Supreme Soviet proclaiming a "Public

Murder Day"? You are a member of the party. Don't you think it's blasphemous?

GARBUZENKO: Although there are some real facts and dates in it, I mentally associated it with an earlier period.[§]

PROSECUTOR: (reads from evidence): "I took it that the story was about the submissiveness of the people and the lack of unity between the people and the leaders." You are a member of the party, the headmaster of a school, responsible for the education of the young. What is your attitude to all this?

Garbuzenko repeats more or less what he had said before—that he had condemned the idea but had kept this to himself, that nobody was killed, etc.

KISENISHSKY: How long have you known Daniel?

GARBUZENKO: Since '46.

KISENISHSKY: Did you see him often?

GARBUZENKO: We used to see a lot of each other, but not so much recently.

KISENISHSKY: What sort of things did you talk about?

GARBUZENKO: About literature, work and mutual friends.

KISENISHSKY: Did you talk about politics? (Reads from Garbuzenko's evidence): "I formed the impression that Daniel stands outside the party. . . . As regards 'The Man from Minap,' I did not give much thought to what this work was about."

JUDGE: (reads B. Filippov's preface to "Hands"): Here you have everything you need—where, when and how it was all published, and Filippov's view of it. How does this strike you—you, a member of the party?

GARBUZENKO: I hadn't read this preface.

JUDGE: How extraordinary! The previous witness said she hadn't read the essay [On Socialist Realism]; now you say you haven't read this preface. Very well, that's all. Next witness.

---

§ I.e., the Stalin period.

Examination of the Witness Khazanov

(Khazanov, Yuri Samoilovich, poet and translator)

PROSECUTOR: How long have you known Daniel? What are your relations with him?

KHAZANOV: I have known him since the end of 1957. He is my friend and co-author.* Recently we have seen less of each other, but were still on good terms.

PROSECUTOR: What do you know about works written by Daniel for publication abroad?

KHAZANOV: I now know a lot, but until September [1965] I knew very little. We once had a conversation about publishing works of a critical nature abroad.

PROSECUTOR: What sort of works of a critical nature?

KHAZANOV: Well, works criticizing certain features, certain periods in the life of our country. This conversation I had with Daniel was in connection with Pasternak. On the whole, our opinions differed. Daniel thought that works critical in the way I have said should be published both here and abroad—wherever possible. But I thought that our problems should be thrashed out at home. Of course, [works on such problems] might be reprinted abroad, but the aim should be to publish them here. Then he said that something of his had been published or was about to be published abroad, but I didn't believe it. I do not remember his reading or showing me any of the works in question. I know his story "Escape," his story about skin,† I am vaguely familiar with the fragment about

---

* Nothing is known of any books written jointly by Daniel and Khazanov—it is presumably a question of joint translation.

† Nothing is known about this. Perhaps the title has been garbled in the transcript. On "Escape," see p. 47.

the waiter in *This Is Moscow Speaking*, but I don't know the works themselves.

PROSECUTOR: Did you talk about Daniel's works being broadcast over the radio?

KHAZANOV: No, we never talked about that.

Prosecutor reads from Khazanov's evidence, in which he stated that Elena Mikhailovna Zaks knew about the broadcast of Daniel's work and that Khazanov got to know about it from her.

KHAZANOV: I remember that I was asked during the interrogation whether I had heard anything from Daniel which would show that he was the author. I replied that I remembered nothing of the kind. I was asked whether I mightn't have heard something to this effect at the Zakses. I said that I might. I was being asked whether I'd had any evidence of something I did not believe. I did not believe that Daniel was the author of these works.

PROSECUTOR: When was this?

KHAZANOV: I really do not remember.

PROSECUTOR: Could it have been in 1962?

KHAZANOV: I don't remember. Perhaps it was later.

JUDGE: (*reads out Khazanov's evidence in full*): Do you stand by this evidence?

KHAZANOV: I don't remember it very well. (*He confirms some of it and denies other parts of it.*)

JUDGE: This is a statement to the KGB in your own handwriting. Do you confirm that you wrote this statement to the KGB?

Khazanov says something it is impossible to make out.

JUDGE: (*holds up a sheet of paper*): Here is a statement in your own handwriting to the KGB. Do you confirm that you gave this evidence?

Once again the answer cannot be made out.

JUDGE: Come up here and see for yourself that this is a statement in your own handwriting to the KGB.

Khazanov, looking more dead than alive, comes up to the judge. The judge repeats several times over: "Statement in your own handwriting to the KGB." Khazanov mumbles something.

DANIEL: (*to Khazanov*): Can you say where I first told you that I was writing works which were published abroad?

KHAZANOV: I don't remember.

DANIEL: (*to the judge*): May I prompt the witness?

JUDGE: No, you may not.

DANIEL: Very well, I will describe the circumstances. The circumstances were peculiar, Khazanov should remember them. I will say what they were, and Khazanov perhaps will confirm whether it was so or not. It was in the winter of '62–63, out of town.

KHAZANOV: Yes, that's right, I remember that it was in the winter of '62–63, out of town.

DANIEL: Can the witness definitely say that he remembers the conversation about the broadcast and has described it exactly?

KHAZANOV: No. I don't remember it well at all, only very approximately.

The judge again reads out Khazanov's evidence. Khazanov can neither confirm nor deny it.

DANIEL: If it is clear to the court that this evidence can't be relied on for its accuracy, then I have no more questions to put to the witness. Khazanov is a nervous person; he might in the circumstances either have forgotten or have followed the prompting of his interrogators. I simply put this question to him so that this should be clear to the court. The mention of a third person, Elena Mikhailovna Zaks, is quite irrelevant here, in this context. (*Someone shouts:* "*Good for you! The witness is a coward.*")

VASILYEV: (*to Khazanov*): Are you a member of the Union of Writers?

KHAZANOV: No.

JUDGE: Next witness.

Examination of the Witness Khmelnitsky

(Khmelnitsky, Sergei Grigoryevich, architect)

In 1963, at the defense of his dissertation, his former friends Kabo and Bregel stood up and told how in 1949 they had been arrested and sentenced on his denunciation. Shortly after this Khmelnitsky left Moscow. His appearance at the trial was a surprise to the defendants. When Khmelnitsky's name was called out, Sinyavsky smiled and Daniel leaned forward. Khmelnitsky went into the witness box, turned his head to the right and looked with vacant eyes over the top of his glasses at his former friends, Sinyavsky and Daniel. Then he looked straight ahead, raised his chin and began to answer the questions.

PROSECUTOR: How long have you known Daniel and Sinyavsky? What are your relations with them?

KHMELNITSKY: I have known Sinyavsky since '33 and Daniel since '47. Our relations are friendly.

PROSECUTOR: Did you ever have any conversation with Daniel about a radio broadcast of *This Is Moscow Speaking?*

KHMELNITSKY: There was never any conversation about that.

PROSECUTOR: Wasn't it you who suggested the plot of this story to Daniel?

KHMELNITSKY: I gave Daniel a paradoxical idea I had about the study of people's psychology.

PROSECUTOR: Your idea was . . . There was something about who permitted the murders?

KHMELNITSKY: I had no intention of writing it up, I was just interested in the idea, the outline. So I didn't work it out in detail.

JUDGE: But was there something in your outline about a decree? A decree of the Supreme Soviet permitting the murders?

KHMELNITSKY: That was no concern of mine.

PROSECUTOR: But didn't you and Daniel talk about turning it into a story?

KHMELNITSKY: We talked about it twice. On the first occasion I asked Daniel whether he had written the story on the basis of my idea. He answered very sharply that he hadn't. The second conversation took place in the following connection. In a certain house I heard somebody paraphrasing my idea in the form of a story about "Public Murder Day." I exclaimed that the idea was mine and that I'd given it to Daniel. I told Daniel about this, and he rightly gave me a dressing down.

JUDGE: Why "rightly"?

KHMELNITSKY: Well of course it was a rotten thing to do—to mention somebody by name in connection with an anti-Soviet radio station broadcasting anti-Soviet works.

JUDGE: The hearing is adjourned.

Session of February 12, 1966 (Morning)

Examination of the Witnesses

Examination of the Witness Golomshtok

(Golomshtok, Igor Naumovich, art historian, co-author with A. Sinyavsky of a book entitled *Picasso*, Moscow, Znanie, 1960)

PROSECUTOR: How well do you know Sinyavsky and Daniel?

GOLOMSHTOK: We are on good, friendly terms.

PROSECUTOR: Do you know Sinyavsky's works?

GOLOMSHTOK: Yes, I know *The Trial Begins*, *Fantastic Stories* and *Lyubimov*.

PROSECUTOR: When did you get to know them?

GOLOMSHTOK: After Sinyavsky's arrest.

PROSECUTOR: Did Sinyavsky show you his works?

GOLOMSHTOK: No.

PROSECUTOR: During the preliminary investigation Sinyavsky said that he did.

GOLOMSHTOK: At our confrontation Sinyavsky said that he read parts of some of his works to me. When I read the works in question, I didn't think I had ever heard these particular parts. Here in court Sinyavsky has said that he may have read me passages which didn't go into the final versions. Perhaps I simply didn't recognize them.

PROSECUTOR: Where did you get his works?

GOLOMSHTOK: After Sinyavsky's arrest I learned why he had been arrested and I made it my business to get his books and read them. I got them from friends.

PROSECUTOR: Name these friends.

GOLOMSHTOK: I refuse to name them.

PROSECUTOR: I would not like you to refuse to do this. By refusing, you are aiding and abetting the dissemination of anti-Soviet literature.

GOLOMSHTOK: I do not regard these works as anti-Soviet.

PROSECUTOR: Answer my question.

JUDGE: Did you read them in a library?

GOLOMSHTOK: No.

JUDGE: So you obtained them illegally?

GOLOMSHTOK: I borrowed them from friends. Is that illegal? I didn't know.

JUDGE: It was wrong of the prosecutor to call these works anti-Soviet. The court has still to determine whether they are anti-Soviet or not. Therefore you can name the friends whom you borrowed them from.

GOLOMSHTOK: I refuse to name these friends because, although I do not think these works are anti-Soviet, my friend here is being tried for . . . well, under Article 70. I don't want to implicate other people as well.

PROSECUTOR: (*makes a statement*): The witness has been warned about liability for refusing to give evidence in court and yet he still refuses to do so. The prosecution begs the court to make a separate decision to charge the witness Golomshtok.

The judge asks both parties whether they have anything to say about the prosecutor's request.

SINYAVSKY: Golomshtok is not refusing to give evidence about matters before the court. He has given full answers to all questions concerning the case of Sinyavsky, in connection with which he has been called, but the question as to where he got my works after my arrest is not relevant to the case. Therefore I regard as improper the request that Golomshtok be charged.

Daniel supports Sinyavsky and says that it would be improper, to put it mildly.

GOLOMSHTOK: I would like to explain why I refuse to give evidence.

JUDGE: Witnesses are not called upon to explain.

KOGAN: Haven't you written a book with Sinyavsky?

GOLOMSHTOK: Yes.

KOGAN: Didn't you discuss the situation of the artist, of the individual, in bourgeois countries?

GOLOMSHTOK: Yes, we did talk about that.

KOGAN: What are Sinyavsky's views on this?

GOLOMSHTOK: I cannot repeat what he said word for word, but his attitude was this: Sinyavsky has a good knowledge of Western culture and has always been fairly critical of it, even by my standards—and I am a specialist in Western art. Sinyavsky regards abstract art as a symptom of spiritual decline. He is rather a Slavophile in his views.

JUDGE: Yet in *Unguarded Thoughts* he writes of the Russian people that they are a nation of drunkards.

GOLOMSHTOK: This does not fit in with what I know about Sinyavsky. He was evidently trying to say something else in this passage.

JUDGE: Well, let's see what he did mean. (*Reads passage about Russian people.*) Is this blasphemy what you call Slavophilism?

GOLOMSHTOK: But you can find things like that in Gogol.

JUDGE: So that's what you mean by Slavophilism?

GOLOMSHTOK: Yes. (*Laughter in court.*)

JUDGE: Answer the questions I am putting to you. What do you think of Sinyavsky's attitude to Russian culture?

GOLOMSHTOK: The whole of Sinyavsky's work is concerned with Russian culture—the whole of it.

JUDGE: And is sending books to the West a service to Russian culture?

GOLOMSHTOK: I am talking now about his outlook, not about his actions.

JUDGE: Sinyavsky has also written about Mayakovsky, and Mayakovsky once said, "Soviet people have their pride." A lot of pride it shows to act like this!

Next witness. (*Addressing Golomshtok*): You will stay in the courtroom until a decision has been taken in your case, that is, till the end of the trial.[†]

Examination of the Witness Petrov

(Petrov, Alexander, an engraver)

Coming in, he cheerfully greets the defendants, answers questions loudly and defiantly.

PROSECUTOR: How well do you know Sinyavsky and Daniel?

PETROV: Very well. They are my best friends.

PROSECUTOR: What do you know about this case?

PETROV: I know a great deal, now that such a rumpus has been raised all over the world.

PROSECUTOR: I am not asking you what you know now, but what you knew previously.

PETROV: I knew the works of Tertz, but whether Tertz was Sinyavsky or Daniel or somebody else, I had no idea.

PROSECUTOR: How did you come to read the works of Tertz?

PETROV: The fact is that we and the Sinyavskys are great friends—almost like members of the same family. We visit each other quite freely—they have the key of our flat and we have the key to theirs, so I take down any book I like from their shelves. Well, I just picked them up and read them. I was interested by the title *Fantastic Stories*. I suppose I just got to know them on my own.

PROSECUTOR: And did you notice who had published them?

PETROV: Well, I saw they'd been published abroad, but so have lots of other books.

JUDGE: Next witness.

[†] For Golomshtok's subsequent fate, see note on p. 8.

PETROV: Can I stay in the courtroom?

JUDGE: I see no reason for you to stay.

PETROV: I haven't seen Sinyavsky and Daniel for ages, I'd like to have a good look at them.

Petrov is removed from the courtroom.

Examination of the Witness Duvakin

(Duvakin, Victor Dmitrievich, lecturer of Philological Faculty of Moscow University, the only defense witness at the trial)

KOGAN: When and where did you get to know Sinyavsky?

DUVAKIN: I have known Sinyavsky since 1945. In the autumn of 1945 I examined a student in a shabby greatcoat, who had been taking a correspondence course. I picked him out as a person of great quality. He started coming to my seminar and I found that my first impression had not been mistaken. At first our relations were those of teacher and pupil, but gradually we became friends.

KOGAN: Can you describe Sinyavsky's academic and professional qualities?

DUVAKIN: Sinyavsky's academic and professional qualities are outstanding. I think his colleagues would agree with this.

JUDGE: These digressions are not necessary.

DUVAKIN: Very well. I know his books on Soviet literature. We sometimes argued; we talked mainly about art. For two years he lectured in Moscow University and was very popular. At first I used to look over his lecture notes, but then I realized it wasn't necessary. I felt that he was a better lecturer than I was. I felt like a . . . well, like a duck which has hatched out a swan. He was an ugly duckling who grew up into a swan.

JUDGE: Some swan! More like a goose! (*Laughter in court.*)

DUVAKIN: Of course, one can joke about it, but I am trying to give my impression of Sinyavsky's qualities. He is a person who seeks the truth and is sincere and honest in his search.

JUDGE: Sincere and honest! This man who is being tried here now?

DUVAKIN: Yes.

JUDGE: And you think his books are also sincere and honest?

DUVAKIN: May I now speak about the books?

JUDGE: No. It's for the court to pronounce on them.

DUVAKIN: But it's the books I was asked about during the preliminary investigation.

JUDGE: This question is of no interest to the court.

KOGAN: Well, let's go back and look at the facts. During the preliminary investigation you talked about the autobiographical nature of "Graphomaniacs," and another time you said that Sinyavsky's undoing had been his obsession with words, his craving to be published.

DUVAKIN: Sinyavsky once said to me that it is impossible to draw the line between a writer and a graphomaniac. Evidently, his . . .

JUDGE: (*interrupts*): We don't need words like "evidently." Stick to the facts. What do you mean by autobiographical?

DUVAKIN: He leads a very ascetic life, the life of a man engrossed in Russian art, in love with Russian art, but whose life is not easy. That's how Sinyavsky lived. And in "Graphomaniacs" there is also an author who lives on bad meat.‡ Well . . .

JUDGE: (*interrupts*) Next witness.

The Judge rejects a previous request of the defense to call the witnesses Yakobson and Voronel, saying that they are not required in court.

---

‡ See p. 183 of *Fantastic Stories*.

PROSECUTOR: (*applying for formal permission*): I should like to read out the record of the confrontation between Daniel and the witness Azbel.

Reads record of confrontation, at which Daniel said that he had read his works to Azbel. Azbel said that this was perhaps so, but that he didn't remember it.

PROSECUTOR: (*to Daniel*): Do you confirm what was said at the confrontation?

DANIEL: I do and I would like to explain it. In the autumn of 1962 I read something to Azbel every day: passages from "Escape," stories which have been mentioned here, and others as well. He cannot have remembered what exactly I read to him, because two or three weeks later he went away, and after that his wife fell seriously ill, and she was an invalid for a year and a half. So that all this must have made him forget what exactly I read to him. I read him "Atonement" at a time when he was very ill. This was not so much to acquaint him with the work as to take his mind off his illness. (*Makes a formal plea.*) I should like to be allowed to make a further statement concerning the charges against me.

JUDGE: It's not what you want to say in your final plea?

DANIEL: No, it's not what should come in my final plea. I want to say something about the nature of the charges and my attitude to them. I don't understand the point of the prosecutor's questions. I reply to these questions, but . . .

JUDGE: (*interrupts*): Your disagreements with the prosecutor are of no interest to the court.

Speeches by the Prosecution and Defense

Speech by Public Accuser A. Vasilyev

I would like to begin with a quotation from Sinyavsky's article on Maxim Gorky in the first volume of the *History of Soviet Literature*.§ Comparing Sashka Epanchin, Mechik and others to Klim Samgin, Sinyavsky writes: "They have all the marks of moral and spiritual degradation—there is a conflict between what they do and what they say; they are not what they would like to make themselves out to be, and many of them dream of a third way." I don't intend to compare Sinyavsky and Daniel with Klim Samgin—they are much smaller fry —but the point is that Sinyavsky and Daniel are not what they would like to appear to be. It has come out during the trial that Candidate of Sciences Sinyavsky was always hanging around in editorial offices and in the Institute of World Literature. Part of the time he passed himself off as a Soviet literary scholar. I could read out many quotations from Sinyavsky's articles. He even quoted Lenin in them. But now we know that he spent most of his time writing books and articles filled with spite and hatred. Daniel was a visitor to any editorial office whose budget provided for the payment of fees. While working away on manuscripts for Madame Zamoyska, he existed on money which he got for his translations. Nobody asked him why he had to

§ Sinyavsky's article is on p. 99 of this work (*Istoria Russkoi Sovetskoi Literatury*, izd. Akademii Nauk SSR, Moscow, 1958). Epanchin is a character from Alexei Tolstoy's novel *Manuscript Found under a Bed* and Mechik is from Fadeyev's novel *The Rout*.

153

sit at home and write poetry—they were sorry for him and didn't question his need to make a little extra money here and there. Yet while signing receipts for Soviet money, he was working away for Madame Zamoyska.

Certain persons abroad describe them as honest and decent people, but they are double-dealers. What a strange notion of honesty! Tarsis* wasn't a double-dealer at least. Tarsis is a gentleman compared to them. Sinyavsky and Daniel deliberately set out on the path of treachery. It is quite possible that their clients did not know what sort of people their authors were. Filippov writes: "Our author, hiding behind a pseudonym . . ." Perhaps Filippov doesn't know, but we know where these pseudonyms come from—from underworld songs. Both purveyors—though I fear Sinyavsky won't understand this word, just as he didn't understand the word "intermediary"—both purveyors of goods to Madame Zamoyska found their nicknames in the rubbish heap of underworld slang.† What's in a name? These are the people whom foreign writers describe as representatives of the Soviet intelligentsia. By Soviet intelligentsia we mean such people as Academician Kurchatov, Keldysh, Tovstonogov, Landau‡ —we mean thousands, hundreds of thousands of doctors and engineers. Sinyavsky and Daniel have no connection with such people.

A lot of time has been spent on the question as to whether they acted misguidedly or by intent. Daniel has said that he now regrets what he did. But he talked about it with his friends, with Khmelnitsky and Garbuzenko. These discussions show that he knew what he was doing. Take *This Is Moscow Speaking*: everybody who has read it understands what the author means—everybody, that is, except the author. I would like once again to read out this passage. (*Quotes the*

---

* Valeri Tarsis: Soviet writer who for several years openly published work abroad (*The Blue Bottle* and *Ward 7*) and who was allowed to leave the Soviet Union at the time of the trial of Sinyavsky and Daniel. Tarsis was subsequently deprived of his Soviet citizenship and is now an émigré in the West.

† See note, p. 76.

‡ Igor Kurchatov (1903–1960), Soviet atomic physicist; Mstislav Keldysh (born 1911), mathematician and President of the Soviet Academy of Sciences; Georgi Tovstonogov (born 1915), famous Soviet theater director; Lev Landau (born 1908), physicist and Nobel Prize winner.

passages about murder from This Is Moscow Speaking.) The fact is that the defendants are like-minded not only in their choice of pseudonyms but also in their ideas. This is not literature, but a direct incitement to murder, and we know who it's directed against. And what does Tertz have to say? (Quotes passage about bloody hyperbole.)* Who does he mean by "they"? The Soviet authorities. And who are "we"? The likes of Arzhak and Tertz.

In his evidence [under preliminary investigation] Sinyavsky says: "I realize that I was being too pessimistic, but the fact is I sent out my manuscripts and I now regret it." Daniel also says that he has seen the light, but only after reading Filippov's preface. Sinyavsky tried to wriggle out by saying, "This is a literary device, it's satire, extravaganza." Satire, is it? It's low abuse, it's spitting on the Russian people. Just have a look at Gogol and Shchedrin—you won't find a single bad word about the people. But Abram Tertz talks about "a nation of thieves and drunkards, incapable of creating a culture." And here's what he says in Lyubimov. (Quotes.) That's from Lyubimov, his pride and joy as he calls it, or, as one of the witnesses put it, "his swan song." That's the way in which White Guards and enemies of the Soviet Union would like to see our people. (Quotes passage beginning "The history of the backwoods town of Lyubimov . . ." from Filippov's preface.) There is nothing holy for Sinyavsky-Tertz. He has no respect for the precious word "mother," he jeers at mothers. On the last page [of Lyubimov] they are given comfort by a semiliterate priest: "The mothers were here, close at hand. . . ."

In the bourgeois press Tertz is described as "the author of masterpieces." Let me quote one passage which illustrates his "talent." (Quotes: One woman had a miscarriage. . . .")

His liking for bad language and pornography is something pathological. Perhaps it's this that they find attractive about him in the West. Sinyavsky says that an author is one thing and his characters are another. I will now quote something that will deeply offend those present, but it can't be helped. (Quotes passage about Lenin from Lyubimov.) That's from Lyubimov. And now here is something from his essay "Taking a Reading." (Quotes passage about [Lenin's]

---

* The Makepeace Experiment, p. 150.

"innocuous bookkeeper's appearance," "Lenin, the statistician of the revolution," etc.)

This article is not mentioned in the indictment. I am only quoting it to show in what soil the characters [in *Lyubimov*] were nurtured. In both we have references to bookkeeping, statistics, etc. Sinyavsky has tried to suggest that he is concerned with the cult of Stalin. This is untrue. (*Quotes from "Taking a Reading"*: "*Stalin is cozier and easier to understand than Lenin.*") The whole of Sinyavsky's hatred is directed against Lenin. Even Lenin's serious illness is for Sinyavsky only an excuse to make fun of him. (*Quotes from the same essay a passage about sclerosis of the brain.*) Lenin's most humane qualities infuriate Sinyavsky more than they do our sworn enemies. What might appear to be the best qualities frighten him. (*Quotes: "There is something sinister in this humaneness and simplicity."*)

I must digress here. Yesterday it came out that Sinyavsky received from his clients two jackets, two sweaters, a white shirt and some rubber boots, as well as something for his wife and for his son. Not very much, you might say. But I think it's a lot. His masters might well not have paid Sinyavsky at all, considering that his "works" were cribbed from the Menshevik newspapers of 1918, which are to be found in the Lenin Library. We have established that Sinyavsky had access to the Lenin Library. How can one talk of his honesty if even in working for his masters he behaved like a petty swindler?

Comrade Judges! All the evidence shows that the men in the dock are violent opponents of the Soviet regime and deliberate slanderers. The whole of the expert and material evidence shows that we have here two men who are anti-Soviet and who know what they are doing. They understood and they knew.

I am speaking as a representative of the Union of Soviet Writers, of which, I am ashamed to say, Sinyavsky was a member. There's a black sheep in every family. In the name of all our writers, I accuse them of the gravest possible crime and I beg the court to punish them severely. Anyone who enters the Central Writers' Club sees a marble slab on which are engraved in golden letters the names of writers who fell in the Great Patriotic War. I accuse them in the name of the living and in the name of the dead. Their crime must be punished. (*Applause*).

Speech by Public Accuser Z. Kedrina

CITIZEN JUDGES,

For several days running, there has been an attempt in this court-room to create the mystical atmosphere of a realm of psychic magnetism in which wonders never cease. They [the defendants] don't understand the term "intermediary," they assure us that in a critical article the words are not those of the author and the author is therefore not responsible for them. As the Russian proverb says, "What is written with a pen can't be removed with a hatchet." Their writings speak for themselves.

Sinyavsky has assured us that his writings are innocuous philo-sophical essays on such subjects as means and ends or the philosophy of power. What interests him is to mingle fantasy and fact—the result is no concern of his. This, allegedly, is pure art, without any political purpose. But "art for art's sake" is a fiction. To believe in it is itself a hostile attitude. . . . The fact is, however, that Sinyavsky's writings do have a political meaning. To portray [Soviet] people in the guise of witches, thieves, graphomaniacs and drunkards is tantamount to active rejection of our form of government. It's because Sinyavsky has this attitude to Soviet life that he rejects what is genuine in modern literature.

This is how Sinyavsky deals with the tradition of Russian writing: "It's the classics I hate more than anything," declares his hero in "Graphomaniacs." The hero dismisses classical literature. These words are the hero's, but they were put into his mouth by Sinyavsky. Duvakin calls this passage autobiographical. The same attitude to the classics is expressed in Sinyavsky's essay [On Socialist Realism]. All the classics, according to Sinyavsky, are God-seekers and failures.

Rejection of the very basis of socialist realism, rejection, above all, of Marxism, is the foundation of Sinyavsky's "theory of art." (Sum-marizes the essay On Socialist Realism—on such questions as the goal aimed at and the goal achieved,§ the contrast between Western writers and ours, etc.)

All the greatest achievements of Soviet literature are reassessed by Sinyavsky. Look at what he writes about Leonov's *Russian Forest!†* He claims that Soviet literature is regressing. And his attacks on Gorky!

Irony is one of Sinyavsky's main disguises. He attacks Blok, he attacks Mayakovsky. In his own stories, he doesn't miss a chance of smearing Lenin. In his article "Taking a Reading," he jeers at Ilyich [Lenin]. Mayakovsky also gets it in the neck—Sinyavsky describes him as an opportunist. . . . He contrasts Russian realism with "phantasmagoric art."

Fantastic Stories shows a debauched imagination and paints a false picture of life. There are werewolves, witches, water spirits, thieves, drunkards. . . . Together with Colonel Tarasov [in "The Icicle"], the hero, who, without his wanting it, becomes a clairvoyant, plans future Communist aggression. . . .

Kedrina goes on to repeat most of her article, "The Heirs of Smerdyakov," printed in *Literary Gazette*, January 22, 1966.

All this is pretty poor stuff.

In his articles about science fiction* he wrote about space flights, but all he has in his *Lyubimov* is a woman flying about on a broomstick, and then only by a trick of the imagination. (*Laughter in court.*)

Every Russian writer of the realistic school has his positive hero. In Shchedrin the hero is the [Russian] people. He mentions the people in his introductory note to *History of the Town of Glupov*. And doesn't the "Story of the Peasant Who Fed Two Generals"¶ show how gifted the Russian people are? But what do we find in Tertz? The only worker in his stories turns into a thief.‡

Again paraphrases her article.

---

§ *On Socialist Realism* (Pantheon edition), pp. 38–39.

† *Ibid.*, p. 54.

* There was an article by Sinyavsky on this subject in *Literary Gazette*, January 5, 1961 ("*Realism Fantastiki*").

¶ See note * on p. 190.

‡ This must refer to "At the Circus," one of the *Fantastic Stories*.

Speech by State Prosecutor O. P. Tyomushkin

Before you in the dock are the Soviet citizens Sinyavsky, a candidate of philological sciences, a senior research fellow of the Institute of World Literature, a member of the Union of Soviet Writers, and Daniel, a poet and translator.

The Soviet public knew Sinyavsky as a literary critic and Daniel as a translator. What has brought them to the dock? It turns out that Sinyavsky is not Andrei Sinyavsky but "Abram Tertz." This was the name—that of the hero of a pornographic underworld song—with which he signed himself. Daniel is "Arzhak."

An author is entitled to write under a pseudonym, or even anonymously, but under these names they published work that had nothing in common with their publications in the Soviet Union, with what they did here. In these works they give vent to their complete dissatisfaction with the Soviet system and Soviet society. They make it out to be like a lunatic asylum.

Sinyavsky and Daniel are people with "secret compartments";* they are internal émigrés.§ They have been charged under Article 70 of the Criminal Code of the R.S.F.S.R. (*He reads out the text of the article.*) The evidence, after exhaustive examination, gives reason to state that they are guilty and that their guilt has been proved.

Adopting a hostile attitude on a number of questions, they have been writing, ever since 1956, works maligning the Soviet system of government. Sinyavsky established contact with Zamoyska, the daughter of a French naval attaché, and illegally sent out of the country both his own and Daniel's manuscripts. They were published everywhere by reactionary, and even émigré, publishers. They have been taken up and actively exploited.

---

* This term can be applied to a suitcase used by a smuggler, or, metaphorically, to a person.

§ A standard Soviet term (*vnutrenni emigrant*) for persons who have the mentality and attitudes of émigrés, even though they remain physically in the Soviet Union.

In 1956 Sinyavsky wrote *The Trial Begins* and *On Socialist Realism*, in which he makes direct attacks on our ideology, slanders the party and the state, and makes fun of our people. In 1961 he wrote *Lyubimov* and sent it out in 1963.

In 1956–57 Daniel wrote his story "Hands," a slanderous account of the policy of class warfare in the years of the Civil War. In 1961 he wrote *This Is Moscow Speaking*, a malicious lampoon on Soviet life in which there is incitement to terror, and "The Man from Minap," which is against our way of life, against our morals, against our ethics. "Atonement," written in 1963, gives a picture of moral decay and decadence.

Sinyavsky introduced him [Daniel] to Zamoyska, thereby helping him to get his works abroad, and handed some of them over himself. He helped Remezov to send out four works.* Furthermore they are both guilty of circulating their works among people close to them.

The defendants have not admitted their guilt, but neither have they denied writing works which they illegally sent abroad. They have explained this by a desire to have their works published, but they have denied malicious intent. The proof that they wrote these works and were guilty of sending them abroad is contained in the evidence of Garbuzenko, Khazanov and Azbel, who knew that these works had been written and sent out of the country. Garbuzenko read them and saw them in their published form. From the evidence of Petrov and Remezov it is clear that they had read Sinyavsky's works. Dokukina, who kept his manuscripts for him, had read the essay [*On Socialist Realism*] and *The Trial Begins*.

There is an expert report on the works themselves. Of Sinyavsky it says: "All the works are characterized by pretentiousness, affectation, the exploitation for literary effect of dreams and hallucinations, and by an obsession with demented states of mind. The typical ideas expressed in these works range from Freudism through anti-Semitism and sex to 'God-seeking.' " The expert evidence makes it clear beyond all doubt that they were written with the intention of putting over an anti-Soviet message. These clearly are political writings.

The expert report on the works of Arzhak (this was Daniel's

---

* Only two appear to have been published in the West. See note on p. 41.

pseudonym) says: "They were written from a desire to give expression to an anti-Soviet idea. The literary technique is crude and hackneyed, and the writing is pedestrian. It is political writing to which a literary framework has been given." Remezov's evidence proves that Sinyavsky helped to send out his [Remezov's] anti-Soviet works.

The circumstances in which the works were written and sent out of the country are quite clear, but proof of purpose and anti-Soviet intent can only be obtained through close and painstaking analysis. The content of the works of Tertz and Arzhak is witness to their hostility to the system, the party and the state. They are full of slander and attacks on the party and government, and this is the only reason they were published abroad, poverty-stricken as they are from a literary point of view. They were printed abroad for propaganda and for no other reason. These works have a clearly anti-Soviet character.

Take *Lyubimov*, for example. (*Quotes the passage where people eat pepper instead of meat.*) [In other words] the Soviet Government thinks nothing of making a fool of the people. They are shown here as starving. It's supposed to be about the city of Lyubimov, but it's really about Communism.

Comrade Judges! How cynical one must become and to what depths one must sink in order to give such a picture of Communism, of our shining goal, to blaspheme and make fun of all progressive ideas, of Campanella, Fourier and Owen! Everything of value is dismissed out of hand. Russia is depicted as a poor and hungry backwoods, and the people as downtrodden and worn out by hard work. (*He quotes the passage in which Lenya speaks from the balcony:* "Hold up your heads. . . .")†

The novel is full of insultingly garbled phrases borrowed from Lenin. (*Quotes passage about the* "breathing space.") The room covered with hundred-rouble notes alludes to what Lenin said about the role of money. What savage hatred! There is even more spite in his picture of Lenin's last days in Gorki. I will spare you the need to

---

† *The Makepeace Experiment*, p. 102. This is a speech in which the people of Lyubimov are hypnotized into believing that they themselves want to work harder for less reward.

listen to it once again. It is difficult to believe that a Soviet citizen who was educated in a Soviet school and university, became a candidate of sciences and got on his feet here, could have written anything like this.

Well, then, the Communist idea fails in Lyubimov. (Reads description of the town.)[‡]

In other words, a reading of Lyubimov leads one to the conclusion that it is a militantly anti-Soviet work every line of which is against Soviet ideas and against the Soviet system. Fantasy is just a convenient device, allegory is used to describe our economy and everything else, and there is even something about military aggression. . . . This was how Lyubimov was understood in the West. Our enemies received exactly what they wanted. Radio Liberty didn't make three broadcasts out of it for nothing. Tertz's stories [i.e., Fantastic Stories] do not figure in the charges against him. They are peopled with schizophrenics, alcoholics, outcasts and criminals. Everything in this country appears conducive to crime, alcoholism and mental illness. But among these stories it is The Trial Begins that stands out particularly. In content it is a vulgar piece of work on the level of the cheap novelette. It is full of malicious slander on Marxism, and it is peopled with anti-Soviet rabble. This is what Sinyavsky, speaking through the mouth of one of his characters, has to say about our glorious future. (Quotes passage about the fish.) What extraordinary cynicism! Isn't all this shot through with open hatred for everything Soviet? And who are the men of the future? Tolya and Vitya.[§] These two figures fill the author with horror and he turns them into a symbol. (Quotes the epilogue.) Is this meant to be about the Stalin cult? No. The author is saying that nothing has changed since the death of "The Master." . . . The epilogue is very important for an understanding of the anti-Soviet essence of The Trial Begins. (Quotes lengthy passages from the epilogue—the one about how the author was caught, about the way bread was shared in the camp in Kolyma.) So

---

‡ For the references in this paragraph, see ibid., pp. 110–111. Gorki was Lenin's country residence near Moscow where he died. For the allusion to Lenin's last days, see p. 22. The description of the town of Lyubimov after "the Communist idea fails" is on pp. 176–177 of The Makepeace Experiment.

§ The two secret police agents referred to in note § on p. 95.

we see that by a demagogic use of certain literary commonplaces the author slanders our system. Even such a thing as the sharing of the bread in the camp becomes a symbol, a model for the Communist distribution of goods. Innocent people sitting behind barbed wire and sharing their bread—that is our society and its ideals.

In his essay Sinyavsky attempts an analysis of socialist realism, but this is just a blind. If it were nothing more than this, the author wouldn't be sitting here. Behind all the talk about the failure of socialist realism there is a political creed, a study of which enables one to understand the other works and what the characters in them say, as well as what the author means. This leaves no doubt that Sinyavsky's attitude is very anti-Soviet. (*Quotes passage about hyperbole.*) Hyperbole—that's what his works published abroad are. With the purpose of rebutting Communist ideas and proving that they are unscientific, Sinyavsky writes: (*quotes: "the ape got up on its hind legs," "the dirt of the whole world," "so that prisons should disappear forever. . . ."*).* This is blasphemy on the part of the author.

Sinyavsky equates the demand for *partiinost*† with a demand for religious devotion to duty, with dogmatism: "He who will not believe must go to prison."‡ He alleges that the Soviet system is changing its nature, that the ideals of the Revolution are the opposite of today's. He slanders Lenin, and maliciously and hypocritically expresses his sympathy for Mayakovsky. The height of blasphemy is what he says about Lenin baying at the moon, and the passages in "Essay in Self-Analysis" ["Taking a Reading"]. (*Quotes "ideal type of scholar," "symbolism of his life and death—massive sclerosis of the brain, and nothing but sclerosis."*) Lenin always charmed people by his humanity, straightforwardness and sincerity [*quotes Gorky on Lenin*], but in this essay Lenin is called "a sinister cybernetic machine," "a statistician of revolution." Lenin's most attractive features, combined with his capacity for logical thinking, frighten Tertz. These are malicious and slanderous statements. Sinyavsky hypocritically ex-

---

* *On Socialist Realism* (Pantheon edition), pp. 31, 37 and 38.
† This term denotes the idea of submission to the party and acceptance of its ideology.
‡ *On Socialist Realism* (Pantheon edition), p. 41.

presses his regret that it is impossible to create a cult of Lenin. He argues that Stalin must be deified because our society depends on fraud.§

Sinyavsky showed all his anti-Soviet works to Daniel, who followed his example and, with Sinyavsky's help, sent "Hands" abroad.

"Hands" is about the misfortunes of a man who worked for the Cheka. (Summarizes the story.) As though to confirm the truth of Arzhak's story, Filippov, in his preface to "Hands," tells of a similar tale he heard when he was in a camp in Ukhta. The policy of the young [Soviet] state [is thus made out to be] inhumane, crippling people physically and mentally.

"The Man from Minap" is a crude lampoon maligning our society, our morality and our ethics. (Summarizes.) It's a fit subject for a vulgar anecdote, as even Filippov says, but Filippov welcomes it all the same, because of the anti-Soviet undertones, and because, as he puts it, the author tells this vulgar story so brilliantly. . . .

So it appears, Comrade Judges, that Soviet society, in Arzhak's account, is hypocritical and degraded. The author never misses an opportunity to poke fun at it. (Quotes: "But you are a Komsomol, too.") The final part is full of anti-Soviet jibes.

Comrade Judges, I stress that I am not denying an author's right to paint the seedy side of life. I stress that we have hypocrites and some immoral individuals among us. But does the author—like Mayakovsky, Mikhalkov and others—seek to extirpate these vices, or does he collect them, exaggerate them and send this picture abroad, passing it off there as a true picture of Soviet society? In this case, it is a cheap and vulgar invention which in our days shows anti-Soviet intent, for he passes this off as the truth about our life.

Still more anti-Soviet is the plot of "Atonement." (Paraphrases the plot.) The present phase of the life of our country is represented as a period of decadence, in which the people have no faith in the aims of the party.

The whole thing reads like the ravings of the sick, of lunatics, interspersed with anti-Soviet verses. (Quotes: "We are Russians. . . .") How this echoes Tertz's maxims in Unguarded Thoughts! This idea of claiming that the people as a whole are guilty of inertia.

---

§ The references to the cult of Lenin and Stalin are on p. 92 of On Socialist Realism (Pantheon edition).

(*Quotes:* "Brother will rise against brother. . . .") The reader is inevitably led to the conclusion that passivity during the purges needs to be atoned for; the nation is shown as intimidated. (*Quotes:* "Prisons have not been closed down. . . .")

This is being used by the anti-Soviet press. No wonder the publisher draws his conclusion about universal, collective responsibility for evil.

But the most outspoken and wild of all Arzhak's stories is *This Is Moscow Speaking*, in which the author shows himself capable of Jesuitically mocking at anything you can think of—even the growth of prosperity. This is what a character, an educated man, says. (*Quotes.*) The question arises, why did the author need to invent such nonsense? He invented it so that, against this background, slanderously passed off for reality, he could shout outright terroristic slogans and libel everything Soviet—our way of life, our press, our socialist principles. He starts with the press. (*Quotes.*) Next he turns to Soviet writers, whom he and Sinyavsky bitterly hate and describe as "Black Hundreds"—Sofronov, Bezymensky, Mikhalkov.* And how do Soviet intellectuals behave [in the story]? (*Quotes.*) He slanders Soviet people, describing them as anti-Semites who are only waiting to start a pogrom. (*Quotes the passage about "Babi Yar."*) † Who are "they"? I'd like to ask you, Daniel. Who was doing the shooting at Babi Yar? To whom are you comparing your countrymen? To Fascists?

Daniel makes out that the Armenians, Georgians, Azerbaijanis, Central Asians, Russians are all at daggers drawn, that they slaughter each other, and that the whole of this massacre is supervised by the party. Attacking the Communist Party and the people, the author asserts, through his characters, that such happenings are characteristic of our system, that 1937 followed organically from the nature of the Soviet system. What a monstrous invention!

The hero addresses a number of incendiary speeches to the reader. The hero says who is to be murdered. Daniel has tried to convince us

---

* See notes on p. 62 and 124. See also p. 17 for the reference to "Black Hundreds."

† A Jewish character in *This Is Moscow Speaking* fears that "Public Murder Day" might lead to a massacre of Jews as at Babi Yar in 1941. See *Dissonant Voices*, p. 273.

that his hero never meant to commit a murder and did not do so in fact, but we know what it says in that epigraph.‡ (*Quotes.*) I can't read the whole of the epigraph—some of it is unprintable. But who are the targets of all this hatred? Who are these people—who are these "fat-faced masters of our destiny"? If this isn't plain incitement to terrorism, what is it?

In order once again to stress the logical link between the different parts [of the story], he shifts the stage to the Mausoleum,§ and the whole of this wild, lunatic invention is joyfully seized upon in the West and put forward by Filippov as the truth.

I have given much thought to what could possibly have led Daniel to perpetrate this outrage. Why was he attracted to this date, the tenth of August, 1960? I looked up the issue of *Pravda* for that day. The *Pravda* of the tenth of August carried a resolution about the building of schools, items about the harvest in the Kustanai Region, the story of a collective farmer who rescued six children. (But there was also a page about Powers.)* That's what fills our life. How monstrously can it be slandered?

To come to the artistic merits of the two authors: both are equally feeble, equally trashy. They pour mud on whatever is most holy, most pure—love, friendship, motherhood. (*Quotes.*) Their women are either monsters or bitches. Their men are debauched. (*Quotes:* "A *wife is cheap, but it's better to pay too much.*")†

And I should like to quote one more epigraph from Arzhak's story *This Is Moscow Speaking.* (*Quotes:* "*They are in the water from the shower. . . .*")¶ And here is one from Tertz. (*Quotes:* "*In the lavatory, you are by yourself. . . .*")**

And this is exactly what can be said of their work—[it's like] water gurgling in a toilet bowl.

No bourgeois publisher would have touched this mixture of bad taste, vulgarity and pornography with a barge pole, but thanks to its anti-Soviet character, purchasers were found. Sinyavsky and Daniel have much in common—their ideas, their methods of sending their

---

‡ See note on p. 57.
§ I.e., the Lenin Mausoleum on Red Square. See pp. 64–65.
* I.e., Gary Powers, pilot of the U-2 shot down over Russia in 1960.
† Reference to the story "You and I" (*Fantastic Stories*, p. 12).
¶ *Dissonant Voices*, p. 284.
** The reference is to "Pkhentz" (see *Encounter*, April, 1966).

manuscripts out of the country, the discussions they had together, the way foreign publishers made a political judgment of their work. There is also the important fact that neither kept his manuscripts at home and that both used pen names. All this proves their outright anti-Soviet purpose. Here in court they have tried to prove either that they did not know what was said about their work abroad or that they learned of it too late. But it has been established that the press comment on their work both here and abroad was known to them at least since 1962. I am referring to the radio broadcast of *This Is Moscow Speaking* and to Ryurikov's article. Yet even after this, not only did they fail to take any [preventive] measures, but they sent out four more stories—*This Is Moscow Speaking,* "Atonement," "The Man from Minap" and *Lyubimov.* They put all their spite and hatred into their writing. They knew that it was slander, they acted deliberately, with the purpose of discrediting our system. Article 70 applies directly to this.

The social danger of their work, of what they have done, is particularly acute at this time, when ideological warfare is being stepped up, when the entire propaganda machine of international reaction, connected as it is with the intelligence services, is being brought into play to contaminate our youth with the poison of nihilism, to get its tentacles into our intellectual circles by hook or by crook, to sow the seeds of antagonism through such individuals as Sinyavsky and Daniel, to entangle in their nets if only a few people who have sold their pens, their honor and dignity as Soviet citizens, for dollars, for pieces of silver. With the help of these filthy scribblings, they are trying to discredit everything they can. Our enemies have understood the nature of the poisoned weapon handed them by these renegades. This is shown by what the bourgeois press has said about them, by all the praise showered on them and the money put aside for them in a bourgeois bank. If the enemy praises someone to us, there can be no good in such a person.

Their works have been printed by many publishers, by organizations of postwar émigrés, by intelligence agencies, etc. Now that they have lost their accomplices because the state security authorities have put them out of action, these bodies have raised a frantic howl. It is not for them to accuse us of having no freedom of the press. We don't have to say at this time what sort of a freedom of the press *they* have.

Freedom of the press is not an abstract notion. We have real freedom, we have freedom to march with and behind the people, to educate the people, particularly the young people through literature, we have the freedom to glorify the deeds of our people. I should like to quote the Greek patriot Theodorakis. (Quotes.)*

I accuse Sinyavsky and Daniel of activities directed against the state. They have written and have published under the guise of works of literature dirty lampoons calling for the overthrow of our system; they have disseminated slander, dressing it up as literature. What they have perpetrated is not the result of a chance error; it is an action tantamount to treason. The court must take a number of circumstances into consideration. Taking into account the fact that neither of the two men has admitted his guilt and that Sinyavsky has played the leading role, I must ask the court to sentence Sinyavsky to the maximum term: seven years' detention in camps of the strictest category, to be followed by five years in exile (applause), and Daniel to five years in camps of the strictest category to be followed by three years in exile.

Daniel ended his lampoon with the words: "This is Moscow speaking." No, Moscow speaks a different language. Moscow speaks to the world, Moscow speaks of the first moon rocket, and the same voice pronounces shame on renegades and slanderers. (Applause.)

Recess.

Session resumes in afternoon.

Speech by Defense Counsel Kogan
(Summary)

Sinyavsky faces three charges:
1. That he produced, harbored and disseminated his own works.
2. That he passed on those of Daniel.
3. That he passed on those of Remezov.

---

* Mikis Theodorakis: Greek composer (he wrote the music for Zorba the Greek) and left-wing politician.

The charge that Sinyavsky passed on Daniel's manuscripts is baseless. Sinyavsky denies that he passed them on, and Daniel denies that he got them out through Sinyavsky. Thus there are no grounds for the second charge.

As regards the third charge, Remezov should not in fact have been a witness at this trial; he should have appeared as a defendant, since he is as guilty as the other two. There is no reason for treating them differently, the one as a witness and the other two as defendants. The difference in their treatment can have only one explanation: a witness binds himself not to give false evidence, whereas a defendant can say anything he likes. Hence a witness is more readily believed, being bound to speak the truth. Although Sinyavsky's evidence deserves to be given at least as much weight as Remezov's, the fact of Remezov's speaking from the witness stand enhances the credibility of his evidence from a legal point of view.

Sinyavsky says that he did not pass on Remezov's manuscripts, but Remezov says that he sent his manuscripts out through Sinyavsky. However, Remezov's evidence in court is rather contradictory: he muddles dates and at first he said nothing about his friend Busseno, a publisher with whom he had been in touch, or that he himself had been abroad, or that he had friends with foreign contacts. Now, one may assume that he admitted his authorship [of the Ivanov MSS] because he did not know what was in Sinyavsky's evidence—he may have thought that it had already been revealed by Sinyavsky. And so, since Sinyavsky had already been arrested, he might have thought it was all right to blame him for sending out the "Ivanov" manuscripts as well as his own—perhaps in order to cover up for another person who is still unknown. Remezov thus has reasons for not speaking the truth and his evidence is confused. But it so happens that his evidence has greater authority than Sinyavsky's in law. This is not right, and this particular charge against Sinyavsky should be withdrawn.

As regards the main charge in the indictment, the defendant has undertaken to speak about his work from a literary point of view, and it is difficult for a lawyer to do this. It was therefore Sinyavsky who spoke about his ideas under examination and he will do so again in his final plea, while I, as a lawyer, will now deal with the legal aspects of the case.

Sinyavsky's mystical bent and his interest in the fantastic are borne out by the expert opinion of a psychiatrist. The end of the psychiatrist's report mentions a tendency toward exaggeration and the construction of fantasies. It says that Sinyavsky is a person who lives to a certain extent in an unreal world devised by himself. Therefore, what the prosecution often describes as slander is a way of looking at things peculiar to this psychological type. Sinyavsky's personality is certainly not pathological, but within the bounds of the normal he has certain peculiarities. Although he was not charged with it, his interest in sexual matters and in describing sexual scenes was quoted as adverse evidence about his moral character. The judge spoke of his "savoring" such scenes. Given Sinyavsky's mental makeup, this is not "savoring"; it is true that he has a heightened interest in this subject, but only because of its connection with sin. The problem of sin, as we know, looms large in the minds of religious people. Sinyavsky's approach to this question is analytical. In fact, in these scenes he emphasizes the element of sinfulness or "black magic." Sinyavsky even says outright in one place: "Woman is the black magic of the Russian people, and its white magic is vodka."

Of the nine works sent abroad by Sinyavsky, only three figure in the charges, only three are held to be anti-Soviet. The prosecution bases its case on the fact that these works were sent abroad. Why was this done [the prosecution asks] if not with the intent of undermining or weakening the Soviet regime and the power of the Soviet Union, and for purposes of ideological subversion? Yet not only the three works mentioned in the indictment were sent out—there were nine altogether and Sinyavsky didn't differentiate between them. This immediately raises doubts as to whether there was intent of any kind whatsoever.

Then there is the very complexity of his work. If there had been an intention to undermine the Soviet regime, then it would have been necessary to appeal to simpler tastes in order to undermine anything at all. But in fact Sinyavsky's work is very complicated. It isn't easy for literary experts, never mind for simpler readers. There has been argument about the ideas expressed in it. It is not clear what the author wanted to say. Each of these works can be interpreted in at least three different ways, all of them completely authoritative. (*Kogan quotes several foreign interpretations of Tertz's work, all* different and none of them attaching any anti-Soviet meaning to the work.) And even if Sinyavsky's works were anti-Soviet, they would necessarily have failed in their purpose, since they are not available to [Soviet] readers.

Thus, for a person to be judged guilty under Article 70 of the Criminal Code, there must be proof, not only of the anti-Soviet nature of his work but also of his intent to undermine or weaken the Soviet regime. But such intent has not been proved during the trial. I ask the court to take this into account.

(It should be noted that Kogan draws no conclusion as to the guilt or innocence of the defendant, nor does he touch on the character of the work itself. He simply asks the court to take his words into account.)

Speech by Defense Counsel Kisenishsky

(Summary)

Four of Daniel's works, that is, everything he published abroad, figure in the charges against him.

At least three of these works are not anti-Soviet in nature, and cannot be regarded as such. These are "Hands," "The Man from Minap" and "Atonement."

"Hands"—originally entitled "An Occurrence"—is a simple story about an incident in somebody's life. It is a story of psychological interest and has no political angle at all. It could be used to illustrate some set of political views or other, it could be interpreted in such a way, but since there is no one interpretation, it cannot be considered anti-Soviet.

"The Man from Minap" is an anecdote pure and simple, it has no political message of any kind, and no general conclusion can be drawn from it.

The idea of "Atonement" is that every man is responsible not only for himself but for all around him—this is not anti-Soviet.

As regards *This Is Moscow Speaking,* there is certainly no malicious intent on the part of the author. This is borne out by the fact that the basic principles of socialism, of the Soviet regime and of Communism are frequently held up for admiration in this book. Thus three of the four works are not anti-Soviet, while there is no malicious intent in the fourth.

At the same time, Daniel's military career and his hard-working life should be taken into account. I ask the court to do so.

Objection by Kedrina

Kogan says that the obscurity of Sinyavsky's work precludes its use for anti-Soviet propaganda. There are two forms of propaganda—the propaganda of the poster and propaganda through art which plays on the emotions. The latter kind is sometimes more effective.

Kogan says that Sinyavsky is not a Marxist but an idealist, both in his stories and in his articles. But when he published articles here he wrote as a Marxist and as such, objectively, he was on the other side of the fence from Tertz, though he himself was Tertz. Such double-dealing is intolerable and inadmissible, and it is a matter for criminal proceedings.

Kogan says that Sinyavsky always avoids polemics, appealing to moral rather than political standards, calling for the restoration of love to people's hearts, and telling them to find God. Where does God come in here? Take that scene where mothers are depicted as wizened mushrooms. What sort of love is that? Or his description of Lenin—is that an example of love for one's neighbor?

About Arzhak and Kisenishsky's speech: The defense counsel says that "Hands" has no political meaning. If I write something about picking flowers in a meadow, no political meaning can be read into it, however much one tries. But once a political meaning is read into "Hands," its anti-Soviet nature shows up.

Kisenishsky says that the author's sympathies are on the side of Malinin, the hero of the story. But one cannot say that in fact. How can one talk of sympathy when Malinin is presented as a stupid man with a limited outlook? The sympathy is aroused not for him but for his predicament. This is why the story is anti-Soviet.

One only has to see how vividly the execution is described. Daniel does not usually write with such literary power, but what force he puts into this! This is the scene that attracts him most of all, and it is here that he shows how essentially anti-Soviet he is.

Objection by A. Vasilyev

Sinyavsky's Defense Counsel Kogan has read out a letter from two French literary experts, Frioux and Aucouturier.‡ But he didn't read it out to the end. I will now say what is in it. It says that the two professors don't believe that Sinyavsky and Tertz are one and the same person. But since it has now been proved that they are one and the same person, there is no point in referring to this letter.

---

‡ There is no trace of this in the transcript of Kogan's speech.

Final Plea by Andrei Sinyavsky

It will be rather difficult for me to speak since I had not expected that I should be called upon to make my final plea today. I had been told that it would be on Monday, and I have not had time to prepare. It will be even more difficult in view of the special atmosphere that one can feel here fairly keenly. I am not convinced by the arguments of the prosecution, and I stick by my previous attitude. The arguments of the prosecution give one the feeling of being up against a blank wall, on which one batters one's head in vain, and through which one cannot penetrate in order to get to some kind of truth. The arguments of the prosecutor are the same as those of the indictment and I heard them many times during the preliminary investigation. It is always the same quotations, over and over again: "One round and another and another . . . firing from the hip";* "to do away with prisons, we built new prisons."† It is always the same hair-raising quotations from the indictment, repeated dozens of times and mounting up to create a monstrous atmosphere that no longer bears any relation to any kind of reality. It is an artistic device to keep on repeating the same phrases over and over again, and it is a powerful one. It creates a kind of shroud, a peculiar kind of electrified atmosphere in which the boundary between the real and the grotesque becomes blurred, rather as in the works of Arzhak and Tertz. It is the atmosphere of a murky anti-Soviet underground hidden behind the

---

* From Daniel's *This Is Moscow Speaking*. See p. 18 of Introduction.
† From Sinyavsky's *On Socialist Realism*.

bright faces of the candidate of sciences Sinyavsky and the poet-translator Daniel, who hatch plots, nurture plans for *putsches*, terrorist acts, pogroms, assassinations, assassinations, assassinations . . . in general, a real "Public Murder Day"—but with only two actors: Daniel and myself.

It really is very strange that literary images suddenly lose their make-believe character and are interpreted by the prosecution literally —so literally that these court proceedings merge into a literary text as a natural sequel to it. I unfortunately put the date 1956 at the end of the epilogue to my short novel *The Trial Begins*, and I am now accused of having misrepresented that year in a slanderous way, and so they say, "Aha, you saw what was coming to you . . . now, in 1966, off you go to a camp!"‡ There are unmistakable undertones of gloating over this in the speeches for the prosecution.

But there are other notes as well. There are additional touches to the picture by means of which our political underground is also made into an underworld of degenerates, cannibals with lurid instincts, who hate mothers and their own people, who are Fascists and anti-Semites. Since it is difficult to make Daniel out to be an anti-Semite, the Fascist Daniel, hand in hand with the anti-Semite Sinyavsky, trample on everything that is sacred, including the notion of motherhood.* It is difficult to break through this atmosphere—no arguments, however circumstantial, about the nature of the creative process, are of any avail here. I already realized under interrogation that all this is of no interest to the prosecution: they are not concerned with artistic concepts, but only with certain quotations which are repeated over and over and over again.

I am not going to try to explain the literary purposes of our works, or deliver a lecture, or beat my head against the wall, trying to prove something—that would be futile. All I want to do is to repeat a few elementary arguments about the nature of literature. The most rudimentary thing about literature—it is here that one's study of it begins—is that words are not deeds, and that words and literary

---

‡ In the epilogue to *The Trial Begins*, the fictional narrator describes how he is arrested and imprisoned in a camp for having been discovered as the author of his novel!

* See p. 179.

images are conventions: authors are not identical with the characters they create. This is an elementary truth, and we tried to talk about it. But the prosecution stubbornly rejected the idea as an invention, a means of evasion and deceit.

If you read the story *This Is Moscow Speaking* attentively—or even in the most cursory way—as long as you are not afraid of words, you will see that the story is one long cry of "Thou shalt not kill!" The hero says, "I cannot and do not wish to kill—a human being must remain human in all circumstances." But nobody pays any attention to this. "Aha," they say, "you wanted to kill, you are a murderer, you are a Fascist." There is a kind of monstrous perversity about all this.

The hero of my *The Trial Begins*, Globov, is perhaps not a bad man, but in accordance with the requirements of the time§ he makes a display of anti-Semitic sentiments and utters certain anti-Semitic words: "Rabinovich is slippery, like all Jews." My story is clearly *against* anti-Semitism, it is about the "Doctors' Plot"—but no, the author is an anti-Semite, and so put him next to the Fascist Daniel!

At this point logic breaks down. The author also turns out to be a sadist. Anti-Semitism is generally combined with nationalism and chauvinism. But we are dealing with a particularly perverse author: he hates the Russian people, and the Jews as well. He hates everything, he hates mothers and the whole of mankind. The question arises: Where did these monsters come from, out of what bog, out of what underground did they emerge? Apparently a Soviet court (I know this from books) usually concerns itself, in coming to its decision, with the origin of the crime, with its cause. In the present case this is of no interest to the prosecution. So where did we come from, Daniel and I? We must have been dropped by parachute from America and immediately begun to wreak havoc—scoundrels that we are! I have been compared here with Gratsiansky—a man with an obscure past who later turns out to be a spy.* Has the prosecution

---

§ The story is set in 1952, the time of the Jewish "Doctors' Plot," and of an officially inspired campaign of anti-Semitism.

* Gratsiansky is a character in a novel by the leading Soviet writer, Leonid Leonov, *The Russian Forest* (1952), who pretends to be a fervent Soviet patriot, but who had worked for the Czarist secret police before the Revolution and at the beginning of World War II becomes a spy for the Germans. This comparison with Gratsiansky is not in the transcript of the speeches for the prosecution.

really not pondered the question about our origin? How could a Fascist arise in our midst? Surely, if you come to think of it, this is a far more terrible matter than that of a couple of books, however anti-Soviet they may be in content. The prosecution has not even raised this question. Here you have two outwardly respectable persons, but in their heart of hearts they are Fascists, only waiting for a chance to raise a revolt and throw bombs. Or were these words thrown into our faces just in order to insult us?

I think I have made it clear during the trial, with the help of quotations, that Karlinsky [in *The Trial Begins*] is a totally negative character and that there can be no doubt whatsoever about my attitude, as his creator, toward him. But no, once again the prosecutor reads out the blasphemous words—these terrible cynical words —about the little fishes which are extracted from mothers' wombs, and exclaims with great feeling: "Now isn't this anti-Soviet propaganda through and through? Isn't this disgusting?" Yes, it is disgusting; yes, it is anti-Soviet through and through, like the words of the same character: "Socialism is free servitude." But the character is an anti-Soviet one, who is exposed as such. There is not the slightest doubt about this. But nobody would listen to this, or perhaps it made no difference. That's probably it—it made no difference.

I can even see the prosecutor's point of view. His tasks are of a broader nature; he is not obliged to take account of all kinds of literary matters regarding authors and their characters, and that kind of thing. But when similar things are said by two members of the Union of Writers, one of whom is a professional writer and the other a critic with a university degree—when they identify the words of a negative character with the author's own sentiments, here one really throws up one's hands.

Let's take that passage about the classics in "Graphomaniacs." How can one possibly suppose that because it is written in the first person about an unsuccessful writer (in whom there might well be certain autobiographical features) that I, the author, hate the classics? This might not be understood by somebody who has just barely learned to read. For such a person, of course, Dostoyevsky would be his own "man from the underground," Gorky would be Klim Samgin and Saltykov-Shchedrin would be Yudushka. In this way everything can be turned upside down.

The prosecutor raised in passing the question of the "compartment."† Vasilyev even mentioned, without embarrassment, the diapers which were given to me for my new-born son—incidentally, not by Madame Zamoyska but by another Frenchwoman. Even underclothing was brought into play in order to show up the dark interior behind the bright front presented to the world by me and Daniel. There were quotations from my articles showing how in one place I wrote about socialist realism from a Marxist point of view, and in another place from an idealist point of view.‡ If I were able to write from an idealist point of view here, I would do so.

Often when I was asked to write about something here, I would refuse, and try to write about authors with whom I have something in common. Kedrina knows this very well—we worked together in the same Institute. She knows that I didn't play the hero, didn't speak at meetings, didn't beat my breast and never spoke in slogans. And quite often I was hauled over the coals for "mistakes," "deviations" and "inaccuracies." In the report on me from the Institute of World Literature, which came to the KGB [security police] after my arrest (even my interrogator was indignant when he saw that in this report I had been retrospectively demoted from senior to junior staff member), some things are true: It said that my ideological attitude was vague, that I wrote about Tsvetayeva, Mandelshtam and Pasternak, that this was my bent.* This was my bent, these were the people I wanted to write about. I did everything I possibly could to express my real thoughts under my own name of Sinyavsky. As a result I have had a lot of trouble, I have received reprimands, I have been attacked in the press and at meetings.

Apart from my salary, I have enjoyed no particular benefits. Vasilyev says that I was "always hanging around in the Union of Writers." Did I ask for any loans there, or travel allowances, or free vacation vouchers? Vasilyev enumerated all the birthday presents that

---

† See note * on p. 159.

‡ "Idealist" is used here, as opposed to "materialist," in the philosophical sense.

* All three of these poets were distinctly un-Soviet in style and content. Marina Tsvetayeva (1894–1941) was a Russian poetess, and friend of Pasternak, who returned from emigration to the Soviet Union in the late thirties, and committed suicide there. Mandelshtam died in a Soviet concentration camp.

various friends have given me in the last ten years.¶ If I had ever received a free vacation voucher, one can imagine what he would have made of that! . . .

Is there really any point in my trying once again to explain a few simple things? I am reproached for having insulted mothers. But in *Lyubimov* I say explicitly: "Do not dare to harm mothers." And then Lenya Tikhomirov was stopped by a magic force when he attempted to do violence to his mother's soul.† How can it be said that I insulted mothers? Is it because I describe the old women [in *Lyubimov*] as being like wrinkled, worm-eaten, forest mushrooms? Should I have put halos round the heads of these old women prostrate on the floor of the chapel?‡ It is a time-honored device in literature to write in a deliberately low key. One cannot expect the prosecution to go into this sort of thing, but that *writers* should not understand it!

To sum up: everything is camouflage, everything is deceit, a cover, like my candidate's degree. My "feeble" literary form§ is simply a vehicle for counterrevolutionary ideas. Idealism, hyperbole, fantasy— all this is of course nothing more than the trickery of a dyed-in-the-wool enemy of the Soviet system who uses every conceivable form of camouflage! Well, let's admit that here I camouflage myself and that I had good reason to, but over there, abroad, couldn't I have thrown off my mask, and really let myself go? . . .

Hyperbole, fantasy—does this mean that art itself becomes a device, a cover for anti-Soviet ideas? Very well, but there are phrases, ideas and images which point in a completely opposite direction, even though they are lost in the dense thicket of the other quotations. I could repeat them, but it doesn't make sense. Side by side with the sentence that has been quoted here dozens of times, "In order that there should be no prisons, we have built new prisons," there is another sentence which I have asked you to read: "Communism is a luminous aim." But nobody wanted to read this. And then there is my passionate defense of the Revolution—nobody was

---

¶ This point is missing in the transcript of Vasilyev's speech.

† He tries to hypnotize her into giving up her faith in God.

‡ At the end of *Lyubimov*, all the old women come to pray for the souls of the dead and the living, the fathers and sons, after the reign of the lunatic dictator in the town of *Lyubimov* has come to an end.

§ See p. 221.

interested in this, nobody was concerned to analyze it; they were interested only in certain expressions and anti-Soviet clichés which could be branded on the forehead of Daniel and myself, just as they could be stamped on our works.¶

The Public Prosecutor has said (I was so struck by this sentence that I made a note of it): "Even the foreign press says that these works are anti-Soviet." If you think about it, the logic of this is that for the prosecutor the highest standard of objectivity is provided by the foreign press, i.e., if even *it* has said something or other, then surely we are in duty bound to believe it! I was particularly struck by the word "even." I could use this "even" in a different context: "Even" a section of the foreign press has written that my works are *not* anti-Soviet. . . . There is, for instance, Karl Miller,‡ who writes about my almost unshakable faith in Communism, or the following, for instance: "Tertz looks back on the revolution with nostalgia, but his attitude to what came later is not orthodox." Now why did these bourgeois characters say that Tertz looks back with nostalgia to the Revolution, if we are Fascists?

As proof of our guilt, the prosecution quotes Filippov, but the others, like Milosz and Field, are fools, are they? In fact, they are worth much more than Filippov; they are more serious authors, after all.

As a result, we are accused of "malevolence which even a White Guardist might envy," and things printed on our books have been quoted at us (such things as "Fight the Communist Party of the Soviet Union" and something else I don't remember). What is printed on the book is equated with the book itself. I can imagine that just such things have been put on the works of Zoshchenko, Solzhenitsyn, and on Akhmatova's *Requiem*. No distinction is made between propaganda imprints and the literary works.

The question arises: What is propaganda and what is literature? The viewpoint of the prosecution is that literature is a form of propaganda, and that there are only two kinds of propaganda: pro-

---

¶ This evidently refers to things said about their work abroad, or added in prefaces, etc., to editions of their work published abroad. All the references in the above paragraph are *On Socialist Realism*.

‡ Reviewer in the *New Statesman*.

Soviet or anti-Soviet. If literature is simply un-Soviet, it means that it is anti-Soviet. I cannot accept this. It is a poor business if writers are judged and categorized by such standards, but what would be done with somebody who printed manifestoes? He also comes under Article 70 of the Criminal Code. If a work of literature has to be judged in the light of the maximum penalty provided for by this Article, then what would happen in the case of a political pamphlet? Or is there no difference? For the prosecution, there is no difference.

The literary specialist Kedrina has said here that nobody would read political significance into butterflies in a meadow. But reality cannot be reduced to butterflies in a meadow.§ Wasn't an anti-Soviet meaning read into Zoshchenko? Indeed, is there anybody into whom such a meaning hasn't been read at one time or another? I know there is a difference in that they published their works only here. But everybody, particularly if they wrote satire, has had anti-Soviet intentions imputed to them. Ilf and Petrov, for example, were also accused of slander. Slander was even discovered in Demyan Bedny.* True, this was in a different period. But I don't know of a single leading satirist who hasn't had anti-Soviet ideas read into him. It is also a fact that until now nobody has ever been held criminally responsible for his creative activity. In the whole history of literature I know of no criminal trial like this one, even of authors who also published abroad, and in a sharply critical way at that. I do not wish to make any comparisons between my case and those of other people,† but am I right in believing that Soviet citizens are supposed to be equal before the law?

---

§ In the transcript of Kedrina's speech, it is "flowers in a meadow" (p. 172).

* Ilya Ilf (1897–1937) and Evgeni Petrov (1903–42) were joint authors of the famous satires *The Twelve Chairs* and *The Golden Calf*. These two works were virtually banned in the last years of Stalin's rule.

Demyan Bedny (1883–1945) was an orthodox, "proletarian" poet who nevertheless on one occasion was severely criticized for the libretto of an opera which displeased Stalin because it satirized Russia's conversion to Christianity by St. Vladimir. By 1937, when the opera (*Bogatyri*) was put on, it had been decided that this event had, after all, been "progressive." All this was in line with Stalin's decision to appeal to Russian patriotism.

† Perhaps Sinyavsky is here referring to Remezov, who had also published abroad under a pseudonym but was not put on trial because he had turned state's evidence. Remezov's work is much more political than Sinyavsky's. See pp. 131–36 for Remezov's testimony.

The arguments which have been flung at me are such that it is impossible to explain anything. If I write in an article about my love of Mayakovsky, then they quote at me Mayakovsky's words: "Soviet citizens have a pride all their own," but you, they say, sent your manuscripts abroad. But why, inconsistent and un-Marxist as I am, may I not express my admiration for Mayakovsky?

At this point the law of "either-or" comes into operation. Sometimes it is justified, but at other times the results are terrifying. He who is not with us is against us. At certain periods—in revolution, war or civil war—this logic may be right, but it is very dangerous in times of peace, when it is applied to literature. I am asked: "Where are your positive heroes? Ah, you haven't got any! Ah, you are not a socialist! Ah, you are not a realist! Ah, you are not a Marxist! Ah, you are a *fantaisiste* and an idealist, and you publish abroad into the bargain! Of course, you are a counterrevolutionary!"

In my unpublished story "Pkhentz"‡ there is a sentence which I feel I can apply to myself: "Just think, if I am simply different from others, they have to start cursing me." Well, I am different. But I do not regard myself as an enemy; I am a Soviet man, and my works are not hostile works. In this fantastic, electrified atmosphere anybody who is "different" may be regarded as an enemy, but this is not an objective way of arriving at the truth. Most of all, however, I do not see why enemies have to be invented, why monsters have to be piled on monsters by means of a literal-minded interpretation of literary images.

I feel deeply that juridical standards cannot be applied to literature. The nature of an artistic image is complex, and even the author himself cannot always explain it. I think that if Shakespeare (I am not comparing myself with Shakespeare, nobody should imagine that) had been asked: "What is the meaning of *Hamlet*, or what is the meaning of *Macbeth*, is there some insidious meaning in them?" —I think that Shakespeare himself would not have been able to give an answer to such questions. You lawyers are concerned with terms which, the more narrowly defined they are, the more precise they are. By contrast, in the case of a literary image, the more precise it is, the broader it is.

---

‡ It has since appeared in the April, 1966, issue of *Encounter*.

Objection by Prosecutor

(Summary)

The gist of the prosecutor's objection is that he rejects what Kogan says about the counts in the indictment. He insists on retaining the charge that Sinyavsky passed on Daniel's and Remezov's manuscripts. He says that since Remezov has clearly and unambiguously defined his own views, there can be no doubt of his truthfulness. Sinyavsky's evidence, on the other hand, was evasive and vague. Remezov's evidence was therefore the more credible. Neither did he doubt that Sinyavsky had also helped Daniel to get his manuscripts out. He based this belief on the confused nature of evidence given during the preliminary investigation.

As regards the question of intent: even if one were to ignore the facts and believe that the two men just wanted to be published, then how is one to explain that they did not pay attention to the clear and unambiguous article by Ryurikov in 1962?† It is quite impossible that Sinyavsky should not have read the journal. Lawyers regard anything published as a matter of general knowledge. We must take it that they knew this article. Yet even after this article, they wrote further works and sent them abroad. This is proof of direct intent.

---

† See p. 123.

Final Plea by Yuli Daniel[*]

I KNEW that I should have the right of making a final plea and I wondered whether I should waive this right altogether, as I am entitled to, or whether to limit myself to the usual generalities. But then I realized that this is not only my last word† at this trial, but perhaps the last word that I shall be able to say to people in my life. And there are people here, there are people sitting in the courtroom, and there are also people sitting at the bench. It is for this reason that I decided to speak.

In the final plea of my comrade Sinyavsky there was a note of despair about the impossibility of breaking through a blank wall of incomprehension and unwillingness to listen. I am not so pessimistic. I wish to go over the arguments of the prosecution and the defense once again.

Throughout the trial I kept asking myself: What is the purpose of cross-questioning? The answer should be obvious and simple: to hear our replies and then put the next question, to conduct the hearing in such a way as finally to arrive at the truth.

This has not been the case.

To make my point clear I will remind you once again of the way things have gone.

I shall talk only about my own works—I hope my friend Sinyavsky

---

* The transcript of this session, at which the sentences were pronounced, is evidently incomplete, since it contains only this "final plea" by Daniel.
† "Final plea" in Russian is "last word."

will forgive me, he talked about both of us—it is simply that I remember my own things best.

I was asked all the time why I wrote my story *This Is Moscow Speaking*. Every time I replied: Because I felt there was a real danger of a resurgence of the cult of personality. To this the answer was always: What is the relevance of the cult of personality, if the story was written in 1960–61? To this I say: It was precisely in these years that a number of events made one feel that the cult of personality was being revived. This was not denied; I was not told, "You are lying, this is not true"—my words were simply ignored as though I had never said them. Then the prosecution would say: You have slandered your people, country and government by your monstrous invention about "Public Murder Day." To this I would reply: It could have happened—one only has to think of the crimes committed in the days of the cult of personality; they are far more terrible than anything written by me or Sinyavsky. At this point the prosecution stopped listening, did not reply to me and simply ignored what I had said. This refusal to listen to what we were saying, this deafness to all our explanations, was characteristic of the whole of this trial.

It was the same story with another of my works. Asked why I had written "Atonement," I would explain: Because I think that all members of society, each of us individually and all of us collectively, are responsible for what happens. It may be that I am wrong or that this is a fallacy, but all the prosecution said is: "This is a slander on the Soviet people and the Soviet intelligentsia." They did not argue with me, but simply paid no attention to what I was saying. "Slander" was the easiest reply to anything said by the defendants.

The "public accuser," the writer Vasilyev, said that he was accusing us both in the name of the living and in the name of those who fell in the war and whose names are engraved in gold on marble in the Writers' Club. I know these lists engraved on a marble tablet. I know the names of these people who fell in the war. I knew some of them personally, and their memory is sacred to me. But why does Vasilyev, quoting from Sinyavsky's article: ". . . so that not one drop of blood should be shed, we killed and killed and killed . . ." why, in quoting these words, did not Vasilyev remind us of certain other names, or are they unknown to him? I mean the names of

Babel, Mandelshtam, Bruno Jasienski, Ivan Katayev, Koltsov, Tretyakov, Kvitko, Markish, and many others.§ perhaps Vasilyev has never read their works or heard their names? But perhaps the specialist in literature Kedrina knows the names of Levidov and Nusinov?* But even if they are so phenomenally ignorant in matters of literature, perhaps the name Meyerhold† rings a bell with them? Or, if they are in general unversed in matters of art, perhaps they have heard the names of Postyshev, Tukhachevsky, Blücher, Kossior, Gamarnik, Yakir.‡ Evidently these people must have died in their beds from a cold in the head, if we are to believe the assertion that we did not kill. Well, what is the truth of the matter—did we kill or didn't we? Did all this happen or didn't it? To pretend that it didn't happen, that we didn't kill these people, is an insult. It is—forgive me for putting it so bluntly—like spitting at the memory of those who perished.

> JUDGE: Defendant Daniel, I must interrupt you. Your offensive expression is out of place.
>
> DANIEL: I beg the court's pardon for the bluntness of my expression. I am under great strain and it is difficult for me to pick and choose my words, but I shall try to be more restrained.

The prosecution says to us: Judge your works yourself and admit that they are depraved and slanderous. But we cannot say this. We wrote about what was happening as we saw it. No alternative views have been offered to us: we have not been told either that these

---

§ Bruno Jasienski (1901–1941), a Polish Communist writer who went to live in the Soviet Union in 1929; Ivan Katayev (1902– ?), novelist well known as a militant Communist in the twenties and thirties; Mikhail Koltsov (1898–1942), journalist and writer best known for his "Spanish diary" (1938); Sergei Tretyakov (1892–1939), author of *Roar, China!*; Leib Kvitko (1890–1952) and Perets Markish (1895–1952), Yiddish poets who were shot, together with other Jewish writers, in 1952. The other writers mentioned here died in concentration camps.

° Mikhail Levidov (1892– ?) and Isaak Nusinov (1889– ?), prominent literary critics who disappeared in purges under Stalin.

† Vsevolod Meyerhold (1874–1942), famous theater director who was arrested in 1937 and died in a camp.

‡ Prominent party and army leaders murdered by Stalin.

crimes took place or that they did not take place; nobody has said to us: It is not true that people are responsible for each other and for their society. There has simply been silence on these points; nothing at all has been said. All our explanations, as well as the works written by us, are left hanging in the air and are not taken into consideration.

In her speech here the "public accuser" Kedrina repeated, with a few lyrical digressions and additions, almost the whole of her article "The Heirs of Smerdyakov" published in *Literary Gazette* before the trial. I should like to dwell on this article for a moment, since it has been produced at the trial as a speech for the prosecution, and for another reason which I will mention later. At the beginning of her "literary analysis" of my story *This Is Moscow Speaking* Kedrina says of the story's hero: "He wants to kill. But the question is, who?" Now the fact is my hero *doesn't* want to kill, as is perfectly clear from the story. Incidentally, I am not alone in this opinion—the president of the court agrees with me. During the cross-questioning of the witness Garbuzenko he asked: "How do you, as a Communist, view the fact that the hero of the story is ordered to kill, but refuses to do so?" I am grateful to the president of the court for this accurate definition of my hero's attitude.[§] Of course I do not think that the opinion of the president of the court should be binding on the literary specialist Kedrina—she has a perfect right to her own interpretation of my work—but the question is: On what does she base it? This is what she writes: ". . . the hero has a daydream about Studebakers—one, two, eight, forty of them—going over the corpses." I shall come back to this passage, which was quoted in Kedrina's article and here in court.

By the way, this passage is different from the way it has been quoted here; it has never been quoted in full: "And how about these people who sit in judgment and have power, what are we to do with them? What about 1937, when the country was in the throes of mass purges, and what about the madness after the war? Can all that be forgiven?" (I am quoting from memory.) This sentence is always carefully passed over in silence. Why? Because it gives the motives for the hero's feelings of hatred, and this would have to be argued

---

§ This point is missing in the transcript of Garbuzenko's questioning.

about and explained in some way, so it is much simpler to ignore it. It's after this sentence that we have what has been quoted in court: "Do you still remember how to do it? The fuse . . . pull out the pin . . . throw. Lie flat on the ground. Lie down! Now it's exploded and now run forward, firing from the hip—one round after another, and another and another!" Then everything gets blurred and mixed up in the hero's mind: "Russians, Germans, Georgians, Rumanians, Jews, Hungarians, tunics, placards, medical corps, spades . . ." I am quoting the whole of this passage, where there is indeed a bloody melee and where all the details are very unpleasant: "Why is he so thin? Why is he wearing a padded coat, bedecked with medals? . . . Over the body runs a Studebaker, two Studebakers, eight Studebakers, forty Studebakers, and you will lie there flattened like a frog; we've had all that before!"

This is what Kedrina calls "dreaming" of Studebakers that will crush bodies! The hero's horror and revulsion at this picture in his mind's eye is interpreted as the hero's "dream," something for which he longs! This is what Kedrina calls "straight Fascism"—these are her exact words. But she has to support her contention that this is Fascism, so she writes: "The 'hero' of the story tries to justify this program of 'liberation' from Communism and the Soviet system by assertions to the effect that the idea of 'public murder' is rooted in 'the very essence of socialist doctrine' and also that antagonism among people is in the nature of society in general."

Here I should say that there is not a single word in the story about liberation from the Soviet regime. The hero of the story invokes the name of Lenin, as though taking refuge in it: "He did not wish this, he who was first laid to rest within these marble walls."[†] Now who is it who is trying to "justify a program of 'liberation,'" the hero of the story or one of the other people in it? When I first read Kedrina's article, I must admit that I thought there had been a misprint, a typographical error, that she had really meant some other character in the story, and that this explained why it looked as though Kedrina was talking all the time only about my main hero. But no, the same thing has been said again here in court. In fact, the hero does not say

---

† See p. 297 of *Dissonant Voices*.

that the "notion of public murder lies at the very root of socialist doctrine." What happens is that the hero of the story is approached by his acquaintance, Volodya Margulis, a stupid and narrow-minded person: "He [Margulis] came to me and asked me what I ('I' is the hero of the story who talks in the first person) think about all this."*
Volodya Margulis "began to argue that it all sprang from the very essence of socialist doctrine."

Now then, is it the hero who says this or another character in the story? What the hero says is actually quite different: "We must stand up for the real Soviet system." He goes on to say that our fathers made the Revolution and that we must not think badly of it. Is this a "justification" by the hero of the story of a "program of liberation from Communism and the Soviet system"? Of course it isn't! And who is it in the story who says that "everybody would drown each other in a spoonful of water," and that "before long animals will be the only link between people"? According to Kedrina these words are also spoken by my hero. This also is not true! These words are spoken by a half-demented and misanthropic old man with whom the hero argues.§ So what is left of the ideological justification of my supposed call for terrorism and liberation from Communism and the Soviet regime? Kedrina has read the story not in the sense in which it was written but in a deliberately prejudiced way, in a way in which it cannot be read.

Sinyavsky and I are accused of all manner of things, including the fact that we do not have "positive" heroes. Needless to say, a positive hero makes things easier—you can contrast him with your "negative" hero. When we refer to other writers who do not have positive heroes, this is taken as an attempt on our part to compare ourselves with great writers or we are told—as in the case of Shchedrin—that there *is* a positive hero in his works, namely, the People. Clearly the "positive hero" in this case is invisible, since the people who are depicted in *The History of the Town of Glupov* arouse pity rather than admiration. And is the People the "positive" hero of *The Golovlev Family?* As for the reference to the tale about how one

---

* I.e., the Supreme Soviet's decree announcing "Public Murder Day."
§ See p. 286 of *Dissonant Voices.*

peasant fed two generals,* this is quite shameful. Kedrina seems to think that this peasant who made snares out of his own hair in order to catch birds for the generals to eat and who voluntarily accepts slavery provides a "positive" image of the Russian people! Shchedrin would never have agreed with this!

I would not have bothered to refer to Kedrina's article if it were not for the fact that the whole of the prosecution's case is on the same level.

How did they try to prove the anti-Soviet nature of Sinyavsky and myself? Several procedures have been used. The simplest and most head-on form of attack has been to attribute to the author the ideas of his characters. One can do all kinds of things by this method. Sinyavsky need not think that only he has been declared to be an anti-Semite. I, Yuli Markovich Daniel, a Jew, am also an anti-Semite—all this by virtue of the fact that one of my characters, an old waiter, says something about the Jews, and so the following entry goes down in my dossier: "Nikolai Arzhak [Daniel] is a consummate and convinced anti-Semite." Do you think this was written by some inexperienced consultant? No, this report was written by Academician Yudin. . . .†

Then there is another procedure: quoting out of context. All you have to do is to take a few sentences, make a few cuts here and there, and you can prove anything you like. The best example of this is the way in which This Is Moscow Speaking has been made into a call for terrorism.

There have been constant references to the émigré Filippov as a person who has made a correct assessment of our works. It appears that he is the highest arbiter of truth for the Public Prosecutor. But even Filippov failed to exploit this particular possibility. One can imagine that if there really were a call for terror, then surely Filippov, of all people, would have leaped at this and pointed it out ("Just look how the underground Soviet writers call for assassination and terror!"). But even Filippov was not able to say this.

---

* This is one of Saltykov-Shchedrin's Fairy Tales (Skazki, 1869–86), a collection of bitterly satirical fables. To illustrate the inertia of the Russian peasant masses Shchedrin writes about a peasant who, stranded on a desert island with two generals, continues to feed them and fetch and carry for them.

† Presumably Pavel Yudin, a Soviet philosopher who edited the Cominform journal in Belgrade before the split with Yugoslavia in 1948.

Yet another procedure has been to make out critical remarks about characters in the books to be remarks directed against the Soviet regime; i.e., the author says something intended to expose one of his characters, and the prosecution takes this as applying to the Soviet system. Here is an example. Most of the indictment is based on expert testimony supplied by Glavlit. Now this report of Glavlit has a passage which reads literally as follows: "The author regards it as possible to hold in our country a 'Homosexuals' Day.'" In fact, however, this refers to the opportunistic and cynical artist Chuprov, of whom the main hero of the story says that he would design posters even for a "Homosexuals' Day" as long as he could make a bit of money out of it.‡ What is my hero condemning here, the Soviet system or another character in the same story?

In the indictment, in the Glavlit report and in the speeches for the prosecution we find identical quotations from my story "Atonement." And what are these quotations? "Our prisons are within us!" exclaims the hero of the story, Volsky. Yes, this is a powerful accusation addressed to the world at large, and I have not tried, as Vasilyev here has alleged, to make out that my only concern is with literature pure and simple. I do not wish to deny the political content of my works, and there is a political aspect to these words of Volsky's. But what happens after he has shouted out these words, and what sort of a man is it who shouts them? They are shouted by a madman, a man who has gone out of his mind, and is shortly afterward put in a lunatic asylum.

Then there is still another very simple, but extremely effective way of "proving" anti-Soviet intent: This is to invent something on the author's behalf and say that a work has anti-Soviet passages, even though there are none. Take my story "Hands." My defense counsel, Kisenishsky, gave a well-argued proof that the basic idea of the story is not anti-Soviet, in whichever way you care to interpret it. In her reply to Kisenishsky, Kedrina said: "Just look with what expressiveness and vividness, which are otherwise uncharacteristic of him, Daniel has described the episode of the execution!" I beg you, I implore you to think of the implications of this remark, namely, that vividness and expressiveness of description can serve as proof of the

---

‡ See p. 282 of *Dissonant Voices*.

anti-Soviet nature of something. This was the answer to my defense counsel's remarks about the story "Hands"—and this was all that was said about it.

As regards this story of mine, I beg you all to do one thing. This session of the court will shortly come to an end, and you will all go home. Go to your bookshelves, take down a certain book, open it and read about how a certain commander of the Red Army was assigned to an execution squad. He returns home, dark and haggard from his work, staggering like a drunken man. He has been shooting not priests, but peasants. There is even one detail which I remember particularly well: He keeps thinking of the hand of one of the men he has shot, a hand as hard and horny as a horse's hoof. He feels sick and horror-struck. When he is alone with the woman he loves, he even finds that he has become impotent. Now one of the points made against us in the indictment could be applied to this passage— the point about the policy of class warfare against the Soviet people crippling people morally and physically. . . .

> JUDGE: What sort of nonsense is this! What policy of class warfare?
> DANIEL: I'm quoting from the indictment, here it is (reads): ". . . a supposed policy of class warfare against the Soviet people." That's what it says in the indictment.

As you have probably guessed, I have just summarized a chapter from Sholokhov's *And Quiet Flows the Don*, and the characters to whom I have referred are Bunchuk, the Red Army commander, and Anna.*

What other methods are used to accuse us? Criticism of a certain period is made out to be criticism of a whole epoch; criticism of a five-year period is passed off as criticism of fifty years; even if you write about as short a space of time as two or three years, you are accused of writing about the whole Soviet era. The prosecution tries to close its eyes to the fact that the whole of Sinyavsky's essay [*On Socialist*

---

* *And Quiet Flows the Don*, book 2, chapter 20.

Realism] is concerned with the past, that even all the verbs in it are in the past tense: "We killed"—not "We kill," but "We killed." And except for the story "Hands," all my works, too, are set in the fifties, in a period when there was a real danger of a revival of the cult of personality. I have said this over and over, and it's quite plain from the book itself, but everybody turns a deaf ear.

Finally I should mention one last procedure: the assertion that criticism of the part applies to the whole, so that disagreement with certain things is made out to be a rejection of the system as a whole.

These, in brief, are the ways and means by which our guilt has been "proved." Perhaps they wouldn't have seemed so terrible to us if we had been listened to. As Sinyavsky rightly asked: Where are we supposed to have materialized from, we two werewolves and vampires; do they think we fell from the sky? The prosecution's reply to this is to say what scum we are. The arguments used are unusual: Vasilyev says we sold ourselves for thirty pieces of silver, some diapers and nylon shirts; that I gave up my honest work as a schoolteacher and started going round editorial offices with outstretched hands, begging for translation work. If I were to ask my wife, she could bring a whole pile of letters from poets asking me to translate their verse. I didn't give up the security of my work as a schoolteacher in order to make easy money as a translator, but because I had dreamed from child-hood of doing something connected with poetry. I did my first translation at the age of twelve. As regards the "easy money," any translator will tell you how "easy" it is! I abandoned a life of security for one which is precarious. I consider translation as my life's work and I have never treated it as hack work. Some of my translations may be bad or indifferent, but this is from lack of skill, not because of carelessness.

It is strange that in matters where a lawyer should be absolutely scrupulous, the Public Prosecutor refuses to recognize facts. At first I thought it was a slip of the tongue when he was talking about how we were aware of the nature of our works, and said that in 1962 there was a broadcast [by Radio Liberty], but that *after this* we sent abroad *This Is Moscow Speaking* and *Lyubimov*. But what was the broadcast? What was broadcast was, in fact, the text of *This Is Moscow Speaking*. Am I supposed to have sent out the manuscript of this story a second time? I thought this must be a slip of the tongue, but later on we had the same thing again: referring to Ryurikov's article, the Public Prosecutor said we had been warned, we knew of [Ryurikov's] opinion, and yet we sent abroad *Lyubimov* and "The Man from Minap." When was Ryurikov's article published? In 1962. And when were the manuscripts in question sent abroad? In 1961.† A slip of the tongue? No, this is the Public Prosecutor adding a new touch to his portrait of me as a malevolent, anti-Soviet person.

Our every utterance, even the most innocent, even things that could be said by anybody sitting here, has been misrepresented. In *This Is Moscow Speaking* there is something about a leading article in *Izvestia*—"Aha, so you're making fun of the newspaper *Izvestia*, are you?" When I reply that I'm not making fun of the newspaper as such, but of newspaper clichés and journalese, they come back at me with malicious glee: "Now at last you're talking in your real voice!" Do you really think that to talk about newspaper clichés is anti-Soviet propaganda? I just don't understand it. Or rather, perhaps I understand it all too well.

Nothing here has been taken into consideration—neither the testimony of literary experts nor the evidence of witnesses. They say, for instance, that Sinyavsky is an anti-Semite, but why, in that case, has nobody wondered why he has such friends? There's me, for instance, but of course I'm an anti-Semite myself; but then there's my wife, Brukhman, the witness Golomshtok or the lady with the nice Jewish accent who was on the witness stand here yesterday and said, "What a nice man Andrei [Sinyavsky] is."§

It's simpler just to turn a deaf ear to all this.

All I have said should not be taken to mean that I regard myself and Sinyavsky as shining and impeccable paragons of virtue, and that the court should release us from detention immediately after the trial and send us home in a taxi at its own expense. We are guilty—not for what we have written, but for having sent our works abroad. There are many political indiscretions, exaggerations and gibes in our books. But isn't twelve years of Sinyavsky's life and nine [eight?] years of

---

† In his evidence, Sinyavsky says he handed *Lyubimov* over in 1963. This may be a slip on Daniel's part.

§ It was presumably Dokukina who said this. "Yesterday" must be a slip.

mine a rather excessive payment for our frivolity, thoughtfulness and misjudgment?*

As we both said under preliminary investigation and here, we deeply regret that our works have been exploited by reactionary forces and that thereby we have caused harm to our country. We did not wish this. We had no ill intentions, and I ask the court to take this into consideration.

I wish to ask forgiveness of all my near ones and friends, to whom we have caused distress.

I also wish to say that no articles of any criminal code nor any accusations against us will deter us—Sinyavsky and me—from feeling that we are persons who love our country and our people.

That is all I have to say.

I am ready to hear the sentence.

---

* These were the maximum terms demanded by the prosecutor. In the upshot Sinyavsky was sentenced to seven years and Daniel to five. Seven years is the maximum period of detention, but Sinyavsky was not given the additional five years of exile provided for under Article 70 of the Criminal Code under which the two men were charged.

II. APPENDIX

Yuli Daniel's Letter from Corrective Labor Colony to Izvestia[*]

To Izvestia:

I ask you to publish this letter in your paper or at any rate to take account of it should you print anything further about Andrei Sinyavsky and myself.

Throughout the investigation and the trial I had no objective information about the public reaction to the works of Tertz and Arzhak, and the interrogators, the prosecutor and the court did their best to convince Sinyavsky and myself that our books had been read and publicized only by the enemies of our country who had used them as a weapon of ideological struggle. I must confess that five months of this kind of "persuasion" had some effect on me: in the end I pleaded guilty to "thoughtlessness" and expressed my regret for the fact that our works had been used to cause damage to our state.

Since my trial and conviction I have had the chance to read our papers and to get some information about the foreign press. I then realized that the only reason for my expression of regret and admis-

---

* This letter, in which Daniel retracts his partial admission of guilt, was written in April, 1966. It was first published in the Italian journal *L'Espresso* of May 29, 1966.

sion of guilt was the misleading information given me at the time. I also realized that the readers of our newspapers (*Literary Gazette, Izvestia* and others) have been misled about the meaning, the ideas and even the artistic character of the novels and short stories of Tertz and Arzhak. I will not list all the underhand methods used, in completely bad faith, by our journalists and critics: I have already spoken of this in my final plea at the trial.

The tendentious accounts in our press of the trial, the works and the personalities of the accused by our press, and on the other hand the expressions of sympathy and the protests against the trial and the sentence from progressive circles all over the world and from a group of Soviet writers, scholars and men of letters, oblige me to express myself plainly and unequivocally about what has happened.

I have now come to the conclusion that our work ought never, in any circumstances, to have been the subject of a criminal prosecution. The verdict is unjust and illegal. I retract my expression of regret for the damage our work is alleged to have caused. The only damage which can be associated with the names of Sinyavsky and Daniel is the one caused by our arrest, trial and sentence.

I thank all those who have been concerned about our fate.

I am unable to communicate with or consult Sinyavsky, but I am quite sure that he would agree with every word of this letter.

I would be grateful if you would acknowledge receipt of this letter whether you publish it or no.

YULI DANIEL

April 9, 1966

Statements by Mrs. Sinyavsky
and Mrs. Daniel

The five documents that follow, signed in their maiden names by
Mrs. Sinyavsky and Mrs. Daniel, throw light on the pressures brought
to bear on the relatives and friends of the defendants during the pretrial investigation, which lasted nearly five months from Sinyavsky's
arrest on September 8 and Daniel's on September 12, 1965, to the
opening of their trial on February 10, 1966. Under Soviet law the
preliminary investigation (predvaritelnoye sledstvie) is carried out
by a kind of examining magistrate (sledovatel: the term here is translated as "interrogator") who is appointed either by the Public Prosecutor's office (prokuratura) or, in cases held to involve national
security, by the Committee of State Security (KGB). The interrogator is supposed to conclude his work within a month. By permission of a local prosecutor, this period can be extended by a
maximum of two more months. Any further extension must be
sanctioned by the Public Prosecutor of the R.S.F.S.R. or by the
Prosecutor General of the U.S.S.R. There is no indication whether
the KGB obtained this permission, but it is clear that the authorities
broke the law in other ways, e.g., by not replying to Mrs. Sinyavsky's
first letter: according to Article 219 of the Criminal Procedural Code
R.S.F.S.R., the Public Prosecutor is required to answer any com-
plaint within three days.

Letter from Mrs. Sinyavsky

To the First Secretary of the Central Committee of the CPSU[†]
To the Prosecutor General of the U.S.S.R.
To the President of the Committee of State Security
To the editors of Pravda, Izvestia and Literary Gazette

On September 8 of this year (1965), my husband, Andrei Donatovich Sinyavsky, was arrested by the KGB. The search warrant I was shown stated that he was suspected of "writing, harboring and distributing anti-Soviet literature."

From questions put to me at numerous interrogations and "interviews," and from the statements made by Comrade Kunitsyn at an open party meeting at the Institute of Art History of the Ministry of Culture[‡] I learned that my husband was accused of publishing his work abroad under the pseudonym of Abram Tertz.

In the course of an interrogation I was shown a signed statement by Sinyavsky admitting this fact. At first, as anyone will understand who has lived through 1937, the case of the "Doctors Plot"[§] in 1953 and all the other arbitrary measures of repression under Stalin, my fear and distress were such that I forgot that we have laws—laws written in black and white, beginning with the basic law—the Constitution—and ending with its concrete expression in the Criminal Code.

But when I got over this initial shock, natural in the circumstances, I realized that I was faced with an act of flagrant illegality. I waited a little, thinking the KGB and the Public Prosecutor would correct their mistake, but now over three months have gone by since the investigation began and no one can tell when it will end, and since both the arrest and the investigation are groundless, there is nothing left for me except to write to you.

[†] Leonid Brezhnev.
[‡] The Institute in which Mrs. Sinyavsky is (or was) employed. "Comrade Kunitsyn" must be the head of the Institute's party organization.
[§] See footnote * on p. 95.

The result of this letter may well be my arrest (I am constantly being threatened with it, and, given the illegality of what has already been done, I must be ready for anything), but, frightened though I naturally am by this persecution, I cannot draw back when elementary justice and human dignity are being trampled underfoot.

1. I have read everything published under the name of Abram Tertz and, whether it was written by Sinyavsky or somebody else, I assert, and will always and everywhere assert, that there is nothing anti-Soviet in it—it is literature pure and simple, and contains neither political aspersions nor anti-Soviet propaganda.

2. Tertz's prose, his way of writing, his style, his language, some of his philosophical ideas (which, incidentally, have nothing to do with politics) may be liked or disliked, but a literary disagreement is not a sufficient reason for arresting an author.

So at any rate I had come to believe after the 20th Congress.*

That a writer should be criticized, however harshly, however mercilessly, I could understand, because words, and words alone, are the way to attack a literary work—words, not the arrest of the author, whoever he may be—and I protest against this in the strongest terms because it is an infringement of the clause in our Constitution about freedom of speech and freedom of the press. I protest the more strongly because Sinyavsky is not the first Soviet writer who has published his work abroad. The precedents are known to everyone: Gorky, Stanislavsky, Pasternak, Evtushenko and others.† If all these others were protected by our Constitution, why is Sinyavsky the exception? Does not such a lawless act dishonor our state? I know that it is always difficult to admit a mistake. But it is better to admit it now, before the Sinyavsky affair covers us with shame in the eyes of the whole world, as did the Zhivago affair and the case of Brodsky.‡

I know I will be told that my reasons for defending Sinyavsky so

---

* The Party Congress of 1956 at which Khrushchev made his speech denouncing Stalin and the "cult of personality."

† Maxim Gorky published an essay *On the Russian Peasantry* in Berlin (1922). Evtushenko published his *Precocious Autobiography* in the Paris *L'Express* in 1963 and was subsequently attacked by Khrushchev.

‡ In February, 1964, the poet Joseph Brodsky was sentenced by a Leningrad court to five years' forced labor for "parasitism." After world-wide protests he was quietly released in 1965.

hotly are purely personal: "He is your husband, after all, we understand, we too are human."

In anticipation of this kind of talk, I enclose a characteristic short story of Tertz's, "The Tenants." Those of you who live in communal apartments will know what the story is about and judge whether it is libelous or anti-Soviet. (Personally, I have lived in such conditions for thirty-five years, and Sinyavsky for forty.) Can the author be arrested for "writing, harboring and distributing anti-Soviet literature"? In my opinion, no. And none of Tertz's work is any more "anti-Soviet" than this.

I know the answer to this: "Tertz's work," I will be told, "may not be anti-Soviet in itself, but it's a kind of mystical trash and" (a lot is made of this) "it's published by various anti-Soviet publishers, and thereby does grave damage to 'our Motherland.' " Yet everyone knows that Kochetov's novel, *The Regional Committee Secretary*,§ was brought out by a publisher who could not have been more anti-Soviet, and presented as a book exposing and discrediting the Soviet system. It is also known that a page from *Literary Gazette*,* attacking Pasternak when he was being persecuted, was reprinted in full in several papers abroad. If an author is responsible for whatever use is made of his work by others, then Kochetov, the editor of *Literary Gazette* and the authors of that page on Pasternak ought all to have been arrested. But there is no question of prosecuting them.

Given all this, was the arrest of Sinyavsky legal? No, no, and again no.

3. Various measures connected with the arrest were also illegal:

a. Included in the search warrant was an order to confiscate anti-Soviet literature; books by Tsvetayeva, Mandelshtam, Pasternak, Akhmatova, Gumilev, Remizov and others, none of whom had ever written anything anti-Soviet, were confiscated; with few exceptions, books and manuscripts were confiscated *without any record* being

<hr>

§ Vsevolod Kochetov, editor of the monthly literary journal *Oktyabr*, is an extreme "conservative" who became notorious through his novel *The Brothers Ershov*, a scurrilous lampoon on Soviet liberals. He is mentioned in Daniel's *This Is Moscow Speaking* (see p. 17) and in Sinyavsky's *Makepeace Experiment*.

* *Literary Gazette* of October 25, 1958, denounced Pasternak's acceptance of the Nobel Prize and reproduced a long letter to Pasternak from the editors of *Novy Mir*, in which they set out their reasons for refusing to publish *Doctor Zhivago*.

made, and I was hardly even allowed to see what was being taken away.

b. The methods used in the investigation often have nothing in common with the standards laid down by law; systematic efforts are being made to intimidate me; there are continual insinuations that my liberty is only *provisional*, that I am on the point of being arrested, and at my last interrogation the interrogator said in so many words that he would have me deported from Moscow; my every conversation is listened to, my every letter opened (these letters and conversations are then quoted word for word to me and to other witnesses at interrogations), my every step is watched; several of my friends have been summoned and warned that the fact of seeing me may, at the very least, involve them in trouble with their employers.

c. If such pressure is brought to bear on me, even though I am not under arrest, it is easy to imagine the pressure on Sinyavsky, who is in prison. I have increasing reason to suspect that force is being used. I should like to discuss this point personally with a secretary of the Central Committee or with the Prosecutor General. I have no knowledge of what *exactly* is being done, but I have known Sinyavsky for ten years, and everything the interrogator now tells me about him, or passes on to me as coming from him, is so unlike him that it only leaves me utterly convinced that his situation must be very difficult. Whenever I have asked to see him (even after the investigation is over) permission has been categorically refused, and this gives me still more grounds for the terrible anxiety I feel for him.... To conclude:

I have read the books of A. Tertz;

I greatly admire them and I see nothing anti-Soviet in them;

I agree with every word written by Abram Tertz (whoever he may be).

And if this is a crime, then put me in prison with Sinyavsky, because freedom is useless to me if I can't be with him and if I can't say plainly and honestly what I think.

I have no means and no influence. I have no country house, car, apartment, luxurious furniture or any other treasures. I have never held any exalted posts. At the moment, I haven't even got a job. . . . All I have in the world is my year-old son and my books.

As you see, what I have to lose or to worry about is very little indeed, so I tell you frankly what I think, as very few Soviet people do. Many think as I do, but very few say it. The years of the cult of personality have done their work, people in our country have been cowed into silence, and the Sinyavsky-Daniel incident reminds them all too vividly of past terrors.

This letter is not written in the proper form of a request for aid and protection, but at the moment I find it difficult to choose my words.

MAYA VASILYEVNA ROZANOVA-KRUGLIKOVA

December 24, 1965

Statement by Mrs. Sinyavsky

To the President of the Supreme Court of the U.S.S.R.[†]
Copies to: The First Secretary of the Central Committee of the CPSU
The President of the KGB of the Council of Ministers of the U.S.S.R.

Statement

I hereby inform you that on February 9, 1966, an officer of the KGB, Oleg Vasilyevich Chistyakov, threatened me, through my friends, the Menshutins and N. B. Kishilov, with various unpleasant consequences for me and my year-old son on account of my alleged "intimidation of witnesses in the Sinyavsky case."

I am in constant touch with A. Petrov and I. Golomshtok, and I do not regard it as possible to stop seeing friends merely because they are being called as witnesses.

As regards the third witness in the Sinyavsky case, A. Remezov, I have met him only very rarely in view of the fact that for ten years I have felt nothing but dislike for this person.

I do not think that words of affection spoken to friends can be regarded as an attempt to suborn them. Neither do I think an expression of long-standing dislike can be called "intimidation."

---

† A. Gorkin. See p. 31.

It is the actions of the KGB officials that cause consternation. As early as the middle of December, in my statement to the CC of the CPSU, to the KGB and the Prosecutor's office of the U.S.S.R., I pointed out that the investigation was being conducted by improper means. I have still had no reply to my statement from any of these bodies, but suddenly today I received the above "message" from the KGB in this strange form which violates all legal standards.

I beg you to place this statement in the record of the Sinyavsky case, and also to protect me against illegal procedures.

M. V. ROZANOVA-KRUGLIKOVA

February 9, 1966

Letter from Mrs. Daniel

To the First Secretary of the CC, CPSU
To the Prosecutor General of the U.S.S.R.
To the Editors of Pravda, Izvestia and Literary Gazette

On September 12, 1965, my husband Yuli Markovich Daniel was arrested by the KGB. He is accused of having published works abroad under the pseudonym Nikolai Arzhak. The interrogator has informed me that my husband admits his authorship of these works and confirms that they were published abroad, and that even apart from this admission, it has been established beyond any doubt that he is their author. I have further been told that the works of Nikolai Arzhak are slanderous and anti-Soviet and that Daniel is therefore being charged under Article 70 of the Criminal Code of the R.S.F.S.R.

During my interrogation I was given a brief account of the works of N. Arzhak, but even in this biased and tendentious summary they could not be regarded as anti-Soviet. I have recently read four works by Arzhak—everything that has been published under this name—and I can see nothing in them that could be called anti-Soviet propaganda. I hereby assert and I will defend and stand by this view both in private conversation and in public discussion. I feel that open discussion and open debate (provided that all those taking part have read all the works in their entirety and do not know them merely from specially selected passages and quotations) are the only way of establishing in an objective and unbiased manner what the ideology of a work of literature is, and the only way of bringing pressure to bear on the author, if it is necessary to bring such pressure to bear.

Persecution of writers for their work, even if it has political undertones, is regarded by our literary historians as a wanton act of coercion when it happened in the Russia of the nineteenth century. It is even more inadmissible nowadays. I had thought this was obvious and self-evident. But my husband has been arrested. For three months now he has been in prison because of his literary works. His books are being examined and evaluated by a small group of specially selected people, including the interrogator, who—as I realized during my interrogation—does not know the difference between hyperbole and factual description, between a work of satire or fantasy and a documentary account. Criticism of my husband's work has begun with his arrest and interrogation.

My husband, as I now know, published his work abroad. Whatever one might think of this from a moral point of view, it is not a criminal offense. In our Criminal Code such actions are not qualified as a crime, and the "Declaration of the Rights of Man," which was signed by our country, proclaims in Article 19 "the right freely to distribute ideas by any means whatsoever and independently of state frontiers." In ratifying these words our country recognized this right as morally justified, but then suddenly people who have exercised it find themselves the object of criminal proceedings!

No other reasons for the arrest of my husband have been given. Detention in prison is a "preventive measure" and can be applied to an accused person during the preliminary investigation at the discretion of the interrogator *in case of necessity.* Where was the necessity to apply this measure in the present case? All this is hard to understand, and not only for me. What has to be prevented? The writing of literature? It is now three months since the arrest, and during the whole of this time the KGB has given no information about the case, or about the nature of the charges. The absence of any public statement has naturally given rise to much gossip and many rumors, ranging from the plausible to the most absurd and unlikely. At the same time authoritative persons at official meetings talk about Sinyavsky and Daniel as guilty persons whose criminal activity and even criminal nature are not in doubt. This infringes the basic legal principle of the presumption of innocence. . . . These unsupported but authoritative statements account for the defamatory tone of all the rumors and gossip, influence people's feelings toward Sinyavsky and Daniel in anticipation of the court's decision, and may even influence this decision. It is only natural that I should protest against the illegal arrest of my husband and against the blackening of his character, although the investigative organs have so far, without any grounds, treated my verbal protests as a disclosure of evidence obtained during the investigation, and as an attempt to exert pressure on potential witnesses.

Sinyavsky and Daniel have been accused of acts which are not considered criminal under our laws. They have been arrested, but the only reason for taking this step was in order to intimidate the accused. They have now been held in prison for three months and I have still not been allowed to see my husband. In the course of the investigation the KGB has committed a number of illegal actions—I have written about this in a statement to the Prosecutor General and the President of the KGB (copy enclosed).

All this, together with the failure to make public any information about the case, arouses in me (and probably in many others) the fear that there may be just as little respect for the law, impartiality and justice in the further conduct of the case. Is it possible that my husband's fate has already been arbitrarily decided without reference to the law? The whole business of the arrest and investigation, from the beginning to the present day, goes against the principles of democracy, gives cause for grave anxieties and is reminiscent of the times of the cult of personality which has been condemned by the party.

I demand the immediate release from prison of my husband and Sinyavsky.

LARISA IOSIFOVNA BUKHMAN (DANIEL)

[December, 1965]

Letter from Mrs. Daniel

To the Prosecutor General of the U.S.S.R.

To the President of the KGB

On September 12 of this year my husband Yuli Markovich Daniel was arrested by the KGB on charges of having written and at various times published abroad a number of works printed under the pseudonym N. Arzhak. His arrest on these charges is against the law as laid down in the Criminal Code of the R.S.F.S.R., and I have written a letter of protest to the Central Committee of the CPSU, the newspapers Pravda, Izvestia and Literary Gazette, and the Prosecutor General of the U.S.S.R. I enclose a copy of this letter.

However, apart from this illegal action against my husband, the investigative authorities of the KGB have infringed the letter and spirit of our laws in various other ways.

So long as the investigation is still under way my husband cannot be regarded as guilty, he cannot be regarded as a criminal. Only a court can decide whether the charges have been proven, whether my husband's actions are punishable under our laws and, if he is guilty, to what extent. Yet the senior interrogator, Lieutenant Colonel G. B. Kantov, has alleged in conversation with me and during my interrogation that my husband is guilty and will be punished. This was said not as the interrogator's personal opinion but as a plain fact. Such prejudgment of a case during the course of the investigation makes me doubt the objectivity of the proceedings and whether the laws will be observed at a later stage. Furthermore, I regard a statement of this kind as an attempt to put moral pressure on me, a witness in the case, and I am certain that the pressure being brought to bear on my husband is no less, and probably much greater. The lack of any public announcement and the failure to admit a defense lawyer to the investigation make it entirely possible for the interrogator to commit arbitrary and illegal actions.

G. B. Kantov said to me: "Your husband is guilty and will be punished." He went on to advise me not to retain a defense counsel for the following reasons: (a) I could not afford it and (b) a defense counsel would anyhow be useless in this case and would not affect the court proceedings or the verdict. This was said to me by the interrogator, before the case has come to court!

I nevertheless asked the interrogator to find out from my husband whether he agreed that I should talk to a defense lawyer. I asked him to tell my husband not to worry about the financial side of this or allow the question of payment to influence him. My words were relayed to my husband in this form: "Your wife will go to her friends cap in hand."

The interrogator has made indirect threats: If I behave badly ("You know what I mean"—although I have absolutely no idea what he means), I might have trouble at work "when they find out there." When they find out what? That my husband is under investigation? But he hasn't yet been found guilty. And even if he were found guilty, what kind of trouble might I have, and why? Surely we are not returning to those times when the families of condemned, accused or suspected persons were also made to suffer? But how else am I to understand the interrogator's threats? He talks to me as though I were the accused person. I am not frightened by these or any other threats, not that I don't believe they are serious (the arrest of my husband makes my own immunity doubtful), but because I have nothing to fear. I have nothing to lose. During the whole of my life I have acquired no material goods and I have learned not to set any store by them, while the things of the spirit that I value will always remain with me whatever the circumstances. Nevertheless I am indignant that such threats can be made in our day. I am not asking anybody for favors or privileges. I am only demanding that the normal standards of humanity and justice be observed. I have a right to know from the interrogator, or at least I have a right to be told, where I can inquire about my husband's condition and the approximate duration of the investigation. But it is a vicious circle: the interrogator tells me to go to the KGB, and the KGB tells me to go back to the interrogator. The KGB say they have no information, and the interrogator emphasizes that he would be doing me a favor by answering my questions, but that he is not obliged to do so and doesn't want to.

[December, 1965]

Letter from Mrs. Daniel

To the President of the Supreme Court of the U.S.S.R.

There must be someone in the KGB who is obliged to answer my natural and legitimate questions about the fate of my husband. Who is it?

The investigative authorities are in possession of facts about the private life of myself and my husband. This information has no relevance to the case and is of no interest from the point of view of national security. It was obtained illegally by an examination of my private correspondence and through eavesdropping on conversations in our home. But the most revolting thing of all is that this information has been communicated to other people, to acquaintances of myself and my husband. For instance, Yakov Lazarevich Garbuzenko, a witness in my husband's case, has been told, in an interrogation about my private life, whom I have been on close terms with, and when. This flagrant breach of the law cannot be justified, or even explained, by any practical considerations. The only possible reason for it is to demonstrate how well informed the investigative authorities are, to compromise me in the eyes of my friends and acquaintances, and to induce a state of moral shock in a witness.

I protest against these and similar illegal procedures in the conduct of the case. These facts speak not only of gross infringements of the law on the part of the interrogator, G. B. Kantov, but also of lack of supervision on the part of the heads of the investigative department, and on the part of the Prosecutor's office.

All these infringements of the elementary standards of law and humanity, as well as the illegal arrest of my husband and his detention in prison for three months, give me good ground for fearing that other illegal actions are being committed—actions of which I have no knowledge because I have not once been able to see my husband in prison. What guarantee is there that physical and moral pressures are not being applied to my husband? What guarantee is there that similar illegal actions will not be committed in other cases?

I am attaching a copy of this letter to the above-mentioned one* to the Central Committee of the CPSU, the Prosecutor General and the newspapers.

---

* There is no mention of this letter in the text, the beginning of which is probably missing. The letter in question must be the first one by Mrs. Daniel (p. 205).

Pretrial Newspaper Attacks on the Defendants

The Soviet public first learned about the arrest of Sinyavsky and Daniel from the article in Izvestia by Dmitri Eremin on January 13, 1966. This was followed by Zoya Kedrina's article in Literary Gazette.

Eremin (born 1904) is the secretary of the board of the Moscow branch of the R.S.F.S.R. Writers' Union. He is the author of a number of novels and stories, including Storm Over Rome for which he received the Stalin prize in 1952. In 1964 he opposed the award of the Lenin prize to Solzhenitsyn for his One Day in the Life of Ivan Denisovich. (See Literary Gazette, February 8, 1964.)

Both Eremin and Madame Kedrina had clearly been "briefed" by the authorities who commissioned the articles from them. It is not unusual in the Soviet Union for a case to be presented in the press against people while they are still under preliminary investigation and before their trial, but it has not been common in recent years for writers to perform this function.

The Turncoats

by Dmitri Eremin, *Izvestia*, January 13, 1966

The enemies of Communism are not squeamish. How gleefully they exploit every "sensation" picked up in anti-Soviet backyards! Recently they had a lucky find. The bourgeois press and radio have been talking about the "unjustified arrest" in Moscow of two "men of letters" who had published anti-Soviet lampoons abroad. What a treat for the impure conscience and the still less pure imagination of Western propagandists! With bold strokes, they are already painting the picture of a mythical "purge in Soviet literary circles," which are alleged to be "most disturbed by the threat of a new campaign" against "disaffected writers" and "liberal intellectuals" in general. . . .

What, in fact, has happened? Why all this excitement among the evil cohorts of the enemies of the Soviet Union? And why have certain foreign intellectuals, who look very strange in this company, fallen into their embrace? Why do certain gentlemen pose as our mentors, almost as the guardians of our morals, and claim to defend two renegades "in the name of" the Soviet intelligentsia? There is only one explanation: In the ideological battles between the two worlds, the enemies of the new society are not too fastidious about the means they use, and when two renegades turn up in their trenches, they hurry to acclaim them for lack of a better prize.

For the poor in spirit such turncoats are a precious find. They help them to mislead the public and to sow the poisonous seeds of ideological indifference, nihilism and morbid interest in the more sordid "problems of life."

To put it briefly: The enemies of Communism have found what they were looking for—two renegades for whom duplicity and shamelessness have become articles of faith. Hiding behind the pen names Abram Tertz and Nikolai Arzhak, the two have for several years been sending to foreign publishing houses, and publishing abroad, their dirty lampoons on their own country, the party and the Soviet system.

One of them, A. Sinyavsky, alias "A. Tertz," had also published pieces of literary criticism in Soviet journals, had wormed his way into the Union of Writers, outwardly complying with the requirements laid down in its statutes, namely: "to serve the people, to demonstrate in high artistic form the greatness of the Communist ideals" and "to devote the whole of his literary and social work to active participation in the building of Communism."

The other, Y. Daniel, alias "N. Arzhak," did translation work. But all this was merely a false façade. Behind it something else was hidden—hatred of our system, vile mockery of everything dear to our Motherland and people.

The first feeling you experience in reading their works is disgust. It is revolting to quote the vulgar things with which the pages of their works abound. With morbid prurience, both of them delve into sexual and psychopathological "problems." Both of them present a picture of total moral degradation. Both spatter the pages of their books with everything that is most vile and filthy.

Here are some characteristic examples of their writing: "You see women," writes Daniel, "walking about the streets looking like eunuchs—waddling like pregnant dachshunds or as scrawny as ostriches, with swollen bodies, varicose veins, wadded breasts or tight stays hidden under their clothes."‡

We read of an academician that he "drinks a couple of glasses and, before you know where you are, he is stuffing the silver into his pockets." Or of a secretary in a newspaper office that she is "a wench available to any of the proofreaders." A certain Solomon Moiseyevich is deserted by his wife, "a lascivious Russian slut who had run away, after first robbing him and then deceiving him with a sixteen-year-old hairdresser. He knew women and feared them, having every reason to do so. And what could he understand about the Russian national character, this Solomon Moiseyevich?"§

And one can't help noticing the following detail: Andrei Sinyavsky, a Russian by birth, hid behind the name of Abram Tertz. Why? For a purely provocative reason! By publishing anti-Soviet stories and tales under the name of Abram Tertz in foreign publications Sinyavsky was trying to create the impression that anti-Semitism exists in our country and that a writer with a name such as Abram Tertz has to seek publishers in the West if he wants to write "frankly" about Soviet life. This was a squalid provocation which completely gives away the motives of both the author and his bourgeois sponsors.

They like nothing about our country: nothing is holy for them in her multinational culture, and they are ready to curse and run down

---

‡ This passage is actually by Sinyavsky. See p. 21.
§ The quotations in this paragraph are all from Sinyavsky's *Fantastic Stories*, pp. 13, 160 and 178.

everything dear to Soviet men, both past and present. Imagine what they wrote about Anton Pavlovich Chekhov, the outstanding Russian humanist whose masterly works arouse what is best in man! Only the utmost shamelessness can move the pen which writes such lines: "That Chekhov ought to be taken by his wretched tubercular beard and have his nose stuck into his consumptive spittle." And the Russian classics—the pride of world literature—what is said of them? "It's the classics I hate most of all!"

These "writers" try to vilify and slander our Soviet Army whose immortal exploits saved the peoples of Europe from destruction by the Nazis.

There is no name more sacred to the Soviet people, for the nations of the earth, for the whole of progressive mankind, than that of Vladimir Ilyich Lenin, the leader of our Revolution. The name of Lenin stands for the epoch of socialist revolutions and national liberation movements. It stands for scientific Communism and for the glorious human deeds in which it is enshrined. Even prominent capitalist leaders have bowed their heads before the name of Lenin: they have been forced to recognize more than once that he is the greatest transformer of life in the twentieth century.

Into what a bottomless quagmire of abomination must a so-called man of letters sink for his hooligan pen to cast a slur upon the name we hold sacred! It is impossible to reproduce here the relevant quotations, so malicious is this drivel, so disgraceful and filthy. By these blasphemous lines alone, the authors have put themselves outside the pale of Soviet society.

In Daniel-Arzhak's lampoon *This is Moscow Speaking* there are hypocritical remarks to the effect that "to be printed abroad by anti-Soviet publishers is not so good." But how could the author deny himself the chance of pouring the dirty slops of his slander on the Soviet system? Concluding his vulgar, spiteful, "philosophical" discussion on the subject, the author, through his "hero," turns to the reader and suggests the following course of action:

The fuse . . . pull out the pin . . . throw. . . . Lie flat on the ground. Lie down! Now it's exploded and you run forward, firing from the hip—one round after another, and another and another! . . . They're lying over there, cut to shreds and riddled with bullets!

As we see, there is not much he stops at in his rage against things Soviet. This passage is, in effect, an incitement to terrorism.

In Sinyavsky-Tertz's lampoon *Lyubimov*, the author sets himself no less a task than to prove that the very idea of the Communist transformation of society is an illusion, a vain dream. It isn't easy, through all the welter of sick fantasy with which the lampoon is filled, to grope one's way to the reality it mocks. But its ideological, political message is as clear as daylight:

It is unbridled mockery of the laws of history, mockery of those who gave their lives for our great aims, mockery of our country and our nation. Here the author's impudence reaches truly Homeric proportions. There is no device he overlooks in his attempt to prove that Communist theory and practice are illusion, no heights of bourgeois malice he won't scale in showing us the downfall of the city of Lyubimov, a city in which a certain Tikhomirov strives for universal happiness—with the help of mass hypnosis! How he smacks his lips over the failure of the Communist "experiment" and the return of Lyubimov to the old way of life. He stresses this significant detail: "A gloomy peasant, openly, for everyone to see, stopped and pissed into the foundations, half-full of cement, for a new building" —as much as to say that the peasant knew exactly what he thought of all such things.*

No less typical is the tone of Daniel-Arzhak's above-mentioned "story" *This Is Moscow Speaking*. Briefly, the plot is this: A decree is broadcast over the radio, announcing that "in view of the increased well-being and in response to the wishes of the masses of working people" (the author is capable of jeering at anything!) "Sunday August 10, 1960, is declared"—what do you think?—"Public Murder Day"—on the pattern of the Miner's Day, the Schoolteacher's Day, etc. And there follow monstrous scenes from a way of life alleged to be Soviet, of the mass lunacy of regimented devotion to the "idea" of universal slaughter. People kill each other, husbands and wives settle their accounts, terror reigns throughout the country. And all this, of course, is generously seasoned with vulgar eroticism, drunken debauchery, unbridled immorality and hatred of mankind.

---

* *The Makepeace Experiment*, p. 177.

Sinyavsky-Tertz and Daniel-Arzhak describe as opportunists and "Black Hundreds" all who, openly and with conviction, profess their Communist ideology in their books. They jeer at those who write as active, loyal helpers of the party and as sons of their people. Thus in the Jesuitical little reviews he published in certain Soviet journals, Sinyavsky combed through other authors' works for what distinguishes his own: ideological ambiguity, nihilism, distortion amounting to slander. Here he wasn't sparing in his epithets: "He slanders our life and culture"; his "cynical slander, spiteful invention, stupid insinuations"; "The horrors he describes do not exist, while his characters—though he means the reader to recognize them—are unrecognizable caricatures"; and all this is, of course, "very remote from the real tasks of the ideological struggle facing our art."†

An enemy of things Soviet in the role of mentor to our writers—how shameless! What impudent hypocrisy! What a show of moral degradation! One hand is raised in an assenting vote, the other gestures obscenely inside his pocket.

We Soviet writers who are dedicated to the ideal of the Communist reshaping of life and who regard the party of Lenin as our trusted helper and wise guide in the selfless struggle for [universal] peace and happiness, we Soviet people—all of us—can only feel disgust and anger at the writings of Sinyavsky-Tertz and Daniel-Arzhak. In vain does the overseas sponsor of these renegades, the White émigré poet B. Filippov, try to pass them off in his prefaces to their nasty little books as "well-known Soviet writers"—there are no such persons in Soviet literature!

But enough about the Western patrons of the two lampooners. If there was anything they could bank on, it was only the fact that foreigners are ill-informed about our Soviet life. But lies have short legs and you can't go far on them. I am sure that, putting side by side the facts he knows about the Soviet Union and the lies of the two renegades, every right-minded man in the West will make the proper

---

† This paragraph refers to Sinyavsky's review of Ivan Shevtsov's *The Blight* (see p. 7). The tone of the article is, in fact, very restrained, and Eremin attributes to Sinyavsky "epithets" which are quoted from Shevtsov's book: the words "cynical slander, spiteful invention, stupid insinuations" actually belong to Shevtsov, not to Sinyavsky. (See *Novy Mir*, December, 1964, p. 229.)

choice and throw Sinyavsky-Tertz's and Daniel-Arzhak's lampoons into the slop pail where they belong.

It could not be otherwise. For it is not only Soviet society that the the lampooners attack—they spit poison at the whole of progressive mankind, at its ideals, at its holy struggle for social progress, for democracy, for peace.

Today, many even of those bourgeois journalists who are our ideological opponents speak respectfully of the mighty power of socialism, the "magnet" which attracts Africa, Asia, Latin America, indeed the whole world.

Sinyavsky and Daniel grew up in the Soviet Union. They enjoyed all the benefits of socialism. All those things which were won for us by our fathers and elder brothers in the fiery years of revolution and civil war, in the hard times of the first Five-Year Plans, all these things were at their disposal.

Sinyavsky and Daniel began in a small way: they exchanged honesty for unscrupulousness; literary activity as understood by Soviet people for double-dealing; a sincere attitude to life for nihilism, carping behind people's backs and "picking to pieces" those around them. Once started on these petty tricks they did not stop there. They continued their downward course. In the end they sank so low as to commit crimes against the Soviet system. In so doing they placed themselves beyond the pale of our literature and the community of Soviet people. From petty nastiness to major treachery—this was the course they ran.

During the war many Russian *émigrés* fought with the French Resistance. Struck down by the bullets of the Gestapo, they died with words of love for Russia on their lips—words of love for that faraway Motherland to which they had remained faithful in their hearts. And what about these two? They are *émigrés* of another sort: internal *émigrés*. They locked themselves up in their own little world, a world rotten through and through. There they seethed with their angry passions. There they dipped their pens in poison. There they lived, imagining that this was life.

What irony of fate! A French bourgeois publisher, Hachette, brings out a book entitled *The U.S.S.R. in the Year Two Thousand,* taking as his motto: "If you want to keep up to date, you must understand what goes on around you." The authors of the book know what they are saying and present a picture of a great nation, a picture of the pioneers of our age, whose devotion to Communism they may dislike but whom they cannot help admiring. While these two renegades made up their minds not only not to misunderstand but actively to slander all that goes on around them!

But perhaps it is wrong to talk about this irony. Common sense and moral deformity are not, strictly speaking, comparable. An honest pen and the pen of Judas cannot lie side by side. The outpourings of the turncoats reflect no specific views but only their author's ideological decay, their vanity and lack of principle.

But is this all? We are not dealing merely with the moral degeneracy of two hooligans. We are dealing with renegades, who have entered the service of the most rabid and unbridled enemies of Communism. They are working up this story of Sinyavsky and Daniel in the West for the very reason that these two have, for their part, served as a means of working up psychological warfare against the Soviet Union.

You rejoice too soon, gentlemen. Your turncoats have been turned on their backs. Their true face has been exposed. They are not just moral perverts, but active helpers of those who are stoking up the furnace of international tension, who would like to turn the cold war into a hot war, and who still nurture the crazy dream of raising their hands against the Soviet Union. Such helpers can be shown no leniency. Our people paid too dearly for the gains of October, for the victory over Fascism, for the blood and sweat shed on behalf of our homeland, to be indifferent toward these dregs.

As we have seen, the renegades' "writings" are imbued with malicious slander against our social system and our state: they are models of anti-Soviet propaganda. They are entirely aimed at kindling enmity between nations and at increasing the danger of war. They are, in point of fact, shots fired in the back of a people struggling for peace on earth and universal happiness. Such actions cannot be considered other than hostile to the Motherland.

With the passing of time, no one will any longer recall them.

These pages soaked in gall will molder on the rubbish heap. History has repeatedly confirmed that slander, no matter how rank and malicious it may be, inevitably evaporates under the burning breath of truth. This is what will happen this time as well.

The Heirs of Smerdyakov*
by Z. Kedrina, Literary Gazette, January 22, 1966

Madame Kedrina (born 1904) writes occasionally in Soviet literary periodicals, such as Questions of Literature. She appears to specialize in the literatures of the non-Russian peoples of the U.S.S.R. In what she writes on Russian literature (see, for example, her article in Questions of Literature for August, 1963, where she criticizes Solzhenitsyn's Matryona's Home), she shows herself very clearly to be on the side of orthodoxy, always careful to quote "good" authority for her judgments and showing a distinct predilection for the more conservative writers.

Even before it came to light that A. Sinyavsky and Y. Daniel had been secretly publishing abroad under the pseudonyms Abram Tertz and Nikolai Arzhak, even before they were called to account for their anti-Soviet "literary pastimes," the foreign capitalist press, radio and television had been praising their work to the skies. The London Times for instance, declared the works of Tertz to be "a brilliant experiment in satire . . . worthy of the best Russian tradition," and the New York Times voiced its conviction that "any Russian writer would be proud if he could write such essays, stories and aphorisms as those of Abram Tertz."

In 1962 Radio "Liberty" was already saying that Abram Tertz "pokes fun at Soviet reality. . . ." Quite recently the American news

---

* Smerdyakov is the illegitimate son of the old Karamazov in Dostoyevsky's *The Brothers Karamazov*. He is a degenerate who kills his father. The name, derived from the Russian word for "stink," of this ugliest of Dostoyevsky's creatures is commonly used by Russians to describe somebody who is evil beyond redemption.

agency UPI announced that "Sinyavsky has specialized in works which make fun of Soviet life," and the Italian paper *Giorno* tells us with epic calm that "since 1959, in the U.S.A. and other western countries, pamphlets and books . . . of an anti-Soviet character have been appearing over the signature 'Abram Tertz.' "

The same newspapers and magazines which only yesterday printed titillating articles under headings such as "the elusive Abram Tertz" now blandly give the real names behind the pseudonyms and write of "Tertz-Sinyavsky" and "Daniel-Arzhak."

Bourgeois propaganda has never made any secret of the political value it sets on the writings of Tertz-Sinyavsky and Arzhak-Daniel. It is all the more surprising that in the last few weeks "well-wishers" in the West have voiced their concern at the fate of Sinyavsky and Daniel and asserted that there are allegedly no grounds for their arrest. These defenders and admirers of Sinyavsky and Daniel are now primly silent about the anti-Soviet nature of their works.

Now what have they written, these two men who have been publishing secretly abroad under assumed names? What made them seek the backing of reactionary Western publishers, including *émigré* ones?

I have in front of me the Washington editions of the books by Abram Tertz and Nikolai Arzhak. I have read them carefully and it is quite clear to me that it is downright anti-Soviet stuff which is inspired by hatred for the socialist system. I cannot of course attempt to define the extent to which Arzhak and Tertz are culpable in legal terms—that is a matter for the judiciary. I want to examine another side of the matter. Is it possible that, antagonistic to us as they are in their works, the authors are nevertheless the talented people they are made out to be by their foreign backers? No. Even apart from everything in these books that disgusts one as a Soviet citizen, they are unpleasant and boring to read—sometimes because of their crude singleness of purpose and literary feebleness, and in other cases because of their intentional obscurity, and such a piling up of cryptic images that at times you begin to think that it is all a lot of incoherent rambling.

Making your way through this seemingly endless wasteland of rhetoric, through this jungle of all kinds of symbols, allegories and characters who are reincarnated in each other, you can find a very simple, clear and rational scheme of things—the ideological bare bones, so to speak—in all the works of these people. Tertz's extreme obscurity of form is simply a dazzling disguise for his "basic ideas," and once you have stripped it off you are at first even staggered by the threadbareness of the underlying body of ideas, and you ask: is this really all—just two or three of the most hackneyed anti-Soviet propaganda lines which we know from way back?

The poverty of thought is particularly conspicuous in N. Arzhak's thoroughly slanderous story *This Is Moscow Speaking*. The subject of this "work" is as simple as it is mendacious: It is announced over the radio that the government has decreed a "Public Murder Day"— along the lines of Railway Workers' Day and other such Days. On this day everybody can and must kill anyone he chooses, except certain categories of officials. This "measure," intended to "intimidate" the population, is on the whole a failure.

The reader might well inquire as to the point of inventing such a piece of nonsense. The point is to give the main "positive" character an opportunity of making several "inflammatory" speeches, including one about those who in his opinion really should be killed. After thinking over and rejecting his mistress's suggestion that he kill the husband she no longer loves (though, incidentally, excusing her for this desire, since she hates her husband), the "hero" goes over in his mind all his enemies, everybody who has wronged him from childhood onwards, and decides that it would be all right to teach them a lesson, but not to kill them. Yet he does want to kill. The question is: who? . . . The people who deserve to be destroyed to a man turn out to be those who represent the socialist system and who carry out the policy of the state—people whom the "hero" of the story depicts in the vilest and most scurrilous terms. "What should be done with them?" Here a bloody haze comes over the eyes of the hero-narrator and he yells: "Do you remember still how to do it? The fuse . . . pull out the pin . . . throw. Lie flat on the ground. Lie down! Now it's exploded and you run forward, firing from the hip—one round after another, and another and another! . . ." and feasting his mental gaze on the sight of mangled bodies with their guts spilling out, a bloody melée in which everything is mixed up—"Russians,

Germans, Georgians, Rumanians, Jews, Hungarians, tunics, placards, medical corps, spades," the "positive hero" has a daydream about Studebakers—one, two, eight, forty of them—going over the corpses.

Straight Fascism, you ask? Yes, straight Fascism—illustrations to its program of bloody wars and *putsches*—illustrations which are moreover antihuman not only in content, but in form, in their "aesthetic" of mass murder. The "hero" of the story tries to justify this program of "liberation" from Communism and the Soviet system by assertions to the effect that the idea of "public murder" is rooted in "the very essence of the socialist doctrine" and also that antagonism among people is in the nature of society in general. The sound thing to do is to regard every man as a potential enemy, because "everybody is just waiting for a chance to drown each other in a spoonful of water,"† "soon animals will be the only link . . . between people." The subject of the story illustrates this idea of the total disintegration of human relationships. . . .

I think the reader will agree that with such a subject the question of form doesn't matter very much. This is evidently the feeling of the author himself and of his publishers who state in a preface that "the basic idea of the story" (the declaration of Public Murder Day) is "only a literary device" for the depiction of Soviet society in the required way. The author of the preface goes on to say that "one cannot apply to Soviet life the criteria and standards of European realism: something that seems absolutely improbable in the non-Communist world is completely possible in the world of 'socialist realism.' " In other words one may lie as much as one likes about Soviet society—everything is all right as long as it's against socialism.

Abram Tertz has labored on the same lines, except that he has been more concerned to camouflage his anti-Soviet views. The author of the Abram Tertz stories, candidate of philological sciences A. Sinyavsky, whom the foreign reactionary press has boosted as an "heir of the Russian tradition," is a light-fingered person, never at a loss, and quite untroubled by qualms of conscience when it comes to borrowing from other people's books. The moral nakedness of Abram Tertz, the anti-Soviet "ideas" which he has made his own and longs

---

† For Daniel's own comment on Madame Kedrina's interpretation, see p. 189.

to broadcast far and wide, are clad in the borrowed clothes of a great variety of literary reminiscences and parallels. Plucked wholesale from a great range of other people's works, turned inside out and tacked onto the multicolored patchwork quilt of his anti-Soviet writings, they are characteristic of the literary style of Abram Tertz, a person who battens brazenly, like a parasite, on the literary heritage.

The Abram Tertz essay *On Socialist Realism* is vivid evidence of a "split personality," of a revolting duplicity, since here Sinyavsky reviles everything about which he has published literary studies in the U.S.S.R.

So much for Sinyavsky the "theoretician," but now let's see how he translates his theories into—if one can use the word—literary practice. I have here in front of me the Abram Tertz *Fantastic Stories*, which are about everyday life in the Soviet Union. Now, where do these stories "lead" the reader? What sort of a world unfolds before our eyes? In the story "At the Circus," we have a random crew of thieves and murderers drinking away their ill-gotten gains in restaurants, and living it up with prostitutes, like Moscow merchants in the old days. In "Tenants" there are changelings, witches, rusalkas and all kinds of other ghouls who have got into the town [Moscow] through the water mains and live together in a communal apartment[‡] in a state of bitter mutual hostility. "The Icicle" is about an involuntary clairvoyant who is recruited by the security services and, together with a dimwitted Colonel Tarasov, labors away at the "improvement of history," which amounts to the drawing up of plans for Communist aggression against the world. This is the whole "point" of this extremely long and fatuous story about the misadventures of a superman who can foresee everything but is powerless to avert it, even his own end. It was for this, and also as a further illustration of the "idea" of the everlasting antagonism between people, that "The Icicle" was written.

But however phantasmagorical you may find what you read, you feel all the time that, even though you have never anywhere else come across such dismal malevolence, such slimy filth and utter

---

‡ This is a misrepresentation of the story, which consists entirely of the "internal monologue" of a dypsomaniac who *imagines* that the other inhabitants of the apartment are changelings, witches, etc. See note on p. 60.

cynicism, you are nevertheless already familiar with the externals of the setting, the technique and the main lines of the subject matter. Before you pass dingy hovels inhabited by downtrodden, embittered and humiliated people, and you remember *The Slums of St. Petersburg*.§ Abram Tertz himself and his foreign sponsors are doing everything in their power to trace *Fantastic Stories* right back to Dostoyevsky. You find no clue to Abram Tertz's pretensions [to be the successor of Dostoyevsky] in his power of compassion for the downtrodden and the oppressed, in his depth of psychological analysis and insight into people's souls: Tertz has no time for compassion or any other normal human feelings, and for psychology he substitutes pathology. You recognize Tertz's claim [to be like Dostoyevsky] only by his external, crudely parodied descriptions of damp hovels, by the physical and moral dead ends which loom up in the murky stream of consciousness of the characters in *Fantastic Stories*.

In his essay [*On Social Realism*] mentioned above Abram Tertz declares that Dostoyevsky "was so broad that he combined within himself Orthodoxy with nihilism, and was able to accommodate in his soul all the Karamazovs at once—Alyosha, Mitya, Ivan, Fyodor (and some say—even Smerdyakov), and actually it is impossible to say which of them bulks the largest in him." As far as Tertz is concerned, it is clear to anyone who has read his work that it is Smerdyakov who bulks largest in his, Tertz's, "soul." If Dostoyevsky had not created Smerdyakov, putting into this figure all his hatred for those who pervert the human soul, and if, instead, Smerdyakov had been a writer of novels in which he wrote about life from a "Smerdyakovian" point of view, then it would be very easy to link Tertz with a "literary forebear." For there is no depth of moral depravation which the worthy heirs of Smerdyakov fear to plumb in their eagerness to defile and trample underfoot everything human in Soviet man: friendship, love, motherhood, the family. Only the inflamed imagination of a Smerdyakov could create all these highly refined perversions of hu-

---

§ A long, melodramatic novel by a now almost forgotten author, Vsevolod Krestovsky (1840–1895). It is a blood-and-thunder work, influenced by Eugene Sue's *Secrets of Paris*, which enjoyed a great vogue in the sixties of the last century. It is unlikely that anybody would be reminded of it in reading Abram Tertz.

man interrelationships, situations in which, for example, a woman is unfaithful simultaneously to her husband and her lover—while both of them are also unfaithful to her, and at the same time to the most elementary standards of moral decency, when they all "compare notes" about their intimate experiences.* Only the mind of a Smerdyakov could have inspired the thoughts of one of Tertz's characters about the use of human embryos as canned food in order to prevent the overpopulation of the earth.

The literary parodies and reminiscences of Sinyavsky-Tertz express his vicious hatred for all the institutions, people and life of the society in which Sinyavsky lives, and which he tries to besmirch with all the means available to him, portraying it as an assemblage of loathsome monsters.

You enter his "communal" apartment inhabited by witches and werewolves, and you see flitting before you figures out of Sologub,† the hobgoblins of Klychkov's *Prattler of Chertukhino*.‡ And here's one of his "tenants," a character straight out of Kafka,§ a changeling who crawls into the room without knocking, through the crack under

---

* This apparently refers to "The Icicle."

† Fyodor Sologub (1863–1927) is best known as the author of the novel *The Petty Devil*, 1907, the chief character of which, Peredonov, ranks with Dostoyevsky's Smerdyakov and Saltykov's Yudushka as an epitome of vileness.

‡ Sergei Klychkov (1889–?) is a Russian poet and prose writer, whose novel *Prattler of Chertukhino* (*Chertukhinsky Balakir*), 1926, was part of a trilogy about peasant life before the revolution. In his *Soviet Russian Literature 1917–1950* Gleb Struve writes:

"Written in rich language, now ornately poetical, now colloquial, they combine a realistic portrayal of village life and types with unbridled fantasy rooted in popular legends, and are peopled with all sorts of quaint goblins, wood spirits, and other whimsies, side by side with peasant characters whose intonations and peculiarities of speech are meticulously reproduced. The best of these novels is *The Prattler of Chertukhino*, in which Klychkov gives free rein to his fantasy. Communist critics, while admitting Klychkov's mastery of the peasant *skaz* [story in stylized language], his feeling for Russian folklore, and his clever handling of the plot, stressed his 'arch-reactionary romanticism' and his idealization of old Russia. Klychkov ended by disappearing from literature and there are reasons to believe that he died in a concentration camp."

§ The reference is to Kafka's novel *Metamorphosis*, in which the hero turns into an insect.

Madame Kedrina is being somewhat disingenuous when she contrasts Sinyavsky with Sologub and Kafka. Neither of these authors has ever been favorably regarded by Soviet critics, and until very recently Kafka was always referred to with scorn. Some of his work has recently been published in the Soviet Union for the first time.

the door: "I can walk around inside the premises to my heart's content, on the walls and ceiling if I like. But I can't put a foot over the threshold. My physiology forbids it." But Sologub despised the Peredonov of his own creation. Kafka, despite all the despair of his view of human life, hated the moneygrubbing world of the bourgeoisie, which transforms a human being into a reptile. Tertz, on the other hand, is inseparable from the sordid world of his characters.

"If you take a thread from everyone, you can make a shirt for a naked man," as the Russian proverb says. Next to something purloined from Kafka, without batting an eyelid and in a matter-of-fact way, Tertz puts a sneering parody on Gogol's famous passage about the troika*—all this for the same purpose, to lash out once again at Soviet society:

Train! Train with the wings of a bird! Who invented you? None but a quick-witted people could have given you birth! Although no artful craftsman of Tula or Yaroslavl, but the cunning English Stephenson, they say, contrived you for the good of the cause, you are yet mightily well fitted to our rolling Russian plain and you speed on your way, up hill and down dale, hurtling past the telegraph poles, now faster now slower, till the head spins and the eyes hurt! Yet if one looks more closely, what is it but a stove on wheels or a peasant samovar with a line of wagons in tow? An angry creature at first sight, it's really generous and kindhearted. It puffs and blows and labors up any hill you like, grunting now and then by way of warning, but when it gives that piercing, devil-may-care whistle, you know you'd better watch out, if you don't want to be flattened.

One cannot help agreeing with the changeling in "Tenants" when he says: "No . . . you won't find a single living person among our tenants." Yes, there is not a single person taken from the life which Abram Tertz claims to be portraying, but they are all from other people's books about other times, and even about other countries. It is all borrowed in order to disfigure, defile and besmirch in a peculiar Tertzian way everything Soviet, everything human, and at the same time the source from which it is "loaned."

Even in those instances where Tertz's subject matter is not fantasy, but where he appears to be concerned with ordinary life (as in *The*

---

* This occurs at the end of the first volume of *Dead Souls* and is the famous lyrical digression in which Gogol compares Russia to a troika hurtling in an unknown direction. *Fantastic Stories*, p. 77.

Trial Begins), the development of the story, the images, the way in which the protagonists are ranged against each other, have been borrowed from a great variety of sources, including one type of literature which has now been forgotten in our country—the cheap novelette. It is in the spirit of this literature, for instance, that the prosecutor's wife, the voluptuous *femme fatale* Marina Pavlovna, is presented. One is vividly reminded of the "classics" of trashy literature by the gusto with which the vulgar charms of the seductress are openly paraded. And the detailed description of the manners and customs of the milieu in which the action is set, a milieu of "kindly men of whom perhaps half the world was terrified,"§ also calls to mind the literature of the years of reaction and of even earlier times: Sologub and Artsybashev—they all have their "part" here, unwittingly providing Tertz with mangled odds and ends of their plots and images.†

By putting the Jesuitical doctrine of the ends justifying the means into the mouth of a Soviet man, and mocking Communist ideals for all he is worth, Abram Tertz does his best to illustrate the libelous commonplace of anti-Soviet propaganda that "good socialism" is "free slavery" (*The Trial Begins*).

The novel *Lyubimov* is also intended to illustrate this thesis, and it is the lengthiest of his works, the one which gives fullest expression to the "message" and "literary technique" of Abram Tertz. If in his previous works Tertz had set out to slander our ideals and our society in a piecemeal fashion, so to speak, in *Lyubimov* he tries to "tackle" the problem of the building of Communism as a whole, on the "historical" plane, dealing with it once and for all, if you please! For this purpose he parodies the idea of building socialism in one country by depicting an unsuccessful attempt to build socialism in the

---

§ I.e., the secret policemen in *The Trial Begins*, p. 90.

† Mikhail Artsybashev (1878–1927) was a Russian novelist best known for his novel *Sanin*, which is always held up by Soviet critics as the acme of decadence. It was written between 1901 and 1907, and though it is denounced as "pornographical," it is by no means as "way out" as Madame Kedrina suggests.

"Years of reaction" is a standard Soviet way of referring to the period after the 1905 revolution, when for the first time Russia began to develop the rudiments of a parliamentary democracy, and political parties were legalized, with the result that there was a certain recession in underground revolutionary activity.

backwoods town of Lyubimov, which stands in the middle of woods and bogs, far removed from the civilization of the outside world. The émigré B. Filippov writes in his preface to the Washington edition of the book: "The history of the backwoods town of Lyubimov gives us, as in a drop of water, the history of the whole of the vast communist world, in particular of the U.S.S.R. But it is not Saltykov-Shchedrin's *History of the Town of Glupov*. Saltykov's work is a bilious positivist caricature, completely realistic and flat, which does not delve beneath the surface of things. Tertz's Lyubimov," he adds, "is more topical and more profound. . . ." Of course! Tertz's "opus" is more topical for the simple reason that, having "borrowed" again the purely external outline of Shchedrin's satire with its fantastic hyperbole, Tertz has mixed in some colors from Okurov;‡ but the main ingredient of the whole concoction, which is calculated to appeal to the none-too-demanding tastes of the petty bourgeois, is Zamyatin's *Tales from Provincial Life*.§ For the portrayal of his little backwoods town, the author has also plagiarized certain works of Soviet literature in the twenties, which depict the Russia of the NEP period, borrowing for good measure some of the verbal tricks of "ornamental" prose.*

Tertz is not embarrassed by the fact that the techniques, images and plots he has stolen were conceived for quite different, indeed opposite ideological and artistic functions, and served diametrically opposed social aims. With a feeling of absolute impunity (in Washington they will never know, and even if they do, they won't mind!) this brazen plagiarist has ground all this up, mixed it together, flavored it with a little of the most up-to-date Western modernism,

---

‡ Okurov is the fictional name of a provincial town which figures in some stories by Maxim Gorky.

§ Evgeni Zamyatin (1884–1937) is a Russian writer who is best known in the west for his novel *We*, an anti-utopian novel like Huxley's *Brave New World* and Orwell's *1984*. This work was published only abroad (it appeared in England in 1924), and as a result of consequent persecution, Zamyatin left Russia in 1932 and settled in Paris, where he died. His *Tales from Provincial Life* (*Uyezdnoye*) appeared in 1913 and satirizes the primitive life of the Russian provinces.

* "Ornamental" is a term used for the somewhat ornate, highly stylized manner of writing which was practiced by Aleksei Remizov, Andrei Bely and some early Soviet writers such as Boris Pilnyak. It is a style that is commonly traced back to Gogol and Leskov.

put in a pinch of pepper from Remizov,† and, straining it through his Smerdyakovian colander, he has adapted it to the requirements of his client and of his own unbridled hatred for everything Soviet.

Happening to come across a mystical book of the late landowner Proferansov, *The Psychic Magnet*, and "having read too much for his own good," the bicycle mechanic Tikhomirov [in *Lyubimov*] acquires the gift of hypnotic suggestion and overthrows the party leadership of the town. Then, by the same hypnotic method, Tikhomirov persuades all the citizens, including babes-in-arms, that they would like him to be "czar," and he celebrates his wedding with the local vamp, Serafima Petrovna, by using the same method to turn the water of the nearby river into champagne (even the Gospel has not escaped the attention of the nimble-fingered author). By the same power of suggestion, mineral water is turned into pure spirits and rotten pickles into sausages, etc. Everybody believes—they eat, drink, and praise the newfound miracle maker, and only the dogs cannot be deceived: they will not eat the miraculous sausage.

Thus, using the landowner's treatise as a guide, a usurper rules in Lyubimov, mesmerizing its inhabitants into the belief that they themselves wish to work till they drop, not only without getting anything in return, but actually giving up what they already had. The superman Tikhomirov, with his henchman and chronicler (a *ci-devant* and descendant of the landowner Proferansov, who is made out to be a possible ancestor of Tikhomirov himself), blindly carries out the will of his mystical lord and master. The usurper, abusing the people's trust, which he does not deserve, carries out everything singlehanded —including the defense of the town against a punitive expedition sent "from Moscow" and disguised as a tourist group. His magic power at last begins to wane, coming on without his wishing it to send a woman up into the sky on a broomstick, but failing him just at the moment when he needs it to repulse an enemy attack. Tikhomirov's dictatorship comes to an end. "The magical-materialist hoax, the city of hypnotically induced happiness and well-being—

---

† Aleksei Remizov (1877–1957) was a Russian novelist distinguished by his eccentric style and exploitation of Russian folklore. Although he emigrated after 1921, he exercised a considerable influence on early Soviet prose, and was the most outstanding practitioner of the "ornamental" style.

Lyubimov—is shattered," notes Boris Filippov with satisfaction, at the same time regretting, however, that the socialist way of life has still not been smashed "throughout the whole of the empire," and that one must therefore put one's hope in the "power" of "underground and semi-banned literature," and also in the said Tertz-Sinyavsky.

Fitting comfortably into the Procrustean bed of foreign anti-Soviet propaganda supplied by his "clients," Abram Tertz's handiwork is essentially parasitical and poverty-stricken from an ideological and literary point of view. Nevertheless, he has something that is undoubtedly all his own, something "close to his heart." It consists, in the first place, of pornography by the side of which the raciest parts of Artsybashev look like literature for the kindergarten. In the second place, there is a persistent odor of anti-Semitism, which is given off at once by the provocative choice of the pseudonym "Abram Tertz." Scattered throughout his "works"—and not without design—are such nice little remarks as: "brazen and persistent, like all Jews," "but how could he understand the Russian national character, this Solomon Moiseyevich?"‡ and so forth. All this has an "aroma" of a very specific kind. The indestructible, provocative smell of this "bouquet" is by no means neutralized by the multiple layers of irony, which is intended to enable the author to establish at any given moment his own "detachment" from what he himself has written.

And finally, in the third place, there is the constantly repeated theme, which runs through all the stories, of fear of arrest and premonition of its inevitability. On this subject there is even one entire story—"You and I"—in which insane fear of arrest leads the "hero" to suicide. There is probably not a single work of Abram Tertz without panic-stricken laments like the outburst, in the form of a lyrical digression, addressed by the chronicler of Lyubimov to the long-deceased landowner Proferansov. It shows, incidentally, that Sinyavsky is well aware of the anti-Soviet nature of his work:

---

‡ Madame Kedrina's accusation of anti-Semitism is dealt with by Sinyavsky and Daniel during the trial. Its main interest is that this particular charge is regarded by her as one of the best ways of discrediting Sinyavsky in the eyes of the liberal Russian intelligentsia, which, as under the czars, abhors anti-Semitism because it is connived at by the regime.

I sit and shake for fear that they might search the house and find this manuscript under the floorboards, and then they'll pick up every man jack of us. Listen, professor. You are my co-author. Will you hide this wretched book for the time being? Let it stay for a while in some impregnable safe of yours. . . . You do have some secret place, a hiding-place of some kind. Keep it there for a time. Doesn't it belong to you?§

Yes, the "works" of Tertz and Arzhak do indeed "belong" to the old world, which, as we already know, gladly receives and publishes their "manuscripts," saying for all to hear why it bestows its favors on them. "The intellectual portrait of Sinyavsky-Tertz is just as two-sided as his name," says a writer in the magazine *Espresso*, "open activity as a literary historian and critic . . . and underground stories sent abroad."

We scarcely need add anything to this comprehensive description of the "internal *émigré's*" literary portrait. The heirs of Smerdyakov, not to be tolerated in our midst, have found admirers, publishers and devotees among the forces of reaction abroad, who have still not lost hope of being able to get together a "Soviet literary underground." Your hopes are doomed to disappointment, gentlemen!

---

§ This quotation is the last paragraph of *The Makepeace Experiment*.

Pretrial Protests

The four documents that follow show the reaction of the liberal intelligentsia to Eremin's and Kedrina's articles. There were certainly many similar letters to the editors of Izvestia and Literary Gazette, but none were published. An editorial note in Izvestia of January 17, 1966, said that the paper was receiving "numerous letters of comment." However, it published only three letters denouncing Sinyavsky and Daniel in violent language: "The two traitors belong in the dock" (Suleiman Rustam, People's Poet of Azerbaijan); "Only disgust is aroused by the foul works of these moral monsters . . . they should be severely punished" (A. Lyudmilin, People's Artist of the R.S.F.S.R., and two other signatories); "We must expect Soviet justice to give the criminals their just deserts" (Z. Gulbis, agronomist).

Letter from Y. I. Levin

To Izvestia

DEAR EDITOR,

The article "The Turncoats" by D. Eremin, which appeared in your newspaper, is distressing and bewildering. It recalls such sorry incidents in our cultural history as the recent case of J. Brodsky, the persecution of B. Pasternak and, earlier, of Akhmatova and

233

Zoschenko, the campaign against the "cosmopolitans" and, in a different sphere, the session of VASKHNIL.* Going still further back in time, I was reminded of the death of Mandelshtam, of Babel, of I. Katayev and of many others. Here, in Eremin's article, were the vocabulary, the phraseology, the rabble-rousing appeals to the reader's civic sense, we all remember so well from 1937, from 1946–49 and from 1953.

Yet the whole of Eremin's system of "proof" rests on misleading or, rather, deliberately false premises. He bases his main argument on quotations from the works of Tertz and Arzhak. That quotations torn from their context cannot give a true picture of the whole has been known for a long time and is known to every schoolboy. Yet Eremin does more than quote isolated passages; he quotes the direct speech of the characters or, at best, of the narrator. To identify any of the characters (even the narrator) with the author of a story, to identify their views with those of the author, is a mistake so elementary as to be almost ludicrous (you have only to look at Dostoyevsky's *Letters from the Underground*, or at *My Son and I* by the progressive Swedish author Sarah Lidman in which the narrator is a fanatical racialist); this again is a fact which every schoolboy knows, and such a mistake coming from the writer D. Eremin is all the more unforgivable. Using Eremin's "method" it is easy to prove anything against anyone—quotations from *Onegin* could be used to show that Pushkin, in the intervals of longing for his uncle's death, indulged himself in prurient visions of women's legs and breasts, and enough "anti-Soviet" passages could be extracted from *And Quiet Flows the Don* to make even Radio Free Europe green with envy.

But to come to the substance of the article—by putting such words as "novels," "stories," in quotation marks every time he uses them, Eremin suggests that these works are worthless trash, inspired only by

---

* The campaign against "cosmopolitans" took place in 1948–49 and involved the arrest and persecution of a great many intellectuals, particularly those of Jewish origin. VASKHNIL (*Vsesoyuznaya akademia selskokhozyaistvennykh nauk imeni Lenina*) is the Lenin Academy of Agricultural Science. At a session in 1948 Lysenko denounced the orthodox geneticists (the "Weissmanist-Morganists," as he called them) and claimed Stalin's personal support for his own theories. Many Soviet biologists were arrested, or lost their posts, during the ensuing campaign of persecution.

their authors' hatred of the Soviet regime. I will come back to this "hatred" later. All I want to say now is that a dispassionate analysis of their style shows that, whatever else they may be, they are talented works of literature. One can argue about their literary merits or shortcomings, one may like or dislike their manner, but that they are works of literature, or that their authors are talented, of this there can be no doubt. Tertz has a particularly wide range—from the brisk, matter-of-fact prose of *The Trial Begins* to the ornate, stylized narrative of *Lyubimov*—and his versatility is itself a sign of his remarkable skill. The style of Arzhak's main works ("Atonement" and *This Is Moscow Speaking*) is characteristic of what is known as the "new" school of Soviet writing. Among its members are V. Aksyonov, A. Kuznetsov, etc.,† and Arzhak's style is not at all inferior to theirs. At the same time, he gives the impression of being cramped by this manner. This is shown by his attempt to achieve symbolic effects in "Atonement," by the narrative style of the masterly story "Hands," and by the purely satirical work, "The Man from Minap."

The article systematically misrepresents the subject matter of Tertz's and Arzhak's works. It refers to their "morbidly prurient obsession" with "sexual and psychopathological 'problems.' " This is a lie. Gorky, Sholokhov, Babel, to mention only a few (and not to speak of Boccaccio, Rabelais or D. H. Lawrence), deal with sexual problems quite as frankly and could just as easily be described as "morbidly obsessed." As for psychopathology, Tertz and Arzhak are only moderately interested in this side of life (Tertz in "You and I," Arzhak in "Atonement")—certainly no more so than Gogol, Hoffmann, Bulgakov‡ (*Diavolada*) or Faulkner, to quote the first examples that come to mind.

"They like nothing about our country, nothing is holy for them"— this is another piece of demagogy. The claim is supported (in the above-mentioned manner) by two quotations about Chekhov and

---

† Vasilii Aksyonov (born 1932), a popular young novelist and short story writer. For Anatoli Kuznetsov, see note § on p. 128.

‡ Mikhail Bulgakov (1891–1940), famous Soviet playwright and novelist best known for his play *Days of the Turbines*, which was fiercely attacked when it was first produced in 1926 because of the author's sympathetic portrayal of White officers. *Diavolada* (1925) was a collection of satirical stories, also much attacked at the time of its appearance.

other classical Russian writers—quotations which only the most ingenuous of readers could possibly mistake for an expression of the author's views. The article carefully refrains from quoting such passages as, for instance, the conclusion of *This Is Moscow Speaking*, which shows the depth and sincerity of the author's love of Moscow —yet there are a great many such passages in Tertz's and Arzhak's books.

"These 'writers' try to vilify and slander our Soviet Army"—this again is quite simply a lie. There is nothing of the kind in anything by Tertz and Arzhak.

Eremin misrepresents the plot of Tertz's *Lyubimov*: "Just look how Sinyavsky-Tertz smacks his lips over the failure of the Communist 'experiment,' and the return of Lyubimov to the old way of life!" That the "old way of life" happens to be our existing Soviet order is not even mentioned. What the story, in fact, describes, is the failure of attempts to build an ideal society through the will of one person alone; this, as I understand it, is the point of the book: it is a critique of voluntarism, and I see nothing criminal about it.

This Is Moscow Speaking, by Arzhak, is said by Eremin to "paint monstrous scenes from a way of life alleged to be Soviet . . . of the mass lunacy of regimented devotion to the 'idea' of universal slaughter . . . of terror . . . throughout the country." This again is simply a lie. There are no "monstrous scenes"—even within the convention of a fantastic situation, Soviet life is painted in a realistic way, there is only one murder, there is no "mass lunacy," no "universal slaughter," no "terror"—there is nothing at all of this, any more than there is "vulgar eroticism, drunken debauchery or unbridled immorality."

The most baffling part of the article is the concluding paragraphs which claim that Tertz and Arzhak help "those who would like to turn the cold war into a hot one, those who still nurture the crazy dream of raising their hands against the Soviet Union," and that their purpose in writing their books is to "kindle enmity between nations and increase the danger of war." (An earlier passage accuses them of "spitting poison at the whole of progressive mankind . . . and its holy struggle for social progress, democracy and peace.")

Such statements, utterly irrevelant to anything in Tertz's and

Arzhak's work, are sheer malicious, irresponsible, rabble-rousing slander.

One more point about Eremin's methods. According to the article Sinyavsky "wormed his way" into the Writers' Union. As it happens, in recent years, Sinyavsky has often been mentioned in the press as one of our most gifted younger literary critics, and his book on Picasso (written in collaboration with another author) has been widely acclaimed.

Eremin does his best to represent Sinyavsky as a double-dealer who published one thing in the Soviet press and the opposite abroad. This is another lie. The allegation is based on Sinyavsky's review of A. Shevtsov's novel *The Blight*. This novel is a disgusting piece of pamphleteering against the Soviet intelligentsia. There is plainly a connection between Sinyavsky's struggle against such works as *The Blight* and the critique of certain aspects of our society we find in Tertz—it should be obvious that the one does not contradict the other.

Finally, to come to the most important point: Tertz's and Arzhak's works are described as "dirty lampoons," as jeering at "everything dear to our Motherland and people"; the authors, it is claimed, are filled with "hatred of our system," and have "entered the service of the most rabid enemies of Communism." In other words, Eremin regards Tertz's and Arzhak's writing as anti-Soviet and antipatriotic. He brands the authors as enemies of our system and as men who do not love their country.

As regards "antipatriotism"—I would like to say, first of all, that a man's love for his country is as deeply intimate and private a feeling as his love for a woman or for art. No one has the right to tell anyone else: "Love your Motherland!" It's quite another matter to say that a man who is indifferent to his country—to its language, its people, its landscape—is spiritually wanting, that he robs himself and is as much of a spiritual eunuch as a man to whom art means nothing. But—I repeat—this love is an intimate feeling which should not be advertised and which it is unseemly to shout from the housetops or to publicize in the press. Emotional outpourings on the subject are, as Pasternak said, "morally suspect"; as a rule they point to the absence of love and the presence of intense self-interest. What is certain is that Pushkin, Chaadayev,§ Lermontov—men who never made a show of patriotism and who had many bitter things to say about Russia—were better patriots than either Bulgarin or Benckendorf.*

Chaadayev wrote: "I have never learned to love my country with my eyes shut . . . I consider that no one can be useful to his country unless he sees it clearly . . . the time for blind infatuation is past. . . . I suppose that we have come after others in order to do better than they did, not to fall into their mistakes, illusions and superstitions." These words could have been spoken by many of our greatest writers. They could also have been said by Sinyavsky and Daniel. The only possible reason for painting rosy pictures of reality is indifference to one's country, combined with a strong concern for oneself. The 20th Congress and the denunciation of the cult of personality did more than open the eyes of the nation to the violations of legality under Stalin; they also showed that things were wrong in many spheres of our present-day life. Our papers write of many of them every day, and more radical questions are raised nowadays in our literature. But unfortunately, fear of the written word is one of the consequences of the cult of personality which still survive. In recent years, many subjects have ceased to be taboo and books on them have been published. Writers (creative writers as well as journalists) have written about what happens in the countryside, about the purges under Stalin, etc., and this literature has, of course, played an enormous part in improving the situation in our country. But many subjects are still untouchable—such subjects, to mention only a few, as anti-Semitism, or the responsibility of those who committed crimes under Stalin, as well as of those others who did nothing to prevent them (this is the subject of Arzhak's "Atonement") or the problem of the moral degradation of a part of our intelligentsia (raised by Arzhak in This Is Moscow Speaking and by Tertz in The Trial Begins). It would do our country nothing but good if these and

---

§ Peter Chaadayev (1794–1856), a friend of Pushkin who, after the publication of his Philosophical Letters (1829–30), was officially declared to be mad because of his harsh strictures on Russian conditions.

* Faddei Bulgarin (1789–1859), chauvinist writer and journalist who attacked Pushkin and Gogol, and denounced writers to the secret police. Count Alexander Benckendorf (1783–1844), chief of the gendarmerie and Third Department (secret police) under Nicholas I.

similar taboos were raised—just as nothing but good came of the 20th Congress.

For all these reasons, I maintain that the works of Tertz and Arzhak are inspired by love of their country and its people, sorrow over its past misfortunes and the wish to stop them from ever recurring, as well as by an acute awareness of what is still making things difficult for us today. Deeply sincere and filled with the highest sense of civic duty, theirs is the true literature of patriotism.

A Soviet reader, brought up for the most part on a literature of facile optimism, may well be shocked by many of the things they say. After all, who has ever heard of anything like a "Public Murder Day"? But it surely needs only a moment's thought to appreciate that this "Day" is just an instance of a widely used literary method: the characters are placed in an extreme situation in which their latent moral traits, good or bad, are fully revealed. (Dostoyevsky, for one, used this method time and again.) But why such a monstrous "anti-Soviet" fantasy, why a "Public Murder Day" in our day and age, in our society? The reason, of course, is that this is satire, and it is a truism to say that the use of exaggeration is not merely legitimate but essential to a satirical work. Who, indeed, has ever actually seen a mayor with a stuffed head, as in Shchedrin?[†] And yet, compared to this, a "Public Murder Day" is not so fantastic—one has only to look up the newspapers for 1937 or the beginning of 1953. And isn't it obvious that the story is intended to prevent such things happening again?

Is it true that Tertz's and Arzhak's works are anti-Soviet? Yes, if it is anti-Soviet to write on any subject one is "not supposed" to raise. But at this rate, anything can be branded as anti-Soviet—or as whatever else you like—down to the wall newspaper which complains of the inefficiency of the canteen. Isn't it our canteen, after all? Isn't it our Soviet canteen? As I understand it, anti-Soviet activity is activity the purpose of which is to undermine the foundations of the Soviet state and economic system—its foundations as defined by the Soviet Constitution. It is quite impossible to read anything of the sort into Tertz or Arzhak. What they criticize are certain of our

---

[†] The reference is to Shchedrin's *History of the Town of Glupov* (see p. 13).

institutions, certain features of our society. Usually they criticize the past—the period of the cult of personality (as in *The Trial Begins*); sometimes they touch on the present (as in *This Is Moscow Speaking*, where the author is chiefly concerned with what is happening in literary circles). But with the best will in the world it is impossible to discover in them any revisionist attack against the basis of the Soviet state structure or of the socialist economy, or indeed anything else—such as any indication of a desire to restore capitalism—which would genuinely brand their writing as anti-Soviet.

I apologize for the length of this letter.

Y. I. LEVIN
Candidate of Physical and
Mathematical Science

Letter from Y. Gerchuk

To Izvestia

DEAR EDITOR,

After reading the article by D. Eremin, "The Turncoats," in your issue of January 13 and the reactions to it in your issue of January 17, I feel it my duty to write to you, since I am closely acquainted with the people mentioned in the article, and I have also managed to read the works quoted in it.

It is now many years since our press has published anything in this vein, full of crude abuse, hysterical expostulation and such shameless juggling with quotations torn out of context. This latter is all the easier in that the alleged authors are in prison and have no possibility of answering back, not to mention that the overwhelming majority of your readers do not know their works which have not been published in the Soviet Union. . . .

Eremin uses a very simple technique: he takes the words of a bad character, who is depicted in the worst possible light, puts them in the mouth of the author, and presents them, without more ado, as the author's opinion. There are three quotations from Tertz's "Graphomaniacs," a story written in the first person, as though told by an unsuccessful hack writer who lives in penury and is beside himself with envy and hatred for the "lucky" ones—for other writers, editors and the classics. It is he, and not the author of the story, who hates Chekhov and the classics in general; it is he who sees in an editor's secretary "a wench available to any proofreader.". . .

Can one believe that the writer Eremin didn't realize this? The whole tone of his article makes it clear that this use of quotations is the sleight of hand of someone who knows quite well what he is doing, and who is cynically taking advantage of the fact that his readers cannot refer to the texts.

Then there is another, no less dishonest way of quoting. In Arzhak's *This Is Moscow Speaking* the hero, who has the author's sympathy and who is evidently to a large extent a mouthpiece for his view, thinks aloud about means of fighting evil and tyranny. He wonders whether force of arms may be used: "You pull off the safety pin, throw it and fall on the ground . . . etc." But at the end of this train of thought, the hero rejects terror, he does not want bloodshed and slaughter.

Eremin breaks off the quotation *before* the hero's thoughts take this turn and is thus able to reach the required conclusion that, in his words, "This is, in effect, a call for terrorism!"

After this cavalier use of quotations, Eremin naturally feels even less inhibited when he comes to talk about the general meaning of the works.

Tertz's *Lyubimov* is a difficult work which does not readily yield to analysis. Any attempt to sum it up at one go, in a single phrase, is bound to fail. But for Eremin nothing could be simpler: ". . . the author sets himself no less a task than to prove that the very idea of the Communist transformation of society is an illusion, a vain dream." But this contention, too, is clearly meant for people who do not know the work and have no means of checking up on Eremin.

It is true that this story of Tertz is a satire. It is an extravaganza and fantasy about the failure of attempts to achieve "universal happiness" not by work but by talk, "by means of mass hypnosis," to quote Eremin's expression. . . . Isn't it attempts of this kind which now, after the appearance of the story, have been widely discussed and condemned as "subjectivism and voluntarism"? And if at the end the town of Lyubimov returns to "the old way of life," the way of life in question in the Soviet one. Admittedly, the life of Lyubimov is the not very enviable one of those of our small towns which are far from the main roads and, not possessing an industry, have little prospects of growth. No wonder that the problem of the "small towns" is at the moment of concern to many Soviet writers. And if someone shows that the problem cannot be solved merely by an "effort of the will," is this enough to brand him a criminal?

The same applies, in effect, to Arzhak's *This Is Moscow Speaking*. This is a bitingly satirical work which, despite its fantastic plot, deals with what are, unfortunately, very real problems in our everyday life—including the one exemplified these last few days by the eagerness with which very many people unhesitatingly support any campaign—as, for example, a call to put "paid" to two writers whose works they have never read, on the strength of half a dozen passages quoted out of context in a newspaper (*Izvestia* of January 17).

It is typical that Eremin, concentrating on one or two works by Arzhak and Tertz, ignores other, no less significant ones, such as Tertz's novel *The Trial Begins*, which is about the travesties of justice in the period of the cult of personality and their corrupting effect not only on those directly involved, but even on people who had nothing to do with them. Arzhak's "Atonement" is on a similar theme: the spiritual aftermath of the same period and the tangled web, which has still to be unraveled, of mutual suspicion and recriminations, as well as our collective responsibility for the orgy of purges and denunciations which took place before our eyes. From both these works we get a fairly clear idea of why there is so much satirical fervor in Arzhak and Tertz, and we also see which aspects of our life, which forces and features of the past they deal with in their books. But for D. Eremin any desire to put an end to the dark legacy of the past and to solve still unsolved questions of public morality is merely a "morbid interest in the sordid problems of life"! Isn't it odd that a newspaper which often devotes space to these "sordid problems"—difficult points of morality and the administration of justice —should now find room in its columns for this rabble-rousing article?

No doubt aware of the inadequacy of his arguments as an explanation of the arrest of the two writers and his attack on them, Eremin resorts to more general accusations which are quite unsupported and cannot be substantiated from the works quoted by him. He talks, for instance, about slander on the army "whose immortal exploits saved the peoples of Europe from destruction by the Nazis," forgetting to add that one of the accused, Daniel, took part in these exploits and was wounded in the war, which he went through as a private. There is also something about "kindling of enmity between nations," but no proof is offered for this either.

One more detail typical of Eremin: He writes: "A Russian by birth, Andrei Sinyavsky hid behind the name of Abram Tertz. Why? For a purely provocative reason." I know many Soviet Jewish writers whose pseudonyms sound completely Russian. No eyebrows are raised at this, and I have yet to read any imputation of ulterior motives to such writers. So why should a Russian writer who adopts a Jewish-sounding name arouse such anger and be accused of having done this to prove the existence of anti-Semitism? On the other hand, this innuendo of Eremin's that it is unworthy of a born Russian to call himself by a Jewish name is itself quite sufficient proof of the existence of anti-Semitism, not just anywhere but among contributors of *Izvestia*.

With a great show of feeling Eremin answers Sinyavsky's criticism of a certain writer who according to him, "is an active, loyal helper of the party, a son of his people"; he indignantly quotes from Sinyavsky's article, without, however, saying who it is about. And no wonder, since the name of Ivan Shevtsov, whose novel *The Blight* is the subject of the article in question, is odious, and all the Soviet critics, writing in a great variety of newspapers and periodicals, unanimously condemned this novel with its propaganda for naturalist art and its scurrilous attacks on its opponents. The "positive hero" of the novel knows no other means of fighting people who disagree with him about art than by constantly informing on them. What is so hypocritical about a reviewer who has always openly taken issue with literature of this sort?

Though many readers have to take Eremin's word on the subject of works by Arzhak and Sinyavsky published abroad, they can very easily check on the validity of what he says about Sinyavsky as a critic.

Although I am no expert on literature, I am sure that his numerous and substantial critical articles and studies in literary history are evidence in his favor. One need only mention his long introduction to the recent edition of Boris Pasternak's poetry. This, in fact, is the first study of one of the most outstanding poets of our age. Sinyavsky's remarkably keen and fresh appreciation of Pasternak's verse enables him to bring out the depth and complexity of the great poet's feeling for life.

I have read and reread Eremin's article—it is four columns long—trying to figure out why, when all is said and done, these two writers have now been under arrest for several months. Is it because they published their work abroad? But we know that this is not in itself a crime, that there is no provision in Soviet law forbidding it. Is it because their work is satirical? But satire is an essential instrument of social hygiene, a means of getting rid of shortcomings and doing away with inertia. Without it, society stagnates. There is no doubt in my mind as to the high literary quality of Arzhak's and Tertz's work, and it is clear that the deep feeling behind their critical approach is the product of personal involvement. Furthermore I do not feel that the content of a work of literature can be the object of examination in a court of law. It is true that Arzhak and Tertz did not moderate their satire in deference to official opinion (but then neither did Swift or Saltykov-Shchedrin), and were therefore obliged to publish abroad. Does this warrant the charge of slander against them? Slander is a legal term, something that must be proved, but it should not be confused—either out of malice or ignorance—with literary hyperbole or satirical exaggeration. It is much easier to find slander in Ermin's article with its deceitful technique of quoting passages out of context and twisting their meaning.

One is naturally anxious about the reasons for the publication of such an article just now, after Sinyavsky and Daniel have been in prison for over four months and when their trial is evidently about to take place. What is the reason for printing the "reactions" of people who clearly know about the matter only from Eremin's article, and who can only form an opinion of the two writers from the passages quoted by him in a garbled form? What is the purpose of creating, immediately before the trial, the sort of hysterical atmosphere only too familiar from the notorious campaigns against Pasternak, against the "poisoner-doctors," against the "antipatriotic group of drama critics"‡ and so forth, an atmosphere which is anything but helpful to the court in establishing the truth and doing justice?

The question also arises as to whether this article is not based on materials obtained during the preliminary investigation and whether, therefore, the charges produced in court will not be just as unfounded and biased as those made by Eremin?

It is anxiety on these points that leads me to write you this letter, although the build-up of the Sinyavsky-Daniel case gives me no hope that it will be printed, and the cavalier way in which your contributor handles quotations makes me fear that my letter may be subjected to similar treatment. All the same I am writing to you because I feel it necessary to say that among the Soviet intelligentsia (I think I have the right to speak not only for myself but also for those whose opinions about all this are known to me) there are some who, despite what Eremin says, are deeply disturbed by the arrest of the writers for their literary activities and disgusted by the newspaper campaign against people who have no chance of answering their accusers and refuting the slanders against them, particularly since the dishonesty of Eremin's article is obvious even to those who have no possibility of checking up on his facts.

I had nearly finished this letter when a further lengthy article by Z. Kedrina on Arzhak's and Tertz's work appeared in the *Literary Gazette* of January 22. At first sight it might look like an attempt to discuss them in a more matter-of-fact and fair manner. The article is concerned with a "purely literary," almost academic examination of their works, and with the tracing of literary influences on them. But on closer inspection it is quite clear that this academic tone is hypocritical. The author must know that the fate of the accused will depend to a considerable extent on the view the court takes of their

---

‡ For "poisoner-doctors" see note * on p. 95. The "antipatriotic" group of drama critics was denounced in an article in *Pravda* on January 28, 1949, as the first shot in the campaign against "cosmopolitans."

work, and she does everything she possibly can to deny them a place in art and literature. Therefore, in showing to what traditions they go back—and unlike most of our writers they have been influenced by Remizov, Zamyatin and others, to whom Artsybashev is added for the obvious purpose of discrediting them—Kedrina makes out that Tertz's work is completely devoid of originality and is a patchwork of borrowed fragments, etc. She doesn't even notice that her own words about Tertz's "multiple irony" contradict what she says about the flatness and literary feebleness of his work.

Like Eremin she is also given to the shameless and slanderous twisting of quotations, in particular that same passage in *This Is Moscow Speaking* which is used to reach a monstrous conclusion quite contrary to the whole spirit of the story, and is intended to bring punishment on the heads of the authors. All this makes one feel that Kedrina's article is a further step in the libelous campaign against the arrested writers, and it only increases concern for their fate.

Y. GERCHUK
Art Historian

Letter from N. Kishilov and A. Menshutin*

To the editors of Literary Gazette

DEAR EDITORS,

We feel it our duty to protest in the strongest possible terms against the publication in your newspaper of the mendacious and slanderous article entitled "The Heirs of Smerdyakov" and signed by Z. Kedrina. This article, written in a defamatory and rabble-rousing tone, produces on people who know the works of the two authors the impression of a shameless literary character assassination, concocted in accordance with all the rules of an earlier tradition which we thought was dead and buried.

---

* For N. Kishilov, see note † on p. 43, and for Menshutin, the note on p. 84.

Nobody questions the right of Z. Kedrina and of your newspaper to have their own opinion about any literary work. But it is wrong to replace fair and open criticism with deliberate inventions, to make accusations against an author by attributing to him what his characters say, to tear passages out of context so that they no longer have the sense intended by the author and are arbitrarily interpreted to serve the far from literary purposes of the critic.

We will give a few examples of such blatant manipulation. Attacking Daniel's *This Is Moscow Speaking*, Kedrina quotes the passage in which the hero of the story ponders the question as to whether political assassination is feasible or justifiable. Part of this inner monologue is interpreted in such a way by the critic that the reader is left with the feeling that it is a political manifesto calling for violence and terror. But in fact this part of the monologue refers to memories of the war (in which, incidentally, the author fought), and these memories lead the hero to the conclusion that one should never kill. By deliberately omitting the concluding part of this monologue, Kedrina has turned it into a manifesto saying the exact opposite of what the author meant.

Summarizing Sinyavsky's *Lyubimov*, the critic quotes from a stylized lyrical digression which deliberately parodies the lyrical digresson about the troika in *Dead Souls*. Kedrina begins by accusing Sinyavsky of plagiarism, which is completely inadmissible, since the device of deliberate stylization is not plagiarism—if it were, many eminent writers and poets would lay themselves open to the accusation of literary theft. She goes on to allege that in this passage Sinyavsky "takes pleasure" in jibing at Soviet life. We can agree with her only if she thinks that Gogol is doing something similar in his passage about the troika. It appears that both Gogol and Sinyavsky had no other aim but to blacken the life of our country!

The Jesuitical nature of her criticism reaches its peak at the end of the article when she announces in the tone of a public prosecutor that the poor author cannot be absolved of anything said by any of his characters. Well now, if she is to be consistent, Kedrina will have to accuse Dostoyevsky of sadism and debauchery, Chekhov of cretinism, and Babel of robbery and looting.

When she labels Sinyavsky an anti-Semite, Kedrina carefully conceals the fact that Yuli Daniel is a Jew, that his collaborator on the Picasso book, Golomshtok, is a Karaite,[†] and that there are many other Jews among Sinyavsky's friends.

We are convinced that it is not the works of the two authors which are anti-Soviet and antihuman in the full sense of these words, but the article by Z. Kedrina, which is a disgrace to the pages of the Soviet press. This article does enormous harm to our society by bringing back the smell of corruption and the murderous spirit, which we thought had been done away with forever, of the year 1937.

A savage desire to anticipate and predetermine the course of the court proceedings has made the critic resort to slander, misrepresentation and deliberate untruth. Such practices have often been denounced in our press, and one would not have thought a return to them possible after the article by the President of the Supreme Court of the U.S.S.R. *Izvestia* last year.[‡]

Dear editors, we would like to think that the publication of this article was a silly mistake and that your newspaper will restore its good name by officially dissociating itself from Kedrina's article, or at least by publishing the letters of protest sent to you.

But if the editors are in agreement with the author of this article, then let them remember the dark days of 1937 which saw the destruction of the best part of our literature in the persons of Mandelshtam, Klychkov, Babel, Koltsov and many, many others, and let them try to understand the consequences of aiding and abetting literary gravediggers of the type of Z. Kedrina.

N. Kishilov
artist and restorer

Moscow E-392. Golnovo, Kor. 50, kv. 84.

A. Menshutin
Specialist in literature,
Institute of World Literature

Moscow, ul. Semashko. k. 10, kv. 9.

[†] Member of a small Jewish sect (also regarded as an ethnic group) which does not recognize the Talmud.
[‡] See pp. 30–31.

Letter from I. Rodnyanskaya

To the Presidium of the Supreme Soviet of the U.S.S.R.
Copy to the Editor of Literary Gazette

Izvestia and *Literary Gazette* have each recently published an article—the one by D. Eremin, the other by Z. Kedrina—about the reasons for bringing A. Sinyavsky and Y. Daniel to trial. That any information about the course of the investigation should be published is, of course, a fact which can only be welcomed (although it would have been better for such information to come from an authorized official source). It is, however, the tone of both the articles which makes me turn to so high an authority [as the Presidium of the Supreme Soviet] in my bewilderment and profound concern.

I will not waste time on the style of Eremin's article. I will only note that his expressions of abuse ("bottomless quagmire of abomination," "dirty slops of slander," "spitting poison," etc.) could scarcely be used with decency even in the bitterest polemic or the most outright condemnation, and that they can only disgrace the author who uses them to express his feelings. Moreover, the similarity of Eremin's language to that current in our press during the years when people were illegally persecuted is bound to repel the reader and put him on his guard. But all this is, basically, a question of ethics.

I should like to draw your attention to something else, namely, the attempt made by the authors of both articles—*before* the trial and *in place* of those who will conduct it—to arrive at their own verdict, a homemade verdict, so to speak, and, by publishing it, inevitably to influence the proceedings in court.

Eremin formulates his accusations clearly and precisely: incitement to terrorism, crimes against the Soviet regime, aiding and abetting the most fanatical and ruthless enemies of Communism, assistance to warmongers. Kedrina, who claims that she is not attempting to define Sinyavsky's and Daniel's guilt in legal terms, proceeds a few paragraphs further on to do just that by using the words "anti-Soviet propaganda" and "an illustration to the Fascist program of bloody wars and *putsches*." The court has yet to decide whether anything in the activities of the accused amounts to crimes against the Soviet system and its laws, but the authors of the two articles ignore this task facing the judges, the prosecutor, the defense counsel, the witnesses and all who take part in the complex judicial procedure; no doubt, they regard such "refinements" as unnecessary, for to them everything is clear in advance. It seems to me that this is blatant disrespect for the court and for the important work which faces it—a disrespect bordering on the nihilist view that judicial procedure is nothing but an empty formula. I am amazed that two of the most important organs of the national press should have published such articles without so much as an editorial qualification or comment of any sort.

There is another point I should like to stress. It is clear even to those who have little knowledge of legal matters that an author cannot be liable to prosecution merely for having published his work abroad (the appropriate court for this is *public opinion*), but only for the subversive, illegal character of his work. Hence the most exacting, grave and responsible task before the court is to define the character of the material evidence. This is the point on which the whole investigation hinges and the fate of the accused depends, and it is therefore particularly wrong to try to influence the members of the court in this respect. The court, after all, chooses its own experts and can always call for their assistance.

Yet in their articles Eremin and Kedrina seek to create the impression that there is no such problem here. They equate works of fiction (whatever their artistic merit) with provocative or propagandist appeals, slogans and calls for action, and they do this as lightheartedly as though it were perfectly natural to equate all these things. Thus Kedrina takes all Tertz's artistic devices (mentioning among them such specifically literary ones as the use of fantasy, of multilevel irony, of stylization and parody of the style of famous authors) and, without more ado, describes them as a disguise intended to conceal two or three stock themes of anti-Soviet propaganda. To make her point, Kedrina uses a device which is not admissible even in ordinary literary polemics, where what is at stake is a literary reputation—not a verdict in a court of law: she identifies the author's point of view with the one expressed by the words and actions of his characters. She writes in so many words: "Tertz is inseparable from the sordid world of his characters." Eremin makes use of the same device against Arzhak: "Through the works of his 'hero,' the author turns to the reader and suggests the following course of action." In support of her point of view, Kedrina also quotes an undoubtedly prejudiced witness—the White *émigré* Filippov. We know that even the *Continuation of a Legend* by A. Kuznetsov was published in France with an introduction which recalls Filippov's.§

The memory is still fresh in all our minds of a time when people were persecuted for being followers of Pereverzev or for "Weiss-manism-Morganism,"* and when opinions expressed in literary, scientific or philosophical works were denounced as "anti-Soviet disguises" which had to be "stripped off." And it is in the interests of Soviet legality and of the Soviet social order that every effort—even perhaps very special efforts—should be made to prevent such things from ever occurring in our lives again.

I do not know the authors who are to be tried, I have not read their works (with the exception of essays by Sinyavsky which were published in the Soviet press) and, needless to say, I do not claim to be a judge of the nature or the degree of their guilt. But neither can I refrain from voicing my radical opposition to tactless and indiscreet attempts at meddling with the course of justice and exerting psychological pressure on the judges.

Yours faithfully,

I. RODNYANSKAYA

Member of the Union of Soviet Writers

28 Studencheskaya ul., kv. 26,
Moscow
February 1, 1966

---

§ See note § on p. 128.
* Valerian Pereverzev (born 1882), a Marxist literary scholar. His work was denounced in the early thirties for alleged deviations from Marxism, and the school of literary criticism associated with his name was broken up. For "Weissmanism-Morganism," see note on p. 234.

Statements Offered for the Defense

The following four documents are written testimonials for the defense. None of them was admitted by the court although one of the statements—that of V. V. Ivanov—had been solicited by Sinyavsky's defense counsel.

Statement by A. A. Yakobson

To the Presidium of the Supreme Soviet of the R.S.F.S.R.

I, Anatoli Alexandrovich Yakobson, poet and translator, member of the literary board of the Soviet Writer publishing house,† intended to come forward as an independent witness in the case of Y. Daniel, who is being tried together with A. Sinyavsky. Daniel and his defense counsel, however, thought it best to call me as witness for the defense, and notified the court to this effect. I consider it my duty to give the widest publicity to the statement I had intended to make before the court.

I have known Daniel for ten years. I know him well, closely—he is my friend. I know him professionally—we are members of the same writers' group. Daniel is honorable, sincere, independent of mind and generous. He is disinterested, high-principled, in every sense worthy of his wartime calling as a soldier of the country which defeated

---

† Sovetski Pisatel: The publishing house of the Union of Soviet Writers.

Fascism. Daniel has always loved his country and his people, while being at the same time a convinced internationalist. He always believed that a man who loves his country does not blind himself to what is wrong with it, but actively struggles against it. The writer's weapon in this struggle is the free printed word. I had not until recently read the books Daniel published abroad. But, knowing him, I could not believe they were directed against our people, slanderous or hostile to our society. I could not believe the newspaper articles which said so.

Daniel is a writer, not a professional politician, but his judgments as a citizen were always in keeping with the spirit of the 20th and 23rd Party Congresses.

In view of the forthcoming trial, I found means of reading his books. Article 70 of the Criminal Code of the R.S.F.S.R., under which Sinyavsky and Daniel are being charged, defines anti-Soviet literature as literature which calls for the undermining or weakening of the Soviet regime. Reading Daniel's works, I became convinced that they were not anti-Soviet. They are, first and foremost, works of literature and do not contain any incitement, or statement, or deduction, or program of a political sort, whether anti-Soviet or any other. They do, however, show concern with public affairs and are directed against Stalinism, its aftereffects and all attempts to revive it in our society. This civic message accounts for Daniel's use of satirical narrative as a means of protest, his use of hyperbole, his imaginative treatment of real life. What is good in our society is neither mocked nor insulted in Daniel's stories. If what he describes is not always good, this is not his fault but that of the nature of satire, the art form he has chosen (as it was chosen by Gogol, Saltykov-Shchedrin and, in our days by Zoschenko, or Ilf and Petrov). Evil—not good—is the object of satire. And in accordance with the nature of satire, evil appears in Daniel's stories in a caricatured, grotesque form. But, castigating evil, the author does not give way to bitterness, cynicism or even political scepticism; he has an unshakable faith in the triumph of humanity, justice and goodness. In This Is Moscow Speaking the positive humanist idea, which underlies the whole story, comes out clearly behind the negative satirical images. Someone wickedly plans a "Public Murder Day" to take place throughout the country (let us recall the terror of 1937–38 and the "public" trials of those years, let us recall the lawlessness of the postwar period, the "Leningrad Affair,"‡ the "Doctors' Plot" and the rest). How should a thinking Soviet citizen react to such a "measure"? Just like the hero of the story, who goes out into the street, into the crowd and, by his own example of fearlessness and inner freedom, helps others to remain human in spite of the insane orders they have been given. This is the attitude of the majority, this turns out to be the attitude of the people as a whole, and thanks to this—as the story shows—the whole wicked business comes to nothing.

The individual and collective responsibility of the citizen for whatever takes place in their country—this is the theme of *This Is Moscow Speaking*, and the story shows that this sense of responsibility is already becoming effective in our society.

I will try to sum up the civic message of the other stories Daniel published abroad. I should emphasize that I am talking about them only as social criticism—not about their content as a whole, which is much richer.

"Hands": this story condemns the excesses of the Red Terror§ during the early years of the Soviet regime. We know how harshly these excesses were condemned by Lenin himself. We need only recall how severely he reprimanded Dzerzhinsky and Ordzhonikidze for the violence in Georgia in 1922.*

"Atonement": this deals with the atmosphere of treachery, denunciation and slander which was generated by the cult of Stalin's personality. It describes how, after the air of our country had been

---

‡ The Leningrad Affair (1949–50) was the purge, details of which have still not been disclosed, of the party organization in Leningrad. Most of the city's leading officials were arrested, and some were executed. For the "Doctors' Plot," see note * on p. 95.

§ The official term for the mass reprisals by the Cheka (see note on p. 67) against enemies, real or supposed, of the new Soviet regime. This reign of terror was sanctioned by a decree of the Council of People's Commissars of September 5, 1918.

* Felix Dzerzhinsky (1877–1926), first head of the Cheka; Grigori Ordzhonikidze (1886–1937), prominent Bolshevik leader responsible for Caucasian affairs in the early years after the Revolution. Lenin's reprimand to them (and to Stalin) in March, 1923 (not 1922), is not, strictly speaking, relevant; Lenin was complaining not of violence by the Cheka, but of Ordzhonikidze's "rudeness" toward other Georgian Bolshevik leaders. See V. I. Lenin, *Polnoye Sobranie Sochinenii*, Moscow, 1965, Vol. 54, p. 329.

cleared of this pollution, one honest man could still be destroyed by the fumes of the past suddenly rising around him as a result of a tragic misunderstanding.

"The Man from Minap" has no serious purpose whatsoever. It is playful, mischievous, largely frivolous. What is so frightening about it? Can it really be the fact that the character who is satirized pictures Karl Marx in his imagination "without due respect" and in a not altogether proper context? We find more or less the same kind of thing in Mayakovsky's *Bathhouse*.[†] As a man who was not devoid of humor, Karl Marx himself would only have been amused by this story. The only "sinful" thing about it—as about the others—is that it was published abroad.

Yet the mere fact of having works of literature published abroad is not criminal under Soviet law. Furthermore, the Soviet Government has signed the UNO "Declaration on the Rights of Man," which, in Article 19, states that everybody has the right to disseminate his ideas by any available means, independently of state frontiers.

Is it that publishing a work of literature abroad, though not a crime, is somehow improper or reprehensible from a moral point of view? No, it is not reprehensible from the point of view of any honest man, so long of course as the work itself is honest. Naturally, it would have been better if Daniel had been able to publish his works at home, but this unfortunately was impossible—it was made impossible by the still-persisting fear, our fear of being faced with a frank and harsh exposure of our own failings. It was this impossibility that impelled the writer to disseminate his works "by any available means."

Is it right to blame an author (as is being done in this case) for the fact that a part of the foreign press has used his work for anti-Soviet propaganda? But didn't it make a similar use of the facts revealed by the 20th and 23rd Party Congresses, and is not the impact of facts incomparably greater than that of any work of fiction? Not everything foreigners praise in our life is a discredit to us (e.g., the 20th Congress), nor is everything they attack in it necessarily good (e.g., the campaigns which took place against genetics and cybernetics, or the persecution of "cosmopolitans").

---

† See note † on p. 61.

Works of literature should not be judged by the subjective interpretation someone might put on them, but by what in fact, objectively, they contain. Daniel's stories do not contain anything anti-Soviet. In trying to prove that they did, our papers used dishonest means. Quotations were torn from their context and distorted, the words of the characters were passed off as those of the author. In such a way, any author can be accused of anything. Pushkin can be shown to be a villain (by quoting Salieri);[‡] Saltykov-Shchedrin, a sadist and a hypocrite (by quoting Yudushka Golovev). Chekhov, an obscurantist and a degenerate (by quoting from "The Letter to a Learned Neighbor"); Sholokhov, a barefaced counterrevolutionary (by quoting the words of many of the characters in *And Quiet Flows the Don*, including those of the author's favorite, Grigori Melekhov).

I, too, will quote some passages, but only those which, *taken in the context*, show the author's point of view:

From "Atonement":

"No, the war was not for me what it was to some Fritz or Hans. I didn't have to fight it just because I was called up. The war was my war."

"What were you talking about? Swearing at Russia, were you? We've always sworn at her, all along the way, ever since the times of St. Vladimir.[§] Newspapermen write that those who talk like that bite the hand that feeds them. Idiots! Isn't it my own hand?"

From *This Is Moscow Speaking*:

"You are up in arms on behalf of the Soviet regime? You think that one should stick up for it?" "Of course one should, for the *real* Soviet regime."

My father was a commissar in the civil war and I think he knew what he was fighting for. I have read his letters, and I feel that people of our generation have no right to talk nonsense about those days.

I walk along the street; a quiet homely boulevard—I feel the notebook in my hands and I think how what I have written could have been written by anybody of my generation and background who, like me, loves this wretched, this beautiful country. My judgments about it and its people have been both better and worse than they should have been. But who will hold this against me? As I walk along, I say to myself: "This is your

---

‡ From Pushkin's poem *Mozart and Salieri* (1830).
§ The first Christian ruler of Russia (eleventh century).

world, your life and you are a cell, a particle in it. You must not allow yourself to be intimidated. You must answer for yourself, and you will thereby answer for others as well." And with a soft murmur of unconscious agreement, of surprised approval, they respond to me, these endless streets and squares, embankments, trees and slumbering steamboats of buildings which are sailing in a gigantic convoy into the unknown. This is Moscow speaking.

Doesn't all this show that the author is a true patriot? And I would also like to remind the court of the words of another patriot, Peter Chaadayev: "I have never learned to love my country with my eyes shut, with bowed head and sealed lips. I consider that no one can be useful to his country unless he sees it clearly; I think that the time for blind infatuations is past. . . . I suppose that we have come after others in order not to fall into their mistakes, illusions and superstitions."

I call on the court to listen to the voice of conscience, to the voice of justice, to the voice of the foreign friends of the Soviet Union who have spoken up in defense of Sinyavsky and Daniel. I call on the court to think of the international prestige of our country. I call on the court to acquit Sinyavsky and Daniel.

February 9, 1966

I was not admitted as a witness by the court. None of the witnesses called by Daniel's counsel was summoned to appear.

February 12, 1966

A. YAKOBSON

Letter from I. Golomshtok

To the Supreme Court of the R.S.F.S.R.
Copies to: The Editors of Izvestia
The Editors of Literary Gazette

I ask you to place this letter in the record of the case of A.D. Sinyavsky as evidence in his defense.

I have made a careful study of all the works published abroad under the pseudonym "Abram Tertz," of the criticism of them in our press (Eremin's article in *Izvestia* of January 13 and Kedrina's in *Literary Gazette* of January 22, the reactions of workers to [Eremin's article, in *Izvestia* of January 17], and I have come to the firm conclusion that Sinyavsky's arrest and his forthcoming trial are the result of a tragic misunderstanding brought about by a misinterpretation of the nature of these works (evidently due to insufficient knowledge of them) and also by malice on the part of certain persons. I am convinced that this is so by the treatment of these works as "anti-Soviet," and by the monstrous textual distortions and undisguised slander to be found in the articles of Kedrina and Eremin, who has contrived to discover in these works anti-Semitism, pornography, plagiarism and so forth. If this was a purely literary discussion, then there would be no point in wasting words on it—the absurdity of these accusations would be obvious to anyone who had read Sinyavsky's work. But the affair may have dire consequences not only for Sinyavsky, who is threatened with undeserved punishment, but also for the prestige of our country. It is this that prompts me to put my opinion of his work in writing, if only to show that not everybody in our country thinks the same as Kedrina and Eremin.

A. D. Sinyavsky's writing (published under the pseudonym Abram Tertz) may be described as the fruit of deep and sometimes agonizing reflections on the state of modern civilization, as the work of a mature writer with sharp insights into the contradictions which disturb and torment modern man—and this not only in socialist society. The problems which he raises concern the alienation of the individual from society, the contradiction between technical progress and the spiritual emptiness of man, the relationship between means and ends, etc. These problems stand at the heart of modern culture. They constitute the inner sense of the work of Kafka and Joyce, Faulkner and Hemingway, Böll and Steinbeck, Babel and Pasternak; in another, more indirect guise, they also appear in music, the cinema and the visual arts. We come face to face with these problems when we look at paintings by Picasso and Léger, when we listen to a symphony by Shostakovich or Hindemith, when we look at films by Chaplin, Fellini, Kavalerovich and Eisenstein. These problems are imposed on modern man by the enormous complexity of twentieth-century life, which is shot through with acute contradictions of a sort unknown to any previous age. To deny that these problems confront our society as well is not only to contradict the basic teachings of Marxism, but also to fly in the face of common sense and the facts of our everyday experience. Nobody who claims to call himself a modern writer can afford to close his eyes to them.

Like any other writer, Sinyavsky studies these problems as they affect the scene he knows and loves best. The action of his novels and stories takes place not in outer space, not in some make-believe country, but in the communal apartments and in the small towns of the vast expanses of Russia, of which the author not only has a superb knowledge, but which he also loves in a very real sense. The events and people he describes, whether they are intensely true to life or the product of pure fantasy, only provide the subject matter for his work and do not embody any particular "message." All the same, these two concepts (subject matter and message) are often confused by people who are inclined to see works of art as mere illustrations of political ideas.

It may be that the description of Sinyavsky's work as "anti-Soviet" is the result of some such confusion. To level accusations against Sinyavsky because he uses Soviet life as his raw material is just as ludicrous as, say, to charge Picasso with insulting mankind because in his paintings he breaks up the forms of the human body, or to treat Kafka as an enemy of the Austrian way of life, or to denounce Faulkner for anti-Americanism. The sense of Sinyavsky's work is too complex and deep to be summed up by any general terms. It has to be discussed in specific terms.

The collection of *Fantastic Stories* opens with "The Grapho-maniacs." This is a tale about the eternal human need for artistic expression, which, irrespective of a person's talents, capabilities or qualifications, is stronger than any external circumstances, and which the author rather ironically describes as graphomania. The author talks about creative expression as a kind of spiritual need which has no particular end in view but is just as essential as the need to breathe, and he embodies his ideas about it in material taken from life. It is significant that this is the first story in the collection and that it is subtitled "From the Story of My Life." It was just such a need to express himself and be published, not any political aim, that made Sinyavsky start to write. And he succeeded where the hero of his story failed. Here, as indeed in all Sinyavsky's works, it is impossible to identify the author with his characters, and any attempt, like that of Eremin, to attribute to Sinyavsky himself the wretched graphomaniac Straustin's impotent rage against the classics can scarcely be explained by mere ignorance in literary matters.

The story "At the Circus" is too straightforward and devoid of political undertones to need special comment. However, even here Kedrina and Eremin managed to discover an element of anti-Semitism on the grounds that the story has a character with a Jewish name.

"You and I," "The Tenants" and "The Icicle" convey the tragic feelings of the small man, or of man in general, that his fate depends on obscure and incomprehensible forces which assume the shape of wood sprites and mermaids, of a mysterious eye which looks down from above, reading the hero's thoughts and watching his every move, or of Colonel Tarasov, the policeman who evolves from a simple gendarme to a kind of half-organic crystal in the distant future. In these stories one can see the influence of the tragic world of Kafka, the style of Remizov and images from Russian fairy tales, but there is certainly no anti-Soviet propaganda.

The short novel *The Trial Begins* is more concerned with matters of public interest. Judging by its date (1956) it is the author's earliest work, and it dealt with times by then already past. But even here a specific theme set in the days of the cult of personality is used by Sinyavsky as the raw material for the treatment of a more general idea—the problem of means and ends. This problem is not a new one. Dostoyevsky brooded over it. Marx wrote that evil means can discredit the highest aim. The relationship between means and ends was perverted under the cult of personality, and the Jesuitical slogan about "the end justifying the means" was used as an excuse for mass arrests and the destruction of thousands of innocent people. Criticism of these consequences of the cult of personality is recorded in party documents and in numerous articles published in the Soviet press. *The Trial Begins* is also critical of the anti-Marxist and inhuman attitude [to means and ends] which was revived during the

Ezhov and Beria terror. To call this criticism "anti-Soviet" would be tantamount to saying that the lawlessness, mass arrests and anti-Semitism in the days of the cult of personality were not the result of a perversion of the basic ideas of the Soviet system, but natural manifestations of them. This is a patent absurdity. Unfortunately, it appears in practice that it is possible to resort to literary fraud, as Kedrina has done, and to represent the utterances of a character in the story, the interrogator Globov who is preparing the case against the "murder-doctors," as anti-Semitic outbursts on the part of Sinyavsky himself, and thus to mislead the Soviet judiciary and the Soviet public who have not read the novel. But this sort of thing comes under the article of the Criminal Code on slander, an article which protects Soviet citizens against "arguments" of this type.

It is true that in the epilogue the author describes a camp in Kolyma in 1956, in which he places his narrator who has been accused of writing "pornography and anti-Soviet propaganda." This might give cause to charge Sinyavsky with a distortion of the truth, since, as is well known, political camps were already a thing of the past by 1956. But wasn't Sinyavsky right to see in our present-day life signs of a potential return to the past? After all, the actual arrest of Sinyavsky, which is not a fictional event, only shows how right he was. Isn't this arrest a dangerous throwback to the past? The reasons for it are quite incomprehensible, and the tone of these newspaper articles attacking Sinyavsky and Daniel is far too reminiscent of 1937.

Finally, there is Sinyavsky's last and most important work, the novel *Lyubimov*. This is perhaps his most complicated work, the richest in content and the most accomplished in form. Here, too, the underlying idea concerns the relation between ends and means, and it is this that determines the whole literary fabric of the story.

. . . By means of hypnosis the bicycle mechanic Lenya Tikhomirov overthrows the constituted authority in the town of Lyubimov and sets up his own dictatorship. He is prompted by the good intention of creating an ideal social system in the town, but his only means for the achievement of this aim is the exercise of his own will power. He soon realizes that one cannot create happiness on earth simply by an effort of the will. His will, though employed only to do good, suddenly begins to produce nightmarish effects. The "ideal" society collapses and the dictator himself takes to his heels, anxious only to escape from a situation of his own making, even to hide in his own pocket. This is the fantastic plot of the story. Can the novel be regarded as a caricature of our revolution, of the development of our society? Of course not. Insofar as it is a satire, it is a satire on any one-man dictatorship, on any political mass hypnotism, on any superman who thinks he can exploit the ignorant masses in his own interests; these are things which we have witnessed in various parts of the world in the twentieth century. If this satire applies to our country as well, it does so only insofar as such things have happened here—once again in the days of the cult of personality.

In her article Z. Kedrina quotes the White émigré Filippov, who treats the novel as a satire on Communist society. But let us bear in mind that Saltykov-Shchedrin's *History of the Town of Glupov* is also treated by bourgeois students of our literature as a satire on the Soviet system. And since when have the words of White émigrés become arguments for accusations against Soviet writers? A writer cannot answer for every arbitrary interpretation which may be put on his work. He is responsible only for ideas and facts which he himself states directly. But on this level it is impossible to find anything anti-Soviet in Sinyavsky's writings. On the contrary, *Lyubimov* is full of love for Russia (one only has to think of the nature descriptions, or the scene, tinged with a double irony, of Lenya's meeting with the American imperialists);* it is written in the best traditions of Russian literature and only an unscrupulous critic like Z. Kedrina can talk of plagiarism.

One sometimes finds in Sinyavsky's books secret policemen who fall down on the job, secretaries "available to any proofreader" and failures soured by life. But how can one see in such figures caricatures of the Soviet people and the Soviet system as a whole? The same mistake was made about the work of such writers as Zoschenko, Akhmatova, Pasternak and Babel. Do we have to repeat these old mistakes?

By the very nature of his talent Sinyavsky is very far from being a political satirist or publicist. He is a writer of great philosophical

---

* *The Makepeace Experiment*, p. 108.

range, and the "message" of his works goes far beyond their specific social setting. One may not agree with certain of his views and ideas, and one might well reproach him for being too pessimistic, but no writer has yet been brought to trial for pessimism.

Our literature suffered too many losses in the period of the cult of personality. We should not add to the list of victims.

I. GOLOMSHTOK
Art Historian, Member of the Union of Soviet Artists

Statement by V. V. Ivanov

To the Legal Aid Office[†] of the Bauman District (in reply to their inquiry)

Having recently read the works of Abram Tertz, in connection with which A. D. Sinyavsky is being charged, I hereby state that they contain nothing which could give grounds for criminal proceedings.

Most of the works of A. Tertz are written in the form of the *skaz* (the word is used here in a technical sense), which is traditional in our literature. The main feature of the *skaz* is that the story is narrated in the words of one of the characters, not in the words of the author. Therefore, everything said in the story in the first person (e.g., in *Lyubimov*) comes from the narrator-hero of the story and not from its author. As is clear particularly from the concluding chapter of the novel [*Lyubimov*], the author takes a highly critical view of the fictional character of his own creation. As is usual in prose fiction of the *skaz* type, some of what the narrator says is introduced with the deliberate purpose of showing the reader that the narrator is a substantially different person from the author. The gap between the fictional author (i.e., the narrator in whose words the story and the descriptive passages are written) and the real author is also obvious in *The Trial Begins*—the epilogue of the story is particularly

---

† *Yuridicheskaya konsultatsia*: there are no private lawyers in the Soviet Union and persons requiring legal aid or advice must apply to these offices, which are under the control of the Ministry of Justice.

striking in this respect. For this reason, isolated quotations from these two stories, even if they are written in the first person, cannot be attributed to Abram Tertz, and still less can they be used in criminal proceedings against him. Failure to understand this can only be the result of inability (or refusal) to take account of the distinctive features of literature, and in particular of the *skaz* form which is characteristic of the Russian prose tradition.

This *skaz* form with its fictitious narrator, who is basically different from the actual author, was used by Pushkin in *The Tales of Belkin* and *The History of the Village of Goryukhino*, in both of which the story is narrated by an invented character.

This device was further developed by Gogol and his successors, particularly by Dostoyevsky (who noted in his letters that in his stories it was not he himself but his characters who were speaking), and by Leskov. This form of narrative later reached the peak of its development in Soviet prose of the 1920's, when it was also the object of theoretical study in the works of V. M. Eikhenbaum, M. M. Bakhtin and other researchers into the structure of the literary language. I have already had occasion to write elsewhere about the connection between these theoretical studies and the practical use of the *skaz* in Soviet literature (see my comments in the book by Vygodsky, *The Psychology of Art*, Moscow, 1965, p. 362). After the structural studies by these Soviet scholars one may say that it is normal in works on the language of literature, both in the Soviet Union and abroad, to put special emphasis, when talking about artistic prose of the *skaz* type, on "the speech of another" (Bakhtin's term), of the narrator as distinct from the author. This commonplace of modern scholarship must constantly be borne in mind in any discussion of the work of Abram Tertz, a gifted writer who is carrying on this particular tradition in Russian literature. It should be noted that, in linguistic terms, the forms of the first person singular of the pronoun and the corresponding verbal forms do not, in *skaz* prose, and hence in the works of Abram Tertz, refer to the actual author. To give an example from classical Russian prose, it would be absurd to imagine that Pushkin is speaking about himself in the following lines of *The History of Goryukhino*: "The vocation of a man of letters always seemed to me enviable. My parents, worthy folk, but simple souls of old-fashioned upbringing, never read anything and in the whole house there were no books save for an ABC which had been bought for me, some almanacs and the latest letter writer." Or this, for example: "Thus did my respect for Russian literature cost me thirty kopeks in lost change, a reprimand from my superiors, and I might even have been arrested—but it was all for nothing." It would be just as absurd to imagine that, for example, the epilogue of *The Trial Begins* is actually about the arrest of the novel's real-life author, or that in *Lyubimov* and "The Graphomaniacs" we are dealing with a direct expression of the author's thoughts.

These unquestionable facts about the nature of *skaz* prose make it clear beyond any doubt that quotations from fiction written in this form cannot be quoted in evidence to support criminal charges against their author. Moreover, the scholarly arguments I have mentioned above should be enough to show that prose written in artistic form cannot by its very nature serve as grounds for the prosecution of the author under a law in which the term "literature" is used in a general sense, without any indication that it here applies to creative writing, let alone to literature in the form of *skaz*. Thus, from a scholarly point of view, the very notion of a criminal prosecution of the author is untenable.

In *The Trial Begins* and "The Icicle" there are satirical portraits of officials of the security services and the Public Prosecutor's office which all relate to the period preceding 1953 (except in the epilogue, of which I have spoken above). The activities of these agencies in that period have been the object of more or less severe criticism in our press. These passages in Abram Tertz's work are therefore in no way different from a large number of other literary works, memoirs and articles which have been published in this country since 1956. If it is intended to try the author of the works of Abram Tertz for criticizing the activities of the security services and the Public Prosecutor's office before 1953, then this should be openly stated. It would then have to be said outright that the investigation of [Sinyavsky's] case is an attempt to reverse the judgment on these matters formed by our public opinion during the last ten years.

Lyubimov is not a political work and cannot by any stretch of the imagination be interpreted as such. The plot of the story is based on the acceptance of completely fantastic premises which are quite remote from the facts of real life. It is enough to think of the super-natural psychological powers of the hero and of the miracles he performs with their help, of the introduction into the story of the dead author of an ancient book which is the source of the hero's magic powers. Of course one might take a negative view of this use of fantasy in literature, but it is impossible to put someone on trial for it. If one insists on interpreting the story as being something other than a work of the imagination, then one could make it out to be the story of how a young adventurer vainly tries to change the system in one of our small towns. The young man himself is portrayed in satirical fashion, as a clearly negative character. Why should the portrayal of an enemy of our system of government be regarded as a threat to it? One might argue about whether the author's portrait of Tikhomirov is successful or not, but again there are no grounds here for legal proceedings.

There are also elements of fantasy in *The Trial Begins*—it is part of a cycle of "fantastic stories," and this alone makes it impossible to interpret it on a purely realistic level. I should mention, for instance, the business of the filters in the sewage system,[†] which is needed to motivate the story's epilogue, and only underlines the unreal, purely make-believe nature of this epilogue. Apart from the works men-tioned above and the series of *Fantastic Stories*, which are talented examples of fantasy in *skaz* form and are quite unconnected with politics, Abram Tertz is also credited with an essay *On Socialist Realism* (which I have read in the version published anonymously in the French magazine *Esprit* in 1959). This essay is a critical study of the problems of the history of our literature in the nineteenth and twentieth centuries, and there is a detailed discussion of the origin of the so-called "theory of lack of conflict,"[§] which was heavily criti-cized in the early 1950's. The essay takes issue in a restrained way with some of the things said by N. S. Khrushchev about art and

---

† See note § on p. 95.

§ *"Teoria bezkonfliktnosti."* This was denounced in 1952 as a "distortion" of socialist realism, of which it was a *reductio ad absurdum*. Its proponents argued that, since there were no basic conflicts in Soviet society, there was no need to depict serious conflicts in literature either. (See note † on p. 57.)

literature, but this does not in itself provide grounds for criminal charges against the author. Further, the author writes about distortions of Marxist doctrines on a number of points in the days of the cult of personality, but he insists over and over again that he has no quarrel with the basic principles of the Soviet system, which for him have an aura of revolutionary romanticism. In any case, his way of talking about this question provides no basis for a criminal prosecution. It should be emphasized that the essay notes the triumph of Marxism in our age and the absence of any other ideology that could hold its own with Marxism.

Neither the essay, therefore, nor the works of fiction of Abram Tertz provide grounds for legal proceedings. If A. Sinyavsky is that author, then he has nothing to answer for in a court of law.

As regards the articles on literature and art published by A. Sinyavsky in our press, there is no question whatsoever that they are of very great value. The recently published study of Russian poetry in the early years of the Revolution, of which A. Sinyavsky is co-author, represents, in effect, the first serious treatment of this subject, a subject which is of exceptional importance not only for a scholarly understanding of the early period in Soviet poetry but also for the popularization of its achievements. In addition to this work A. Sinyavsky wrote detailed chapters for a history of Soviet literature,* and last year he published a major article on Boris Pasternak as an introduction to the first scholarly edition to appear in this country of the great poet's work; this essay was a sequel to A. Sinyavsky's earlier articles on Boris Pasternak (it should be noted that Pasternak himself had a very high opinion of Sinyavsky's work about his poetry, picking it out for special praise among all the very numerous Soviet and foreign publications on the subject). Sinyavsky's studies are distinguished by a combination of deep insight into the nature of the actual poetry with painstaking scholarly analysis of the structure of Pasternak's poetry and the laws governing it. In his essay on Pasternak's poetry, and in his other studies mentioned above, Sinyavsky has reached conclusions about the phonetic and semantic texture of poetry

---

* Sinyavsky contributed chapters on Maxim Gorky and the poet Edward Bagritsky to Vols. I and II of a history of Soviet Russian literature published by the Academy of Sciences. See note on p. 153.

which are of exceptional interest for the modern structural theory of poetic language. The book on Picasso, of which Sinyavsky is one of the authors, has great importance for the scholarly study of art, particularly for the semantics of art. In his critical reviews A. D. Sinyavsky has done a great deal by way of distinguishing the real achievements of Soviet literature from stuff that has no literary worth; he is careful to show the difference between real art and trash which is harmful for our society—one only has to remember his criticism of the work by Shevtsov, *The Blight*. For all these reasons an interruption in the literary activities of A. D. Sinyavsky cannot but have negative consequences for the progress of our literature. At the same time, as is evident from the above, there are no legal grounds whatsoever for such an interruption, which would cause nothing but harm to our literature and would be useful only to its enemies.

February 3, 1966

V. V. IVANOV

Candidate of Philological Sciences; Head of the Department of Structural Typology of the Slav Languages in the Institute of Slavic Studies of the Academy of Sciences of the U.S.S.R.; Chairman of the Committee on Structural Linguistics in the Department of Semantics of the Learned Council for Cybernetics of the Academy of Sciences of the U.S.S.R.

Letter from V. D. Meniker

To the Moscow City Court
Copies to: The Central Committee of the CPSU
　　　　　The Supreme Court of the R.S.F.S.R.
　　　　　The Editor of Izvestia

I have learned from articles published in the Soviet and foreign press that the writers A. Sinyavsky and Y. Daniel have been arrested on charges of anti-Soviet propaganda.

Since the documents used to prove this charge (Articles 88 and 83 of the Criminal Procedural Code of the R.S.F.S.R.) at their trial will presumably be the literary works published abroad under the pen names "Abram Tertz" and "Nikolai Arzhak," and since I am acquainted with these works, I consider it my right (Article 70, parts II and III) and my obligation (Article 73 of the Criminal Procedural Code of the R.S.F.S.R.) to put before you everything I know about this case.

I hope that, in accordance with Article 70, part III, and Article 292 of the Criminal Procedural Code of the R.S.F.S.R., the court will make public the following evidence, submitted by me, or will make it possible for me to do so myself.†

A thorough examination of the work published under the pen names "A. Tertz" and "N. Arzhak" shows that

a. These are works of literature.

b. Such political themes as are to be found in them are bound up with the criticism of the cult of personality and its aftereffects, which is in line with the policy of the CPSU and of the whole country, as implemented since the 20th Party Congress.

c. The supposed use of the said works (whether in full or in part) for purposes of anti-Soviet propaganda (in the form of pamphlets, newspaper articles, broadcasts, etc.) cannot be held against the authors if they did not give their consent to it.

On the first of these three points, I cannot claim to be more competent than the average reader, but I venture to draw the attention of the court to the fact that, for all their harshness toward these works, neither *Literary Gazette* (of January 22, 1966), the official organ of the Union of Soviet Writers, nor the article by the writer D. Eremin (*Izvestia*, January 13, 1966) treats them as anything but works of literature. Even the literary expert Z. Kedrina, once she has "struggled through the seemingly impassable jungle of rhetoric," sets a very low value on the "propaganda potential" of these works and, with understandable caution, refrains from defining the guilt of the authors.

---

† The articles in the Criminal Procedural Code (*ugolovno-protsessualny kodeks R.S.F.S.R.*) referred to here cover the use of documents as evidence (Arts. 88 and 83), the right and obligation of private individuals to offer evidence (Arts. 70 and 73) and the requirement that documents admitted in evidence be made public (Art. 292).

This is understandable to any reader of these works who cares for the true prestige and well-being of our country.

The action in the stories of Tertz and Arzhak takes place in the years when the party and the government were headed by Stalin, and the state security services by Beria. They also touch on those years when voluntarism and subjectivism were affecting the conduct of our country's politics, economics and culture.

To the best of my knowledge, there is no party document which claims that all manifestations of the cult of personality ceased with the death of Stalin and the removal of Beria. Indeed, the very opposite is suggested by the minutes of the October (1964) plenum of the Central Committee‡ those of the plenum of 1965, or by the heading of the Central Committee resolution of June 30, 1956, which still remains in force: "On the overcoming of the cult of personality and its consequences." I doubt if any court would think of preferring a charge of anti-Soviet propaganda against comrade Palmiro Togliatti, who wrote that, in the Soviet Union, "the rate at which survivals of the cult of personality are being liquidated is too slow" (Pravda August 18, 1964).

Which manifestations of the cult of personality did Tertz and Arzhak attack in particular? It is difficult to answer this question briefly. Not even Solzhenitsyn or Ehrenburg has drawn so striking a series of portraits of people endowed with the qualities characteristic of the cult of personality; yet these qualities are never ascribed to Soviet life or to Soviet society as a whole. In every case there is an *individual character* who illustrates these features which, it seems to me, Tertz and Arzhak denounce with compelling literary skill. There is, for example, the political demagogue Lenya Tikhomirov (in Tertz's *Lyubimov*) or the cynic and hypocrite Globov (in Tertz's *The Trial Begins*), who preaches that "the end justifies the means" (he is not, as you see, intended to be a typical "Soviet man," as Kedrina asserts); there is also Volodya Zalesski (in Arzhak's "Man from Minap"), as immoral in his attitude to social questions as in his

---

‡ This was the plenum at which Khrushchev was dismissed. Press comment at the time (e.g., *Pravda* of October 17, 1964) stressed the need for a continuing struggle against "the cult of personality," and there was implied criticism of Khrushchev for "voluntarism" and "subjectivism."

daily life; or Colonel Tarasov, a voluntarist in politics (in Tertz's "Icicle"); or the talebearers and informers who thrive around these men, and the cowardly and cynical intellectuals (such as the lawyer Karlinsky, or the history teacher in Tertz's *The Trial Begins*).

But, as we know, "the cult of personality could not and did not alter the nature of our social system" (*CPSU Resolutions*, 7th edition, Vol. 4, p. 231). Accordingly, Tertz and Arzhak also portray characters who illustrate the best qualities of the Soviet people—characters who fight the cult of personality and all its manifestations. Such is the honest youth Seryozha Globov, who is shocked by the violation of Leninist agrarian practice and bewildered by the theory that Shamil's revolt was antipopular;§ such is the old Bolshevik, Seryozha's aunt (in Tertz's *The Trial Begins*); such is Anatoli Kartsev (in Arzhak's *This Is Moscow Speaking*), a man who went through the whole war and who protests against senseless murder. If there are people he would like to destroy, he does not hate them because they "represent the socialist system and carry out the policy of the state"— he hates them because of what they have done to the country.

This recurrent theme—hatred of the personality cult in the name of those truly revolutionary ideals cynically abused by its exponents— fully disproves the guilt of A. Sinyavsky and Y. Daniel. Let us turn to what these writers plainly say:

The image of the Revolution is as sacred, both to those who took part in it and to those who were born after it, as the image of a dead mother. It is easier for us to grant that everything that happened after the Revolution was its betrayal than to insult its memory by reproaches and suspicions. (A. Tertz, *On Socialist Realism*, quoted from *Dissent*, 1960, No. 1.)

Should our enemies conquer us and make us return to the prerevolutionary mode of life (or incorporate us in Western democracy, which would be the same thing), then, I am sure, we would start once more from where we began. We would start from the Revolution. (*Ibid.* My italics. V.M.)

---

§ *The Trial Begins*, p. 17. Shamil (1798–1871), leader of an anti-Russian revolt in the Caucasus. The official Soviet attitude to him has changed frequently: in the thirties he was praised as a rebel against Czarist tyranny, but in the late forties he was denounced as an anti-Russian hireling of British imperialism.

. . . We must defend the true Soviet regime from those distortions which took place after the Revolution. (N. Arzhak, *This Is Moscow Speaking* quoted from *The Reporter* of August 16, 1962.)

Such are the basic attitudes expressed in these works.

Needless to say, anti-Soviet propaganda can use anything, including much that has been published in the Soviet press. Here again we can refer to party statements published since the 20th Congress. The best comment on the subject is the one made in the Central Committee resolution of June 30, 1956, mentioned above:

Schooled in the revolutionary tradition of Marxism Leninism, the Communist Party of the Soviet Union has told the whole truth, bitter as it is. In taking this step, it was guided by considerations of principle. It judged that, even if its condemnation of the cult of Stalin's personality should create certain difficulties in the short run, yet in the long view, from the standpoint of the basic interests of the working class, the result is bound to be an enormous gain. (*CPSU Resolutions*, 7th edition, Vol. 4, pp. 224–225.)

In the light of this very definite party directive, the actions of A. Sinyavsky and Y. Daniel fall under Article 14 of the Criminal Code of the R.S.F.S.R.* and cannot therefore be regarded as crimes, for the damage caused by the personality cult and its consequences is much greater than the harm alleged to have been caused by the publication of these authors' works abroad.

May I draw your attention to the fact that abroad the works of Tertz and Arzhak were called anti-Soviet only in such brief news items and comments as appeared after the arrest of Sinyavsky and Daniel. The only exceptions were the writings of the White émigré Filippov.

As for those British and American reviewers who have read Tertz's and Arzhak's works at all attentively, they say just the opposite:

"There is no doubt that the author [Tertz—V.M.] is a product of the Communist Party of Soviet Russia, and that he accepts the ideology of Marxism-Leninism. . . ." (*Soviet Studies*, 1960, No. 4, p. 434.)

---

* Article 14 provides for exoneration from criminal responsibility in the case of actions undertaken in an emergency, and with the intention of safeguarding the national interest.

"The author [Tertz—V.M.] fully accepts the Revolution, does not wish the pre-revolutionary way of life to be restored, and does not share the ideas of western democracy. All he disagrees with are certain individual phenomena in Soviet life and letters." (*Russian Review*, 1964, No. 4, p. 411.)

"There is no doubt that Arzhak is personally opposed to the pressures which arise in a totalitarian state. But, as with Tertz, to see only this in his work is to miss a great deal.

"There is a strongly pro-Soviet tone in the works of Arzhak." (*New Leader*, November 8, 1965, p. 18.)

Even the Polish *émigré* Czeslaw Milosz points out that Arzhak does not regard himself as divorced from Soviet life and literature and that, in speaking of them he says "we," "our," etc. Milosz sees the essay *On Socialist Realism* as "a contribution to the debate carried on by Soviet writers at home." (*Dissent*, 1960, No. 4.)

Similar views were also expressed in *The New Leader* of May 13, 1963 and July 19, 1965; *The Slavic Review*, No. 3, 1961; *The New York Times Book Review* of November 8, 1964, etc.

Finally, I should like to draw the attention of the court to the fact that the publication of the article "Turncoats" in *Izvestia* of January 13, 1966, was a breach of the law. It is not only that, in accordance with Article 181 of the Criminal Code of the R.S.F.S.R., the article itself can be defined as "fabricated evidence in support of a charge," i.e., a false denunciation. The important point is that *Izvestia* is the organ of the Supreme Soviet of the U.S.S.R., which, through the Supreme Court of the U.S.S.R., controls the activity of all the lower courts in the country (*Directive Concerning the Supreme Court of the U.S.S.R.*, Articles 1 and 2). Consequently, even before the opening of the trial, there has been a violation of Article 16 of the Criminal Procedural Code of the R.S.F.S.R., according to which judges and people's assessors dealing with criminal cases must reach their decisions in conditions which preclude their being influenced from outside.

V. D. MENIKER

Research fellow of the Institute of Economics of the Academy of Sciences of the U.S.S.R.

[Beginning of February 1966]

Letter from A. Ginzburg

Alik Ginzburg is a young Soviet poet who first came into the news in 1960, when he was attacked in Izvestia (September 2) for editing a mimeograph poetry journal Syntax. He was at that time sentenced to two years' imprisonment for "fraud." In June, 1965, the Moscow evening newspaper Vechernyaya Moskva published a letter from him ("A reply to Mr. Hughes") in which he expressed regret for his past activities and denounced attempts by Russian émigrés and "Western intelligence services" to exploit him for propaganda purposes. He now reveals that this letter was written under duress and with the participation of the KGB after his second arrest in 1964. Together with Alexander Esenin-Volpin (the son of the poet Sergei Esenin) he appears to have organized the demonstration on December 5, 1965, of which he speaks in this letter to Kosygin. Le Monde of November 24, 1966, reported that he had also compiled a "White Book" on the Sinyavsky-Daniel case and handed a copy of it to President Podgorny on October 19. According to news reports at the end of January, 1967, he has again been arrested, presumably for his part in organized protests against the imprisonment of Sinyavsky and Daniel.

To the President of the Council of Ministers of the U.S.S.R., Comrade A. N. Kosygin

DEAR ALEKSEI NIKOLAYEVICH,

I write to you, as the Head of the Government, about a matter which has deeply disturbed me for several months past. On December 5, on Constitution Day, I realized that not only I but hundreds of other people as well are concerned about the fate of the writers Andrei Sinyavsky and Yuli Daniel who were arrested in September by the KGB.

Their arrest raises a number of questions which come within the competence of the Head of the Government.

1. *On the nature of the concept "anti-Soviet propaganda" and on the application of this concept*

Sinyavsky and Daniel, who are accused of having published abroad under the pseudonyms Tertz and Arzhak, may be tried under Article 70 of the Criminal Code of the R.S.F.S.R. relating to "anti-Soviet propaganda." But what is to be understood by "anti-Soviet propaganda" in the forty-ninth year of the existence of the Soviet system?

I ask this question because I have myself been charged twice under this article, and on both occasions the investigation of my case was concerned chiefly to convince me that my actions had been directed against the Soviet system. By the end of the first investigation (in 1960–1961) I was ready to agree with this, since the Soviet system as it was understood by my interrogator (Major Ushakov, Senior Interrogator for particularly important cases of the Committee of State Security of the Council of Ministers of the U.S.S.R.) appeared to be nothing more than a machine for the coercion of the individual. The years that followed, however, showed me that his understanding of it was too narrow. In particular, nearly all the verse which had been confiscated from me and kept in the KGB files as "anti-Soviet" has subsequently been published in the Soviet press—in magazines, newspapers and anthologies.

The second investigation (in 1964) had to take account of certain changes in the ideological sphere and was limited to the breaking of my contacts with foreigners. The result was my letter of public self-castigation published in *Evening Moscow* on June 3, 1965, under the heading "A reply to Mr. Hughes." The interrogator succeeded in persuading me that it is a bad thing if you are considered in the West to be an oppositionist. The absurdity of replying publicly to a letter received more than two years previously did not worry the KGB officials, who actively assisted in the writing and publication of this piece.

There have been further changes since 1964. Works which were earlier "anti-Soviet" have now become completely "Soviet" and fit for publication; there has also been a change in attitude toward contacts with the Western world.

All this suggests the impermanent nature of the concept "anti-Soviet propaganda." If criticism of certain faults comes from below, it is "anti-Soviet" propaganda. But similar criticism of the same faults coming from above, if it is embodied in resolutions of party congresses and plenums, is "a guideline for the life of the country." What from below is a "call to undermine or weaken the Soviet system" is, from above, "the strengthening of the power of the Soviet state system."

But the application of the law is unchanging and inexorable. A person who was quicker than others to raise his voice in defense of the honor and dignity of his country is a criminal, "rightly" condemned in accordance with the spirit and letter of the law, and undergoing "deserved" punishment. To this very day people are in prison for having protested against the falsification of the history of the CPSU, against N. S. Khrushchev's abuses of power and other things which have long since been condemned.

If, therefore, their interrogators succeed in convincing Sinyavsky and Daniel that their works are against the current doctrines of the party, then they are doomed to remain in jail until all these doctrines are revised.

2. *On the application of the concept "anti-Soviet propaganda" to literature*

I know Tertz's story *The Trial Begins*, his collection of *Fantastic Stories*, his essay *On Socialist Realism* and I know Arzhak's *This Is Moscow Speaking*. I also know a number of other works which have at various times aroused the indignation of the KGB and have been confiscated as a result. The only reason I can see for their "indignation" is that the authors of the works in question have a fresh approach to reality and the literary treatment of it. One example is Boris Pasternak's *Doctor Zhivago*, a great book which was deservedly awarded the Nobel Prize (it is evidently one of the special duties of the KGB to seize all copies of this book).

It is possible that there is something in the behavior of Sinyavsky and Daniel that constitutes an infringement of some obligation into which they had entered voluntarily. It is possible that the statutes of the Union of Soviet Writers, of which they are apparently both members, have a different interpretation of "socialist realism" than is to be found in Sinyavsky's essay. Perhaps *This Is Moscow Speaking* was written in breach of certain rules laid down in these statutes. It appears that the use of a pseudonym is supposed to be reported to the Union of Writers. Failure to observe these obligations is certainly misconduct, but misconduct which is entirely within the jurisdiction of the Union of Writers, if they are members of it, or of the CPSU, if they are members of the party, or of any other voluntary organization to which they might belong and whose rules they may have broken. But their actions are no concern of the state (Article 70 of the Criminal Code, however, relates to a crime against the state).

The fact that they were born in the Soviet Union does not in itself deprive them of the right to independence of thought. Faithfulness to one's convictions, to one's understanding of what is best for the country, is not a monopoly of those who are in power. Sinyavsky and Daniel also have a right to their anger at past crimes, to their love for their country's traditions and to their view of its future. Sinyavsky's literary activity in his own country (his articles in *Novy Mir*, his books about Picasso and the poetry of the early revolutionary years, his introduction to a volume of Boris Pasternak's verse) shows that Tertz has a right to his own interpretation of, say, socialist realism.

Consequently the right way—but one that has not, unfortunately, so far been tried—of dealing with such a case would be through public organizations, such as those of the writers, the party and the trade unions, rather than through the courts. Fortunately for literature these organizations do not have at their disposal a network of corrective labor camps, but only a carefully devised system for applying public pressure.

3. *On the role of the KGB in the public life of the country*

These are, of course, not the times of Stalin, but even today the KGB is still a serious obstacle to the development of public life. The most recent example is the "participation" of members of the KGB in a peaceful demonstration on Pushkin Square on December 5.

Attempts to display a sign demanding that the action taken against Sinyavsky and Daniel should be made public, and another sign saying "Observe the Constitution," as well as attempts to say this (but no more) aloud, invariably ended in those concerned being frog-marched to the nearest militia station or *druzhina** headquarters. All this was watched, not without approval, by officials of the Moscow branch of the KGB. This is only the most recent such incident. And, on closer inspection, what else but interference in public life can one call the arrest of Sinyavsky and Daniel and their detention in prison, which has now lasted three months?

If the fact of their authorship [of the works of Tertz and Arzhak] has been established and they are going to be tried for the substance of what they wrote, then there is no need to hold them in prison until their trial. Even if it is considered that at the moment Article 70 of the Criminal Code is applicable to what they have written, all their other actions (e.g., the use of pseudonyms or the sending of their manuscripts abroad) are not indictable offenses under Soviet law. Lengthy detention in solitary confinement—I know this from my own experience—has very harmful psychological consequences.

This imprisonment of Sinyavsky and Daniel and the complete lack of any public statements about the case (as in the majority of KGB cases concerning "anti-Soviet propaganda") make it impossible for the public to arrive at an independent judgment about the actions of the accused and to check on the legality, which in this case it would be wrong not to doubt, of the KGB's actions.

4. *On the observance of international agreements*

Article 19 of the "Universal Declaration of the Rights of Man," adopted by the United Nations and ratified in 1948 by the Soviet Union, reads as follows: "Every person has the right to freedom of opinion and to its free expression; this right includes the freedom of adhering without let or hindrance to one's own opinions, and the freedom to seek, receive and distribute information and ideas by any means whatsoever and independently of state frontiers."

Are not these words directly relevant to the case of Sinyavsky and Daniel?

---

* An auxiliary police force intended to deal with "hooliganism."

I consider it both my right and my duty to address these questions to you. I am by no means certain that they too will not be regarded as "anti-Soviet." I have good grounds for my uncertainty. I could also be tried and convicted for using foreign sources of information (I listen to the foreign radio since nothing has so far been published in our country about the case of Sinyavsky and Daniel), for reading the books of these two authors and approving of them, and for taking part in the demonstration of December 5—if somebody takes into their head to denounce it as "anti-Soviet"—and for saying aloud what I have written in this letter. In 1937, 1949 and even in 1961 people were imprisoned for much lesser things.

But I love my country and I do not wish to see its name sullied by the latest unchecked activities of the KGB.

I love Russian literature and I do not wish to see two more writers sent off under guard to fell trees.

I respect Andrei Sinyavsky as an outstanding critic and prose writer.

A. GINZBERG

My address:
B. Polyanka, d. II/14, kv. 25.
Moscow, Zh-180.
[December (?), 1965]

Judgment on Slanderers

The following article is given as a typical specimen of the way in which the verdict was reported in the Soviet press. It will be noted that there is no account of the speeches for the defense.

by B. KRYMOV

Literary Gazette, February 15, 1966

"Anyone who enters the Central Writers' Club sees a marble slab on which are engraved the names of our comrades who fell in battles for the freedom and independence of our Motherland. I accuse Sinyavsky and Daniel in the name of the living and of the dead. Their crime must be punished."

These were the concluding words of the speech by the public accuser, the writer Arkadi Vasilyev. All those present in the court-room warmly applauded his impassioned and indignant speech.

But before this speech, many witnesses had given evidence. They confirmed that all the books in the record had been written by Sinyavsky and Daniel. Yes, they had seen and read these works either in manuscript or as books published abroad; yes, some of the witnesses had warned Sinyavsky and Daniel that these manuscripts were anti-Soviet.

After the examination of witnesses, the court heard the speeches for the prosecution and the defense. Arkadi Vasilyev made his speech by request of the Writers' Union of the U.S.S.R., that of the R.S.F.S.R. and of its Moscow branch. He recalled that in Vol. I of the *History of Soviet Russian Literature* there had appeared an article on Gorky by one of the accused, Sinyavsky, comparing Sashka Epanchin, Mechik and Kavalerov to Klim Samgin. Sinyavsky then wrote: "Like Samgin himself, his literary companions want to play a central role and attention to be focused on them. Yet they are degraded, spiritually and morally degenerate. Their words contradict their actions, they are not what they wish to appear. Many of them dream of a 'third way' between revolution and counterrevolution, but the logic of events forces them into the camp of those hostile to the nation and to socialism."

How well all this fits Sinyavsky himself and his "colleague" Daniel!

Their Western advocates describe the accused as "foremost representatives" of the Soviet intelligentsia. The Soviet intelligentsia, says Vasilyev, indignantly rejects this claim. Soviet intellectuals are people who conquer space. Soviet intellectuals are doctors who save millions of sick people. Soviet intellectuals are those who create works of art worthy of our epoch. With this intelligentsia Sinyavsky and Daniel have no connection whatsoever.

The Western advocates of the accused vie with each other in lauding the "artistic qualities" of the works of Daniel and Sinyavsky. But A. Vasilyev asks how a concoction of murders, sexual perversions and psychic abnormalities can possibly be called a work of art.

"Sinyavsky-Tertz," says the public accuser, "has a sort of pathological inclination toward foul language and pornography. This, it seems, particularly attracted the foreign 'connoisseurs of fine arts.'"

The public accuser goes on to speak of what is most blasphemous in Abram Tertz's and his characters' dirty diatribes—of their jeering at the name which to Soviet readers is more precious than any other—the name of Vladimir Ilyich Lenin. He quotes one passage, then a second, a third. . . . Even the human qualities of Ilyich, those qualities which are admired by the whole world and respected even by his enemies, even these provoke Sinyavsky's spite.

"Here I must make a short digression," says A. Vasilyev. "Sinyavsky, according to himself, has managed to get from his customers two jackets, two sweaters, a white nylon shirt, a pair of rubber boots, a subscription to a periodical and something for his wife and for his son. Not very much! But I still consider it too much. Sinyavsky's masters had every reason to pay him even less."† The point is that

---

† During their interrogation Sinyavsky and Daniel stated that they knew that large sums of money had been deposited in their names in foreign banks. [Krymov's footnote.]

Sinyavsky had cribbed many of his statements about V. I. Lenin from the Social Revolutionaries, from the Mensheviks. This can easily be proved—one has only to look up the issues of *The People's Cause* (*Delo Naroda*) and *Forward* (*Vperyod*) for 1918. What talk can there be of honesty when, even working for his real masters, Sinyavsky acted like a petty swindler!‡

At the end of his deeply felt speech, the public accuser said:

"In the article on Gorky, which I mentioned at the beginning [of my speech], Sinyavsky wrote that it was in vain that Samgin's literary companions, hiding behind their outward respectability, try 'theoretically' to justify treachery, deceit and all kinds of ignoble intentions. Those who act against the nation's interests will inevitably be revealed as antiheroes, as persons condemned by the Revolution to be destroyed. In the name of all Soviet writers, I accuse Sinyavsky (Abram Tertz) and Daniel (Nikolai Arzhak) of the gravest possible crime and I call on the court to punish them severely."

A. Vasilyev's speech was followed by that of the Public Accuser Zoya Kedrina, critic and literary expert. She emphasized that Sinyavsky and Daniel did not merely reject socialist realism; they rejected the very basis of our literature, the very soil by which it is nurtured: socialism and Communism.

It was the active rejection of Soviet life that had led the accused to reject Soviet literature, and it was not by chance that one of Sinyavsky's anti-Soviet articles was an attack on socialist realism. In this context the public accuser recalled the article by B. Ryurikov on "Socialist Realism and Its Critics" published in the journal *Foreign Literature* at the beginning of 1962. The author of the article had discussed the anti-Soviet character of the works which had appeared abroad under the name of "Abram Tertz." B. Ryurikov assumed that Tertz was the pen name of some white émigré—he could not, of course, know that Abram Tertz was here in Moscow!§

---

‡ It is difficult to see what Sinyavsky, in his very few remarks about Lenin, could have owed to Menshevik newspapers of 1918. The passage most complained of by the prosecution about Lenin's having bayed at the moon before his death (see p. 22) obviously could not have come from this source, nor could most of the others.

§ See note on p. 123.

"In supporting the demand that Sinyavsky and Daniel be punished for their criminal acts," said Z. Kedrina, "I seek, at the request of the writers' organization of our country, to protect our country and literature from the dirty attacks of the lackeys of anti-Soviet propaganda."

The next speech was by the Assistant Prosecutor General, O. P. Tyomushkin. He said that the trial had proved the guilt of the accused, it had proved their hostile attitude to the policy of the CPSU and to the Soviet system. He considered that Sinyavsky and Daniel were proved to have acted with deliberate intent; their purpose had been to undermine the Soviet regime. He asked for a sentence on Sinyavsky of seven years' detention to be followed by five years' exile, and on Daniel of five years' detention to be followed by three years' exile.

After the speeches for the defense came the concluding pleas by the accused. Defendant Daniel admitted his guilt in sending what he had written abroad and thereby putting ideological weapons into the hands of the enemies of our country.

Sinyavsky attempted to contradict the agreements of the prosecution but nevertheless said that his works were written "not from the Marxist but the idealist point of view."

The court withdrew to consider its verdict. Those in the courtroom tensely awaited the sentence. Once again, the words rang out:

"Please rise for the court."

The sentence is pronounced.

The court considers that the anti-Soviet, slanderous characters of the works which Sinyavsky and Daniel published abroad has been fully proved by the material evidence and the preliminary investigation. The fact that the accused had carried out anti-Soviet propaganda with deliberate intent had been proved as much by the subject matter of their books as by the actions of the accused.

The Court sentenced A. Sinyavsky to seven years' detention in a corrective labor colony with a severe regime, and Y. Daniel to five years in a similar colony.

Those gathered in the courtroom greeted the sentence with unanimous approval.

Posttrial Protests

These three letters of protest were provoked by the harsh sentences pronounced on Sinyavsky and Daniel. They are clearly the most articulate and widely circulated of many others. The letter signed by 63 leading Moscow writers, critics and literary scholars was angrily attacked by Sholokhov at the 23rd Party Congress, which took place in March not long after the trial. This in turn moved Mrs. Chukovskaya to reply on behalf of the liberal intelligentsia. The third letter is signed by a group of linguists.

Letter of 63 Moscow Writers

To the Presidium of the 23rd Congress of the CPSU
To the Presidium of the Supreme Soviet of the U.S.S.R.
To the Presidium of the Supreme Soviet of the R.S.F.S.R.

COMRADES,

We, the undersigned group of Moscow writers, request you to grant us permission to stand surety for the recently sentenced writers Andrei Sinyavsky and Yuli Daniel. We believe that this would be an act of both wisdom and humanity.

Although we do not approve of the means by which these writers published their work abroad, we cannot accept the view that their intention was anti-Soviet, which alone could have justified the severity of the sentence. At their trial the prosecution failed to prove the existence of such malicious intent.

At the same time, the condemnation of writers for the writing of satirical works creates an extremely dangerous precedent and could impede the progress of Soviet culture. Learning and art cannot exist if neither paradoxical ideas can be expressed nor hyperbolic images be used as an artistic device. In our complex situation today we need more, not less, freedom for intellectual and artistic experiment. From this standpoint, the trial of Sinyavsky and Daniel has already caused us more harm than did any of their mistakes.

Sinyavsky and Daniel are gifted men who should be given the chance to make up for their lack of political prudence and tact. If they were released on our surety and remained in touch with Soviet society, they would soon realize their mistakes and redeem them by the artistic and ideological value of the new literary works they would be able to write.

We beg you therefore to release Andrei Sinyavsky and Yuli Daniel on our surety.

This would be an act dictated by the interests of our country, the interests of the world and those of the world Communist movement.

Members of the Union of Writers of the U.S.S.R.

K. I. Chukovsky
I. G. Ehrenburg
V. V. Shklovsky
P. G. Antokolsky
L. I. Slavin
V. A. Kaverin
E. Y. Dorosh
A. N. Anastasyev
A. A. Anikst
L. A. Anninsky
B. A. Akhmadulina
S. E. Babenisheva
V. D. Berestov
K. P. Bogatyryev
Z. B. Boguslavskaya
V. N. Voinovich
L. A. Levitsky
S. L. Lungin
L. Z. Lungina
S. P. Markish
V. Z. Mass
O. N. Mikhailov
Y. P. Morits
Y. M. Nagibin
I. I. Nusinov
V. F. Ognev
B. Sh. Okudzhava
R. D. Orlova
L. S. Ospovat
N. V. Panchenko
M. A. Popovsky
L. E. Pinsky

Y. O. Dombrovsky
Y. B. Borev
A. V. Zhigulin
A. G. Zak
L. A. Zonina
L. G. Zorin
N. M. Zorkaya
T. V. Ivanova
K. A. Ikramov
L. R. Kabo
Ts. I. Kin
L. V. Kopelev
V. I. Kornilov
I. N. Krupnik
I. N. Kuznetsov
Y. D. Levitansky

S. B. Rassadin
N. V. Reformatskaya
V. M. Rossels
D. S. Samoilov
B. M. Sarnov
F. G. Svetov
A. Y. Sergeyev
R. S. Sef
I. N. Solovyova
A. A. Tarkovsky
A. M. Turkov
I. N. Tynyanova
G. S. Fish
L. K. Chukovskaya
M. F. Shatrov

Letter from Lidia Chukovskaya[†]

To the Board of the Rostov-on-Don Section of the Union of Writers
To the Board of the Union of Writers of the R.S.F.S.R.
To the Board of the Union of Writers of the U.S.S.R.
To the Editors of Pravda
To the Editors of Izvestia
To the Editors of Literary Gazette
To the Editors of Literary Russia
To the Editors of Molot

To Mikhail Alexandrovich Sholokhov, author of And Quiet Flows the Don

When you spoke at the 23rd Party Congress, Mikhail Alexandrovich, you went to the rostrum not as a private person but as "a spokesman for Soviet literature."

---

† The daughter of the venerable Soviet writer, scholar and translator, Kornei Chukovsky. Her letter is addressed to the Rostov-on-Don section of the Union of Writers because of Sholokhov's close association with it.

You thereby made it legitimate for every writer, including me, to pass judgment upon the things you said supposedly in the name of all of us. Your speech at the Congress really can be called "historical." In the whole history of Russian culture I know of no other case of a writer publicly expressing regret, as you have done, not at the harshness of a sentence but at its leniency.

Furthermore, you were upset not only by the sentence; you also did not like the actual court proceedings in the case of the writers Daniel and Sinyavsky. You found them too pedantic, too legalistic. You would have liked it better if the court had tried these two Soviet citizens unhampered by the legal code, if it had been guided not by the law but by its "sense of justice." I was staggered by this suggestion, and I have good reason to believe that I was not alone in this. Stalin's contempt for the law cost our people millions of innocent victims. Persistent attempts to return to the rule of law, to strict observance of the spirit and the letter of Soviet law and the progress made in this direction, constitute the most precious achievement of our country during the last ten years. Yet this is the very achievement of which you wish to rob the people! True, in your speech at the Congress you held up as a model to the court not the comparatively recent period in which Soviet laws were infringed wholesale, but a more distant time, "the memorable twenties," when [Soviet] law and the legal code had not yet come into existence. The first Soviet legal code was introduced in 1922. The years 1917–1922 are memorable for their heroism and grandeur, but they were not distinguished by their respect for the rule of law, as could scarcely be expected, since the old order had been destroyed while the new one was still in its infancy. The habit of trying people on the basis of "rough justice" was fitting and natural during the Civil War, in the immediate aftermath of the Revolution, but there is absolutely no justification for it on the eve of the fiftieth anniversary of the Soviet regime. Who benefits from and what is the point of a return to "rough justice," that is, in effect, to the rule of instinct, now that laws have been established? And whom exactly do you dream of having tried by this particularly severe procedure, which operated outside the framework of the legal code, and was applied in the "memorable twenties"? It is above all writers you would like to see treated in this way. For a long time now, Mikhail Alexandrovich, you have been in the habit, in your articles and public speeches, of talking about writers with crude mockery and scorn. This time you have surpassed yourself. These sentences of five and seven years' corrective labor on two intellectuals, two writers, neither of whom enjoys good health—that is, sentences, in effect, to illness and perhaps to death—seem to you to be too light. You appear to think that if the court had tried them not in accordance with the Criminal Code but in a quicker and more straightforward manner, it would have devised a sterner punishment, and you would have welcomed this. Here are your actual words: "If these fellows with their black consciences had been caught in the memorable twenties, when people were tried not on the basis of closely defined articles of the Criminal Code, but 'in accordance with the revolutionary sense of justice,' then, my goodness, they would have got something quite different, these turncoats! And then, if you please, people talk about the sentence being too harsh."

Yes, Mikhail Alexandrovich, together with many Communists of Italy, France, England, Norway, Sweden, Denmark (whom in your speech you call for some reason "bourgeois defenders" of the condemned men), together with left-wing organizations in the West, I, a Soviet writer, take it on myself to talk about the uncalled-for, completely unjustified harshness of the sentence. You said in your speech that you were ashamed for those who tried to get a pardon for the two by offering to stand surety for them. But, quite frankly, I am ashamed not for them and for myself, but for you. In making this plea they were following the fine tradition of Soviet and pre-Soviet Russian literature, whereas you, by your speech, have cut yourself off from this tradition. It was in the "memorable twenties," that is from 1917 to 1922, at the height of the Civil War, when people were judged in accordance with a "sense of justice," that Maxim Gorky exerted all his authority to save writers not only from cold and hunger but also from prison and deportation. He wrote dozens of letters of intercession and, thanks to him, many writers were able to resume their work. This tradition—the tradition of interceding for people—is nothing new in Russia, and our intelligentsia is rightly proud of it. The greatest of our poets, Alexander Pushkin, said with pride, "I have called for mercy on the fallen." In a letter to Suvorin, who in his paper had dared to blacken Zola, the defender of Dreyfus, Chekhov said: "Even supposing Dreyfus were guilty, Zola would still be right, because it is the business of writers not to accuse or prosecute, but to intercede even for the guilty, once they have been condemned and are undergoing punishment. . . . There are enough accusers and prosecutors as it is."

"It is the business of writers not to prosecute but to intercede. . . ." This is what we are taught by Russian literature through those who represent it best. This is the tradition you have broken by loudly proclaiming your regret that the sentence was not harsh enough.

Consider for a moment the meaning of Russian literature. The books of the great Russian writers have always taught and still teach us that we must never oversimplify, but must try with all the resources of social and psychological insight to understand as deeply as possible the complex causes of human error, misconduct, crime and delinquency. The humanizing message of Russian literature is indeed to be found mainly in this quality of understanding. Think of Dostoyevsky's book about penal servitude, *Notes from the House of the Dead* and Tolstoy's novel about prison, *Resurrection*. Both writers were passionately concerned to fathom the depths of man's soul, to probe deeply into human destiny and social conditions. It was not in order to pronounce a further condemnation on men already condemned that Chekhov made his heroic journey to the island of Sakhalin—hence the great depth of the book he wrote about it.[‡] Last but not least, think of *And Quiet Flows the Don*— with what concern its author treats the mistakes, misdeeds and even counterrevolutionary crimes committed by his heroes. How well he understands the enormous social changes taking place in the country and the slightest impulses of the bewildered human soul. It was startling to hear the author of *And Quiet Flows the Don* reduce a complicated human situation to the simplest and most elementary terms by asking the crude question which you addressed to the delegates of the Soviet Army: "What would you have done if traitors had been found in one of your detachments?" This is nothing less than a call for drumhead justice in peacetime! Why bother, after all,

---

[‡] Chekhov traveled to the penal colony of Sakhalin in 1890.

to wonder which article of the Criminal Code Sinyavsky and Daniel had infringed? Why try to figure out which sides of our recent history had been satirized in their books, what events had led them to write their books and what factors in our life had made it impossible for them to publish in their own country? Who cares about psychological and social analysis? Put them up against the wall! Shoot them within twenty-four hours!

To listen to you, one might think that the condemned men had been distributing anti-Soviet leaflets or proclamations, or that they had sent abroad not works of fiction but the blueprints for a fortress or a factory at the very least. . . . By reducing complex propositions to simple ones, by bandying around the word "treason" in such an unworthy manner, you have once again, Mikhail Alexandrovich, been false to your duty as a writer, your duty always to explain and to bring home to everybody the complexity and contradictory nature of the literary and historical process. Instead, you have played with words, thus deliberately and maliciously oversimplifying, and thereby distorting, the case.

Outwardly the trial of Sinyavsky and Daniel was held with due regard to the legal formalities. For you this was a fault, and for me it was a good feature. Yet, even so, I protest against the sentence pronounced by the court.

Why do I protest? Because Sinyavsky's and Daniel's committal to trial was in itself illegal. Because a book, a piece of fiction, a story, a novel—in brief, a work of literature—whether good or bad, talented or untalented, truthful or untruthful, cannot be tried in any court, criminal, military or civil. It can only be tried in the court of literature. A writer, like any other Soviet citizen, can and should be tried by a criminal court for any misdemeanor he may have committed, but not for his books. Literature does not come under the jurisdiction of the criminal court. Ideas should be fought with ideas, not with camps and prisons.

This is what you should have said to your listeners if you had really gone to the rostrum as a spokesman of Soviet literature.

But you spoke as a traitor to it. Your shameful speech will not be forgotten by history.

And literature will take its own vengeance, as it always takes vengeance on those who betray the duty imposed by it. It has condemned you to the worst sentence to which an artist can be condemned—to creative sterility. And neither honors, nor money, nor prizes, given at home or abroad, can save you from this judgment.

LIDIA CHUKOVSKAYA

Letter from Five Scholars

To L. I. Brezhnev, First Secretary of the CC of the CPSU

DEAR LEONID ILYICH,

We consider it our civic duty to convey to you, and through you to the Central Committee of our party, our views on a matter which deeply disturbs us.

What we have in mind is the case of Sinyavsky and Daniel, and certain other problems which are to some extent connected with it.

Clearly, various courses of action were possible, once Sinyavsky's and Daniel's pseudonyms had been uncovered.

The one chosen was the arrest and trial of the two writers. In coming to this decision, two circumstances ought surely to have been kept in mind.

First, bourgeois propaganda was bound to present this affair in the light of the various mistakes made in our cultural policy over the last decade (before October 1964):* the unfounded criticism of Dudintsev's novel *Not by Bread Alone* (1956); the ill-considered measures against B. Pasternak (1958); the attacks on Y. Evtushenko's *Babi Yar* (1961); the incompetent pronouncements on art and artists, made by N. S. Khrushchev (1962–63); and finally the trial of the poet-translator J. Brodsky, accused of being a social parasite (1964).

We have derived *no* advantage from these steps whatever. We cannot therefore comfort ourselves with the thought that the advantages outweighed the disadvantages of the [propaganda] value to our

---

* I.e., before Khrushchev's fall.

enemies. The result has been a net loss for us both at home and abroad.

The second and major consideration ought surely to have been this:

Never before in the history of the Soviet state has a writer been arrested and *publicly* tried for alleged anti-Soviet, antistate activities which consisted in his having written anti-Soviet, antistate works and published them (whether at home or abroad). M. Bulgakov wrote, and the Moscow Arts Treatre produced, *The Day of the Turbins*, a work which J. V. Stalin judged to be anti-Soviet. Yet Bulgakov was not arrested or tried for this. B. Pilnyak published abroad his anti-Soviet novel *Mahogany*. Yet Pilnyak was not arrested or tried for this. B. Pasternak published abroad his *Doctor Zhivago*—a novel pronounced by us to be anti-Soviet. Yet Pasternak was neither arrested nor tried.

Thus the Sinyavsky-Daniel trial is a case without precedent in Soviet history. Furthermore, never in the history of Czarist Russia, nor—to the best of our knowledge—in that of Europe and America, or of Asia and Africa in modern, recent times, has a writer been arrested and tried on a charge of antistate crimes which consisted in his writing antistate works of literature and publishing them, at home or abroad.

Thus it would appear that this case is unprecedented in world history.

How much care was therefore needed in preparing it, in considering and weighing everything concerned with it! How important it was to choose a competent prosecutor! We know the instructions given to Dzerzhinsky by Lenin in the troubled year 1922—although it was not then a matter of a public trial, but merely of the exile abroad of certain writers and professors who had joined the counterrevolutionary cause:

. . . this must be more carefully prepared. Without sufficient preparation, we'll only make fools of ourselves. Please consider the preparatory steps. Call Messing, Mantsev and others in Moscow to a consultative meeting. Insist that the members of the Politbureau put aside two or three hours a week for the careful examination of [these writers'] publications and books; make sure that this is done; insist on written reports; see that all non-Communist publications are sent to Moscow without delay. Get the opinion of Communist writers such as Steklov, Olminsky, Skvortsov, Bukharin, etc. Entrust the affair to a sensible, educated, efficient man in the GPU (Col. Works, 5th ed., Vol. 54, p. 205.)§

Let us now see how the Sinyavsky-Daniel case was handled.

Before the trial, the official government newspaper *Izvestia* (No. 10, 1966) published an article written in the familiar style of the thirties and forties, in which the accused were described as guilty and their works repeatedly called "anti-Soviet"—although it was for the court to give a decision on this point. Yet in Soviet law an accused person is innocent until proved guilty, and only a court of law has the right to pronounce him guilty and establish the degree of his guilt. It can hardly be for the press to anticipate the decision of the court! Indeed, *Izvestia* itself (No. 61, 1966) stated quite rightly that it is inadmissible for a trial *in absentia* to be held by the press.*

The trial began. Not one foreign correspondent was admitted to the courtroom—not even foreign Communists. Communist journalists were given the same treatment as bourgeois journalists, journalists from countries which for twenty years have been building socialism were put on a par with journalists from bourgeois countries!

Those who are against us were given the opportunity of reminding us that foreign reporters had been admitted even to the public trials of 1936 and '37. They were given the chance to ask: "Why are they not admitted this time? Communist reporters would never slander a Soviet court, they would write the truth. If the procedure is regular, the charge clear, the evidence leaves no room for doubt, if the prosecutor is sure of his case and of his ability to win it, why are foreign journalists not allowed to witness the triumph of Soviet justice?"

In addition to this, our press failed to publish the record or detailed reports of these unusual proceedings and was therefore powerless to neutralize the effect of bourgeois propaganda.

---

§ The group of intellectuals exiled in 1922 included Nicholas Berdyaev. Messing and Mantsev were high officials of the Cheka. Olminsky was head of the historical section of the Central Committee, Steklov the editor of *Izvestia*, and Skvortsov the translator of *Das Kapital*.

* This article, by two Soviet lawyers, stressed the constitutional requirement that Soviet courts should be free of outside influence. (*Izvestia*, March 15, 1966.)

The bourgeois propaganda machine did its work. But even without its help, doubts arose in the minds of unprejudiced people. Unfortunately, their bewilderment was increased rather than lessened by what our papers said. What the papers said was ill-considered, slipshod and at times mistaken to a staggering degree. Yet our press was the only source of information for us and for the world at large. To take a few examples of its inept reporting:

1. The papers claimed that the fact of a literary work being used by our enemies was in itself sufficient to incriminate the author. Yet our enemies will use anything. They used the criticism of the cult of personality and the circumstances of Khrushchev's fall. They used the criticism of subjectivism and voluntarism and the decision of the September and March plenums. They use satirical and critical articles published in our press. The fact of being used by our enemies *cannot therefore be a crime as such.* Whom are these illogical arguments intended to convince? Anyone with a minimum of ability to think for himself can see through them at once. Can they be aimed at people of a low intellectual level? But should our press talk down to the backward section of the population, rather than educate it up to the level of the more advanced?

2. The papers claimed that the mere fact of sending a manuscript (even a work of fiction) out of the country without permission from the authorities, and by hand instead of by post, is a violation of the law. *Pravda* wrote on February 22, 1966, that Sinyavsky and Daniel had secretly and in defiance of the law sent their anti-Soviet manuscripts abroad. Yet we know of no law which forbids a Soviet citizen to send his manuscripts abroad unless by doing so he betrays state or military secrets. If such a law exists, why didn't the papers name it? If there is no such law, why mislead the Soviet public and give our enemies the chance to catch us out in a lie?

3. The papers wrote that it was up to the court to establish the degree of guilt of the accused. Another unfortunate inaccuracy! The court has first of all to establish the guilt of the accused, and only then the extent of their guilt.

4. *Izvestia* of February 10, 1966, quoted Article 70 of the Criminal Code of the R.S.F.S.R. and added that "anti-Soviet literature is literature which incites to action aimed at undermining or weakening

the Soviet regime." But not one paper told us where, in Daniel's or Sinyavsky's writing, such incitement is to be found. Nothing quoted in the press gave grounds for saying that there is any such incitement, let alone on the part of the authors themselves. The few quoted passages could not have proved anything of the sort, even in a work of nonfiction, still less in a novel or short story. As for Sinyavsky's *On Socialist Realism*—the only nonfictional work which, it seems, was held against the author—it was merely described as slanderous and anti-Soviet. Nothing was quoted in support of this charge. Indeed, nothing from this work was quoted at all. This is how our press enlightened us about the substance of the charges. The reader had simply to take it on trust.

But, as we know, the whole problem of Soviet press reporting is anything but simple. We know from our own experience as readers that in the past the press has often made mistakes in its judgment of people and events. We need only recall what the papers wrote in 1936–38, or what they wrote about subversive biologists, about the followers of Weissman and Morgan, about the "great" biologist Lysenko, about the "antipatriotic group of 'cosmopolitan' critics," about Tito—"the watchdog and paid agent of the imperialists"—about the "murderers in white coats";† we have only to recall the praise showered on every one of Khrushchev's decisions and pronouncements. Now that one of the guiding principles of our leadership is a sober and considered approach, free from voluntarism and undue haste, an approach based on an informed evaluation of the facts, we might have expected press reports on the trial to be more serious, convincing and in better taste, especially on so grave and unprecedented a matter.

5. The papers repeatedly stressed that the issue was not what the accused had written, but their criminal activities. Yet the criminal offenses of which they stood accused were contained in their novels and short stories. How could they be tried without a purely literary analysis of the work in question, without a careful examination of their structure, their language, their imagery, their literary devices? This, after all, was the issue around which the trial revolved. How

---

† I.e., the doctors falsely accused in 1952. See note * on p. 95.

could the task before the court be presented by the press in so oversimplified, so facile a way?

6. The papers said that Sinyavsky's and Daniel's guilt was proved by the subject matter of the works they had published abroad, the statements of the witnesses, the opinion of experts and by material evidence. Yet what was the opinion of experts doing in this list since all they were called upon to prove, according to the newspapers, was the identity of the accused? And what material evidence could there be other than their writings? If there was any other, why didn't the papers say so? Undesirable in general, such carelessness is the more regrettable in so serious a case.

7. If *Literary Gazette* of February 12, 1966, is to be believed, the following exchange took place between the presiding judge and Daniel on the subject of slander: "Daniel: 'But how could anyone seriously believe that it [the Soviet government] would decree a "Public Murder Day"? Since it isn't credible, it can't be slander.' 'Slander,' says the judge, 'is the dissemination of information known to be false and damaging. Doesn't this mean that what you wrote is slander?' Silence. 'No,' Daniel says finally. 'It's artistic exaggeration.' "

It is hard to believe that the exchange has been reported correctly. Isn't slander always meant to convince someone? Isn't it therefore clear that an obviously fantastic situation known to be incredible cannot be qualified as defamatory? If, say, Citizen A claims that Citizen B has a mulberry tree growing from his head, or that he has put his mother-in-law inside a rocket and sent her off to Venus, such a statement is incredible and therefore not slanderous. If this is true of a real-life situation, then how much truer it is of a work of fiction!

Pravda stated in its leader on February 22:

Some honest people have been misled by the huge campaign mounted in the West in defense of these two subversive writers. Lacking the necessary information, and accepting the statements of the bourgeois press, which shamelessly puts Sinyavsky and Daniel on a par with Gogol and Dostoyevsky and claims that literary issues and the freedom of the press were at stake in the trial, some honest and progressive people have felt disturbed.

Let us see what this means. *Pravda* writes of "honest and progressive people" who, "lacking the necessary information," have been misled by the bourgeois press. What was the "necessary information" they lacked? Needless to say, they could read Sinyavsky's and Daniel's novels and short stories and form their opinion of these incriminating works. Bourgeois propaganda could not prevent their doing so. Moreover, honest and progressive people in capitalist countries know perfectly well what to think of the bourgeois radio and press. What, then, was the information they lacked? It appears that what they lacked was information about the case, the *trial* itself. Yet they could read our press and, if they were really honest and progressive, they surely did so. Why, then, did they still lack the "necessary information"? Doesn't this mean that our own press failed to supply them with this information, that we ourselves withheld it from them or made it difficult for them to get it, and that, by printing only short and very unsatisfactory summaries of the proceedings instead of the transcript or detailed reports, by excluding the reporters of even the Communist foreign press from the courtroom, we ourselves forced these "honest and progressive people" to accept the statements of the bourgeois press? Another implication of this is that the Soviet public, which had nothing but the Soviet press to go by, had even less information at its disposal than these "honest and progressive" people abroad. How could *Pravda* make such a clumsy and logically vulnerable assertion?

The unfortunate handling of the Sinyavsky-Daniel affair by the press led to public protests, not only from honest progressives but from the most progressive people of all—from our brothers, the leaders of the Communist movement abroad. Thus in many countries we were deprived of the sympathy of even progressive public opinion—to the utmost joy and advantage of our enemies.

So it seems that the Sinyavsky-Daniel case, by the manner in which it was handled, and by the way it was reported in the Soviet press, did greater harm to the world Communist movement, to our country, to our system and our ideology than could have been inflicted by any number of anti-Communist novels, because fiction is only fiction, but *facts are facts.*

In this context, we would like to draw your attention to the views of a certain section of Soviet society, views which were starkly revealed by their attitude to the Sinyavsky-Daniel case.

These people say: "We don't care a damn about the difficulties this may raise for Communists abroad. That's their lookout. Why should we worry?"

Some of these people are Communists. One of them, who holds a responsible post in the Ministry of Foreign Affairs, gave a lecture at Moscow University on March 10, 1966; asked about the statements of Comrades Aragon and Gollan,[†] he replied that these comrades should stick to their own business and not meddle with ours.

Attitudes such as these are significant. They have a long history. As far back as 1925, the leaders of our party warned Soviet people of the danger of certain comrades' forgetting, or failing to understand, their minimum duty as internationalists—their duty to see that the victory of socialism in one country is not an end in itself but the means of supporting and developing the revolutionary movement in other countries. The party told us that people who suffer from this disease fail to see our country as part of the world revolutionary movement as a whole; they see it as the beginning and end of this movement and assume that other countries' interests should be sacrificed to those of ours. This danger has never ceased to exist. This is why our leaders have warned the people and the party against it time and again (e.g., in 1926 and 1931).

It seems to us that our effort to educate the nation in an international spirit should be ten times greater than it is, for there are no other means of fighting this disease.

May we now put forward certain suggestions:

1. It seems to us that philosophers and sociologists should be given the task of investigating the social causes of Sinyavsky's and Daniel's actions. In this context, we should like to recall that Comrade Fidel Castro, writing to the prosecutor in the case of some Cuban counterrevolutionaries, asked him not to press for a sentence of death, adding that the important thing was to discover why former revolutionaries had gone over to the counterrevolutionary camp.

2. We believe that either the case of Sinyavsky and Daniel should be competently re-examined by a highly qualified authority, and explained in a detailed and convincing manner by the press, or that the two men should be graciously pardoned after a full public discussion of their conduct.

[†] See p. 26.

3. It seems to us that we must seriously consider all the mistakes we have made in our handling of writers and intellectuals, as well as the reasons for these mistakes, so that we may radically improve the position and stop, once and for all, handing all the aces to our enemies.

Signatures:
E. KHANPIRA
I. MELCHUK
Y. APRESYAN
L. BULATOVA
N. ESKOV

Protest Against Victimization of Defense Witness V. D. Duvakin

This was one of a number of protests by members of Moscow University against the attempt to dismiss V. D. Duvakin, the only witness for the defense. Some of the signatories are well-known scholars. Zinovi Paperny is an eminent specialist on Russian literature. Mikhail Kazhdan is a professor of ancient history. Vladimir Turok-Popov is an authority on Western European history and Mongait is an archaeologist. P. Yakir is the son of Iona Yakir, the military leader shot by Stalin in 1937. V. Katanyan, like Duvakin himself, is a specialist on Mayakovsky.

It appears that the protest was partially successful, and that Duvakin was not dismissed from the University, though he is no longer allowed to teach.

Telegram of Group of Scholars and Writers

To the Presidium of the 23rd Congress of the CPSU

We, the undersigned scholars and writers, feel disturbed and indignant at the decision, taken on March 25 by the Learned Counsel of the Philological Faculty of Moscow University, to dismiss Assistant Professor Viktor Dmitrievich Duvakin, a well-known and outstanding historian of Russian literature, an experienced and popular lecturer of twenty-seven years' standing and a prominent researcher into the work of Mayakovsky—a decision taken as a result of his appearing as witness for the defense in the trial of Sinyavsky. So illogical a decision is to the discredit not only of Moscow University but of Soviet justice, for in all legal proceedings the presence of witnesses from both sides is provided for, and the court must have full knowledge of the personality of the accused from the standpoint of both the prosecution and the defense. We ask you urgently to intervene to prevent the dismissal becoming effective.

Paperny	Doctor of Philology, member of Union of Soviet Writers
Kazhdan	Doctor of Historical Science
Mongait	Doctor of Historical Science
José García	Doctor of Historical Science
Debets	Doctor of Biological Science, Anthropologist
Gulyga	Doctor of Philosophical Science
Turok-Popov	Doctor of Historical Science
Fyodorov	Doctor of Historical Science
Gorsky	Doctor of Philosophical Science
Vilenskaya	Candidate of Historical Science
Pirumova	Candidate of Historical Science
Ponomaryova	Candidate of Historical Science
Kurnosov	Candidate of Historical Science
Kozlov	Candidate of Historical Science
Markova	Candidate of Historical Science
P. Yakir	
I. Gerasimov	Candidate of Philosophical Science
V. A. Katanyan	Writer

Bibliography of the Works of Abram Tertz (Andrei Sinyavsky) and Nikolai Arzhak (Yuli Daniel) in English and Russian

ABRAM TERTZ

On Socialist Realism

Translation by George Dennis. Introduction by Czeslaw Milosz. New York: Pantheon Books, 1960.
(This work was first published in an abbreviated form in French in *Esprit*, Paris, in February, 1959. This publication was anonymous, and the work was not ascribed to Abram Tertz until later. The Russian original has now been published in *Fantasticheski Mir Abrama Tertsa*, New York, 1967.)

The Trial Begins

Translated by Max Hayward. New York: Pantheon Books, 1960.
(*Sud idyot.* Paris, 1960.)

Fantastic Stories

Translated by Max Hayward and Ronald Hingley. New York: Pantheon Books, 1963.
(*Fantasticheskiye Povesti.* Paris, 1961.)

The Makepeace Experiment	Translated and with an Introduction by Manya Harari. New York: Pantheon Books, 1965. (*Lyubimov.* With an Introduction by Boris Filippov, Washington, 1964.)
Thought Unaware	Translated by Andrew Field and Robert Szulkin. *The New Leader,* New York, July 19, 1965. (*Mysli Vrasplokh.* With an introduction by Andrew Field, New York, 1966.)
"Pkhentz"	*Encounter,* London, April, 1966. (Russian original in *Fantasticheski Mir Abrama Tertsa,* New York, 1967.)

NIKOLAI ARZHAK

This Is Moscow Speaking	In *Dissonant Voices in Soviet Literature,* edited by Patricia Blake and Max Hayward. Translated by John Richardson. New York: Harper Colophon Books, Harper & Row, 1964. Originally published by Pantheon Books in 1962. (*Govorit Moskva.* With an Introduction by Boris Filippov, Washington, 1963.)
"Hands"	*Dissent,* July–August, 1966.

The rest of Arzhak's work has not so far appeared in English. The Russian editions are:

"Hands" and "The Man from Minap"	*Ruki. Chelovek iz Minapa.* With an Introduction by Boris Filippov, Washington, 1963.
"Atonement"	*Iskuplenie.* With an introductory note by Boris Filippov, Washington, 1964.

Index